Roger G. Clarke
TSA Capital Management
Mark P. Kritzman, CFA
Windham Capital Management

Currency Management: Concepts and Practices

The Research Foundation of
The Institute of Chartered Financial Analysts

Research Foundation Publications

Analysts' Earnings Forecast Accuracy in Japan and the United States
by Robert M. Conroy, Robert S. Harris, and Young S. Park

Active Currency Management
by Murali Ramaswami

Bankruptcy Prediction Using Artificial Neural Systems
by Robert E. Dorsey, Robert O. Edmister, and John D. Johnson

Canadian Stocks, Bonds, Bills, and Inflation: 1950–1987
by James E. Hatch and Robert E. White

Corporate Bond Rating Drift: An Examination of Credit Quality Rating Changes Over Time
by Edward I. Altman and Duen Li Kao

Corporate Governance and Firm Performance
by Jonathan M. Karpoff, M. Wayne Marr, Jr., and Morris G. Danielson

Default Risk, Mortality Rates, and the Performance of Corporate Bonds
by Edward I. Altman

Durations of Nondefault-Free Securities
by Gerald O. Bierwag and George G. Kaufman

Earnings Forecasts and Share Price Reversals
by Werner F.M. De Bondt

Economically Targeted and Social Investments: Investment Management and Pension Fund Performance
by M. Wayne Marr, John R. Nofsinger, and John L. Trimble

Equity Trading Costs
by Hans R. Stoll

Ethics, Fairness, Efficiency, and Financial Markets
by Hersh Shefrin and Meir Statman

Ethics in the Investment Profession: A Survey
by E. Theodore Veit, CFA, and Michael R. Murphy, CFA

Ethics in the Investment Profession: An International Survey
by H. Kent Baker, CFA, E. Theodore Veit, CFA, and Michael R. Murphy, CFA

The Founders of Modern Finance: Their Prize-Winning Concepts and 1990 Nobel Lectures

Franchise Value and the Price/Earnings Ratio
by Martin L. Leibowitz and Stanley Kogelman

Fundamental Considerations in Cross-Border Investment: The European View
by Bruno Solnik

Global Asset Management and Performance Attribution
by Denis S. Karnosky, and Brian D. Singer, CFA

Initial Public Offerings: The Role of Venture Capitalists
by Joseph T. Lim and Anthony Saunders

Interest Rate and Currency Swaps: A Tutorial
by Keith C. Brown, CFA, and Donald J. Smith

Managed Futures and Their Role in Investment Portfolios
by Don M. Chance, CFA

The Modern Role of Bond Covenants
by Ileen B. Malitz

A New Method for Valuing Treasury Bond Futures Options
by Ehud I. Ronn and Robert R. Bliss, Jr.

A New Perspective on Asset Allocation
by Martin L. Leibowitz

Options and Futures: A Tutorial
by Roger G. Clarke

The Poison Pill Anti-Takeover Defense: The Price of Strategic Deterrence
by Robert F. Bruner

A Practitioner's Guide to Factor Models

Predictable Time-Varying Components of International Asset Returns
by Bruno Solnik

Program Trading and Systematic Risk
by A.J. Senchack, Jr., and John D. Martin

The Role of Risk Tolerance in the Asset Allocation Process: A New Perspective
by W.V. Harlow III, CFA, and Keith C. Brown, CFA

Selecting Superior Securities
by Marc R. Reinganum

Stock Market Structure, Volatility, and Volume
by Hans R. Stoll and Robert E. Whaley

Time Diversification Revisited
by William Reichenstein, CFA, and Dovalee Dorsett

Currency Management: Concepts and Practices

© 1996 The Research Foundation of the Institute of Chartered Financial Analysts

All rights reserved. No part of this publication may be reproduced, stored in a retrieval system, or transmitted, in any form or by any means, electronic, mechanical, photocopying, recording, or otherwise, without the prior written permission of the copyright holder.

This publication is designed to provide accurate and authoritative information in regard to the subject matter covered. It is sold with the understanding that the publisher is not engaged in rendering legal, accounting, or other professional service. If legal advice or other expert assistance is required, the services of a competent professional should be sought.

ISBN 0-943205-33-6

Printed in the United States of America

January 1996

Mission

The Research Foundation's mission is to identify, fund, and publish research that is relevant to the CFA® Body of Knowledge and useful for AIMR member investment practitioners and investors.

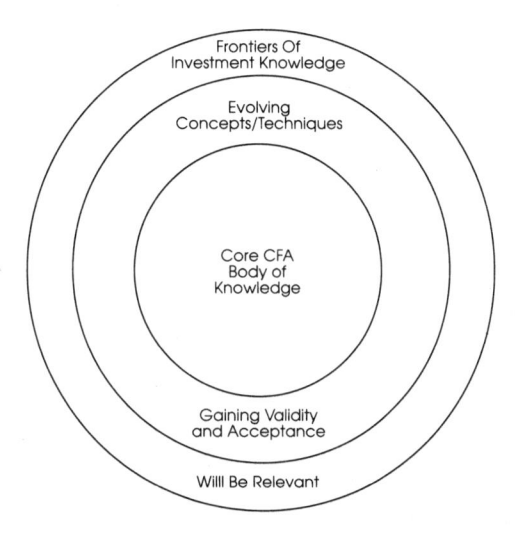

- Frontiers Of Investment Knowledge
- Evolving Concepts/Techniques
- Core CFA Body of Knowledge
- Gaining Validity and Acceptance
- Will Be Relevant

The Research Foundation of
The Institute of Chartered Financial Analysts
P.O. Box 3668
Charlottesville, Virginia 22903
U.S.A.
Telephone: (804) 980-3644
Fax: (804) 980-3634
E-mail: rf@aimr.com
World Wide Web: http://www.aimr.com/aimr.html

Contents

Foreword		ix
Preface		xi
Chapter 1.	Terminology, Conventions, and Basic Relationships	1
	Quotation Conventions	
	Spot and Forward Rates	
	Currency Returns	
	Implied Cross-Rates and Currency Returns	
	Hedged and Unhedged Asset Returns	
	Hedging and Cash Flows	
	Covered Interest Arbitrage and the Forward Premium	
	Statistical Relationships: Expected Returns and Risk	
	Summary	
Chapter 2.	Historical Perspective on Foreign Exchange Risk	29
	Major Historical Events in the Foreign Exchange Markets	
	Empirical Tendencies of Exchange Rates	
	Summary	
Chapter 3.	Hedging Currency Risk	53
	Constructing Symmetrical Hedges	
	Constructing Asymmetrical Hedges	
	Implementation Vehicles	
	Summary	
Chapter 4.	Actively Managing Currencies to Enhance Return	83
	A General Model for Exploiting Views about Currency Returns	
	How to Exploit the Forward Rate Bias	
	How to Exploit Nonrandomness in Currency Returns	
	Technical Analysis	
	Summary	

Chapter 5. Combining Return-Enhancement and Hedging Strategies 91
  Optimal Allocation of Asset and Currency Exposure
  Optimization Relative to a Benchmark
  Combining the Mean–Variance and Benchmark-Relative Approaches
  Extensions beyond Simple Portfolios
  Summary

Chapter 6. Performance Attribution for Actively Managed Portfolios 105
  Performance Attribution When Underlying Asset Composition Is Constant
  Performance Attribution When Derivatives Are Used
  Summary

Chapter 7. Structural Models of Exchange Rate Determination ... 113
  Model Descriptions
  Empirical Tests of Structural Models
  Summary

Chapter 8. Commonly Asked Questions about Currency Hedging 121

Appendix A. Key to Notation Used in the Text 129

Appendix B. Summary of Basic Currency Relationships 131

Selected References 133
  Theory and Empirical Evidence
  Investment Principles and Practice

Foreword

In a provocative presentation delivered in 1989 at an AIMR conference titled *Managing Currency Risk*, Fischer Black asserted that hedging the full foreign exchange exposure of an international equity portfolio is not optimal. He produced a model that showed the optimal hedge ratio to be, instead, 77 percent, and he asserted that this number would be the same for all managers regardless of their unique circumstances! At other sessions of the same conference, James Rhodes concluded that, although the benefits of currency hedging vary with the investor's circumstances, hedging currency risk is beneficial and Michael Rosenberg concluded that hedging strategies are actually counterproductive over long horizons.

That three accomplished professionals could argue so persuasively for such diametrically opposed viewpoints only serves to highlight the complexity of the whole currency management question. Moreover, that all three could actually be correct—given, of course, the assumptions of their underlying models—underscores the tremendous educational commitment practitioners in this field must make to be able to put such findings in their proper perspective. Unfortunately, the path to enlightenment in this important area of international investing has often been blocked by obscure mathematics and the sometimes incomprehensible language and practices of the world's capital markets. It is little wonder that currency management has become a highly specialized function within the investment profession, frequently a function quite separate from the management of the underlying assets themselves.

This monograph by Roger Clarke and Mark Kritzman helps clear that path to a considerable extent. Although the authors note in the Preface that they have not tried to produce "... an exhaustive treatment of the theoretical and institutional details of foreign exchange management," I think you will agree after reading their work that this statement is far too modest. Indeed, what Clarke and Kritzman have done is to give the investment manager a practical and insightful user's guide to the intricacies of the topic. Like any good "how to" manual, it begins with the basics (terminology, conventions, historical overview) and then proceeds to build on that foundation in a careful and logical manner. The topics covered include forward- and option-based hedging strategies, active (that is, return-enhancing) management, and performance attribution. Illustrative examples are given at each critical stage of the exposition, and the authors even package their conclusions cleverly in the form of answers to 17 Commonly Asked Questions about currency management.

What really sets this work apart is the consistency of the Clarke and Kritzman vision. They have provided the reader with an integrated view of the foreign-exchange-exposure question; not only do they offer a thorough analysis of the risk–return trade-off implicit in the currency decision, they also describe how and when this decision should be made within the broad context of asset allocation. Furthermore, the authors, having spent time with these topics in both theory and practice during their academic and money management careers, are uniquely qualified to discuss the issues. You will find evidence of their myriad experiences reflected on every page.

This monograph follows earlier explorations of the options and futures markets and of interest rate and currency swaps as the third in a series of tutorial projects the Research Foundation of the ICFA has published on issues relevant to investment managers. We believe these monographs meet a real educational need by bringing to practitioners who may have had only a passing acquaintance with a certain area what is state of the art in that area. *Currency Management: Concepts and Practices* certainly fulfills that purpose, and we are pleased to present it to you.

Keith C. Brown, CFA
Research Director
Research Foundation of the
Institute of Chartered Financial Analysts

Preface

We have been asked by many clients over the years, "What should we do about our currency exposure?" The answer to that question is not a simple one. It depends to a great extent on what an investor believes about the behavior of currency markets, on how much risk can be tolerated, and on a variety of institutional and legal constraints. Moreover, a discussion of the pros and cons of various approaches to dealing with currency risk is often complicated by unfamiliarity with specialized terminology and concepts specific to the currency markets.

In an effort to clear away some of the confusion, we have tried to clarify the important concepts, principles, and vocabulary related to currency management. Some foundational relationships can be depended on always to hold true because they are part of the fundamental mathematics of exchange rates. Other relationships are tendencies that have been manifest in the past but are not guaranteed to hold true in the future. Anyone formulating a strategy for managing currency risk must distinguish between these two phenomena. Investors will receive fewer surprises after the fact if they know which relationships must hold and which may or may not hold.

Although we have tried to cover a breadth of topics, our effort is not an exhaustive treatment of the theoretical and institutional details of foreign exchange management. We have concentrated on trying to accomplish two things with the material. First, we have attempted to summarize the important concepts and practices concerning currency management. We approached this subject from the point of view of the investment manager rather than the corporate hedger, but most of the principles can be readily translated into the corporate hedging context. Second, we have integrated important concepts into a common analytical framework. This framework is designed to help the investment manager analyze the trade-off between risk and return in the currency decision, and it also allows currencies to be integrated in the asset allocation decision. Some algebra is used to illustrate the basic principles and help the reader understand the intuition that drives the results. To some extent, therefore, the material can serve as a reference source for the solution of simple problems.

Readers need not be discouraged by the algebra, however. Important principles are summarized at the end of each section, and examples illustrating the concepts are shaded. Readers can usually review these shaded boxes without getting lost in the equations. Nevertheless, readers might peek at some of the mathematics from time to time because many important concepts are somewhat clearer with the use of a little algebra. For practical applications of the risk–return framework that involve many different assets and currencies, we recommend using a computer program adapted to solving nonlinear optimization problems rather than trying to arrive at solutions algebraically.

The book consists of eight chapters, two appendixes, and a reference section. Chapter 1 discusses the terminology, conventions, and basic relationships pertaining to foreign exchange rates. Many of the relationships are mathematical and of the type that will persist over time. Chapter 2 provides a historical perspective on foreign exchange risk and currency movements. The chapter points out tendencies in exchange rate relationships that have been empirically true in the past while noting that these tendencies will not necessarily continue for any specific period in the future.

Chapter 3 deals with the two major types of currency hedges, symmetrical and asymmetrical. This chapter also introduces the basic features of futures, forwards, and options contracts that are used to implement currency hedges. Chapter 4 discusses the active management of currencies to enhance return, rather than to hedge risk, and Chapter 5 integrates the goals of return enhancement and risk management into a single framework.

A simple performance measurement framework is presented in Chapter 6. Chapter 7 discusses conceptual economic factors that are postulated to affect exchange rates. Finally, in Chapter 8, we respond to commonly asked questions about currency hedging.

For the reader's reference, appendixes summarize all the algebraic notation used in the text and the most important currency relationships. The reference section lists selected works on issues related to foreign exchange rates and currency management; it is divided into (1) theoretical research and empirical evidence and (2) investment principles and practices.

Special thanks go to our clients and colleagues who have stimulated our thinking and suggested many ideas. We are grateful to Parker King for helping us construct some of the examples and for assembling much of the data. We are also grateful to George Chow for conducting the simulations of the active currency management strategies and Hadas Perchik for supplying some of the graphics. Extra special appreciation goes to Barbara Austin who has typed nearly every word and equation of the manuscript. It could not have been done without her help.

Roger G. Clarke
TSA Capital Management

Mark P. Kritzman, CFA
Windham Capital Management

January 1996

1. Terminology, Conventions, and Basic Relationships

An understanding of the terminology and conventions used in presenting and calculating currency relationships is vital in currency management. The conventions, however, can make interpretation of currency data confusing. This chapter discusses exchange rate quotations, spot rates, forward rates, currency and asset returns, covered interest arbitrage, the forward premium, and the statistical relationships between expected returns and risk.

Quotation Conventions

Exchange rates convert a monetary value denominated in one currency into the equivalent value in another currency. The exchange rate can be quoted either in terms of the home currency/foreign currency (unit of home currency per unit of foreign currency) or in terms of the foreign currency/home currency. We will generally use the convention of quoting the exchange rate in terms of home currency/foreign currency. We make this choice so that from the perspective of a domestic investor, the home currency value of an asset held in a foreign currency will increase when the exchange rate increases.

One way to think about the quotation of exchange rates is to consider the foreign currency as a commodity, like a loaf of bread or sack of potatoes. For example, a U.S. citizen generally thinks of the price of bread in terms of U.S. dollars per loaf. If one already owns bread and the price of bread increases, the bread is worth more, but if one holds dollars and has not purchased any bread yet, the bread will cost more when it is purchased.

The quotation of exchange rates works in a similar way. If the investor has exposure to a foreign currency and the price of the foreign currency increases (home currency/foreign currency increases), the foreign currency exposure is worth more in terms of the investor's base currency and the investor gains. The foreign currency has appreciated in value. If the investor holds the home currency and the price of the foreign currency increases, however, the home currency has depreciated in value and the investor will have to pay more when an exchange is made for the foreign currency.

The Value of Foreign Currency Exposure versus the Exchange Rate

The U.S. dollar (USD) value of Japanese stocks held by a U.S. investor will increase when the USD/yen exchange increases:

Equity Portfolio Value (Yen)	Exchange Rate (USD/Yen)	Equity Portfolio Value (USD)
1,000,000,000	0.0090909	9,090,909
1,000,000,000	0.0095238	9,523,800

Exchange rates quoted using the opposite convention are found by taking the reciprocal of the home currency/foreign currency convention:

USD/Yen	Yen/USD
0.0090909	1/0.0090909 = 110.0
0.0095238	1/0.0095238 = 105.0

The standard convention for quoting exchange rates in the popular press is not always uniform or consistent with the notion that an increase in the quoted rate benefits a home-based investor who holds the currency. Such a convention would require that the quotations always be expressed in home currency units per foreign currency unit. The U.S. dollar has served as an important reserve currency for much of the world, however, so most currencies are quoted relative to the U.S. dollar. Currency quotations expressed in USD/FX (for foreign currency) are referred to as "quoted using an American convention"; when the reverse is used, the quotation is "in the European convention."

The European convention was adopted in 1978 for most currencies as a universal way of expressing foreign exchange rates to facilitate worldwide trading through telecommunications. Among the major currencies, only the British pound and the Australian dollar are typically quoted in the popular press using the American convention. Typical quotation conventions relative to the U.S. dollar are in the box below. Keep in mind that for the many exchange rates that are quoted using the European convention, a decrease in the rate is favorable for a U.S. investor holding the foreign currency.

The result of the mixing of conventions is that an investor can easily get confused about the implications of a change in quoted exchange rates. An increase in the quoted rate could be favorable or unfavorable for the international investor depending on the quotation convention for the particular currency involved.

Currency Quotation Conventions

European convention
Japanese yen	Yen/USD
German mark (deutsche mark)	DM/USD
Canadian dollar	CD/USD
Italian lira	IL/USD
Swiss franc	SF/USD
French franc	FF/USD

American convention
British pound	USD/BP
Australian dollar	USD/AUD

Foreign exchange quotations are also referred to as *direct* or *indirect* quotations. A direct quotation expresses the rate in units of home currency per foreign currency. An indirect quotation is expressed in units of foreign currency per home currency. The American convention is direct for a U.S.-based investor but indirect for a non-U.S.-based investor. Direct and indirect quotations are reciprocals of each other just as American and European quotations are.

Quotations for U.S.-dollar-based futures contracts are more standardized than the foreign exchange quotations. These futures contracts are all quoted in terms of U.S. dollars/foreign currency; so, an increase in the quoted rate implies a profit for a U.S.-based investor with a long position in the foreign currency futures contract.

The investor may sometimes have difficulty knowing which way an exchange rate has changed when certain phrases are used to describe the change. For example, a "weak" or "depreciating" U.S. dollar is used to indicate that more dollars are needed to purchase the foreign currency (that is, the price of the foreign currency has gone up). This increase in the USD/FX exchange rate implies that currency returns are positive for investors holding the foreign currency and negative for investors holding U.S. dollars. A "strong" or "appreciating" U.S. dollar means that fewer dollars are needed to purchase the foreign currency (that is, the price of the foreign currency has gone down). Such a decrease in the USD/FX exchange rate implies currency returns are negative for investors holding the foreign currency and positive for investors holding U.S. dollars. The expressions in each column in the next box are equivalent ways of describing the increase or decrease in an exchange rate from the perspective of a domestic investor (HC here stands for home currency).

One final observation involves the cost of domestic and foreign goods as currency rates change. As a home currency depreciates, consumers need more domestic currency to purchase the same foreign goods. As a result, a depreciating or weak home currency makes foreign goods more expensive than previously for domestic consumers and domestic goods less expensive for foreign consumers. Similarly, an appreciating or strong home currency makes domestic goods more expensive for the foreign consumer and foreign goods less expensive for the domestic consumer.

Spot and Forward Rates

The *spot foreign exchange rate* is the rate used if the foreign currency is to be converted to the home currency at the present time (two-day settlement) rather than a more distant future date. The *forward foreign exchange* rate is a rate the market offers if the conversion is agreed to now but actual conversion is deferred to some point in the future. An individual currency typically has a spectrum of forward rates, each corresponding to a separate date in the future. The spot and forward foreign exchange rates are both quoted using the conventions discussed in the previous section. We will generally use units of home currency/foreign currency (direct quotation) for spot and forward rates.

At any particular time, the forward rate is not likely to be the same as the current spot rate; the forward rate takes into consideration the interest rate differential between the two countries. The difference between the spot exchange rate and the forward rate is usually referred to as the *forward points* (also, the *swap rate*). When the forward points are expressed as a percentage of the current spot rate, the points are referred to as the *forward premium* if the forward rate is higher than the spot rate or as the *forward discount* if it is lower than the spot rate. That is,

$$\text{Forward points} = \text{Forward exchange rate} - \text{Spot rate};$$

$$\text{Forward premium or discount} = \frac{\text{Forward points}}{\text{Spot rate}}$$

$$= \frac{\text{Forward exchange rate} - \text{Spot rate}}{\text{Spot rate}}.$$

If interest rates in the home country are higher (lower) than interest rates in the foreign country, the forward rate will be higher (lower) than the spot rate. The relationship that drives this result is known as *covered interest arbitrage* or *covered interest parity* and is discussed later in this chapter.

Equivalent Conditions from the Perspective of the Domestic Investor

Currency Return > 0	Currency Return < 0
Weak, devaluing, or depreciating HC	Strong or appreciating HC
Strong or appreciating FX	Devaluing, weak, or depreciating FX
Change in HC/FX > 0 (direct quotation)	Change in HC/FX < 0 (direct quotation)
Change in FX/HC < 0 (indirect quotation)	Change in FX/HC > 0 (indirect quotation)

Forward Points and the Forward Premium

For an illustration of the concept of forward points, suppose that the current USD/yen exchange rate is 0.0090909 and the forward rate is 0.0092593. The forward points would be calculated as

$$\text{Forward points} = 0.0092593 - 0.0090909$$
$$= 0.000168,$$

and the forward premium, f, would be

$$f = \frac{0.000168}{0.0090909}$$
$$= 0.0185, \text{ or } 1.85\%.$$

Currency Returns

The percentage change in the spot exchange rate is often referred to as the *currency return*. The magnitude of the discrete percentage change in a spot exchange rate is not the same from each currency perspective. This phenomenon arises from the mathematics of exchange rates, which ties one perspective to another by inverting the exchange rate. The inversion of the rate quotation causes the discrete percentage return to be calculated from a different base for each investor, which alters the magnitude of the percentage change.

Percentage Change According to Investor Perspective

Consider the following illustration of the difference between percentage returns depending on the investor's perspective:

Period	USD/Yen Exchange Rate	Percent Change	Yen/USD Exchange Rate	Percent Change
1	0.0090909	—	110.0	—
2	0.0095238	4.762	105.0	−4.545

Note that the gross discrete percentage changes are reciprocals of each other. The relationship can be written as

$$1 + r_c = \frac{S}{S_o}$$

$$= \frac{1}{S_o/S}$$

$$= \frac{1}{1 + r_f}, \quad (1.1)$$

where

- r_c = percentage change in the spot exchange rate using the domestic perspective (home currency/foreign currency)
- r_f = percentage change in the spot exchange rate using the foreign perspective (foreign currency/home currency)
- S_o = current spot exchange rate (home currency/foreign currency)
- S = spot exchange rate at a subsequent date.

In solving for the percentage return from the foreign investor's perspective in terms of the domestic investor's return, Equation 1.1 becomes

$$r_f = \frac{-r_c}{1 + r_c}. \quad (1.2)$$

The fact that the two discrete percentage changes are not the same in magnitude sometimes causes confusion in analyzing currency movements. To overcome the problem, a simple transformation is often used: The symmetry can be preserved if the analysis is performed in terms of natural logs to represent the continuously compounded rate of return.

Defining a continuously compounded rate of return as r_c^* by using the natural exponent e produces

$$\frac{S}{S_o} = e^{r_c^*}. \quad (1.3)$$

Taking the natural log of both sides of Equation 1.3 gives

$$\ln\left(\frac{S}{S_o}\right) = r_c^*, \quad (1.4)$$

and because of the nature of natural logarithms, we can write the relationship in terms of the foreign investor's perspective as

$$\ln\left(\frac{S}{S_o}\right) = -\ln\left(\frac{S_o}{S}\right)$$

$$= -r_f^*. \quad (1.5)$$

Combining Equations 1.4 and 1.5 gives the relationship between the continuously compounded rates as

$$r_c^* = \ln(1 + r_c)$$

$$= -\ln(1 + r_f)$$

$$= -r_f^*. \quad (1.6)$$

Consequently, the continuously compounded percentage change in the exchange rate from the home currency/foreign currency perspective is just equal to the negative of the continuously compounded percentage change in the exchange rate from the foreign currency/home currency perspective.

Continuous and Discrete Percentage Changes

Continuing with the previous illustration, note the difference in discrete percentage returns between the domestic investor's perspective and the foreign investor's perspective:

$$r_f = \frac{-r_c}{1 + r_c}$$

$$= \frac{-0.04762}{1.04762}$$

$$= -4.546\%.$$

The absolute values of the continuously compounded returns, however, are equal from both perspectives:

$$r_c^* = \ln(1 + 0.04762)$$
$$= 4.652\%,$$

and

$$r_f^* = \ln(1 - 0.04546)$$
$$= -4.652\%.$$

As a result, when maintaining consistency between the perspectives of investors is important, analysis involving percentage changes often uses continuously compounded returns instead of discrete percentage changes. The discrete return from each perspective can then be calculated from the antilog of the continuously compounded return as

$$r_c = e^{r_c^*} - 1$$
$$= 4.762\%$$

and

$$r_f = e^{r_f^*} - 1$$
$$= -4.546\%.$$

The reciprocal relationship between exchange rates gives rise to another phenomenon, *Siegel's paradox*. Siegel (1972) noted that if two investors have the same expectations about the possibilities for future exchange rates, the expected values of the exchange rates from the two perspectives are not reciprocals of each other. This mathematical feature of reciprocal relationships (called *Jensen's inequality*) results in a curious inconsistency when dealing with expected exchange rates (or percentage changes). Apparently, the expected exchange rate depends on whether the exchange rate is expressed in a direct or an indirect quotation convention, even though the investors have no disagreement about the distribution of possible outcomes. Most analysts agree, however, that this inconsistency is more of a mathematical curiosity than a phenomenon of any economic importance.[1]

---

[1]This bias affects primarily the arithmetic mean. The median, mode, and geometric mean are unaffected by how the exchange rate is quoted (Roper 1975).

Illustration of Siegel's Paradox

Suppose the current USD/FX exchange rate is 1.0 and both investors agree that the exchange rate will move up or down with a probability of 0.5; the probable outcomes, then, are

Probability	USD/FX Exchange Rate	FX/USD Exchange Rate
0.5	0.80	1.2500
0.5	1.20	0.8333

> The expected value, $E(S)$, of the USD/FX exchange rate would be
>
> $$E(S) = 0.5(0.80) + 0.5(1.20)$$
> $$= 1.0000,$$
>
> and the expected value of the FX/USD exchange rate would be
>
> $$E(1/S) = 0.5(1.25) + 0.5(0.8333)$$
> $$= 1.0417.$$
>
> From the USD/FX perspective, no change in the exchange rate would be expected, whereas from the FX/USD perspective, the FX/USD rate would be expected to increase. The preservation of exchange rate symmetry would dictate that if rates are expected to remain unchanged from one perspective, they are expected to remain unchanged from the other perspective. Because of the nonlinear property of the reciprocal relationship, however, the symmetry of expected values is not preserved.
>
> Using the natural log transformation of the exchange rates does preserve the symmetry of the expected values: From the USD/FX perspective,
>
> $$E[\ln(S)] = 0.5[\ln(0.80)] + 0.5[\ln(1.20)]$$
> $$= -0.0204,$$
>
> and from the FX/USD perspective,
>
> $$E[\ln(1/S)] = 0.5[\ln(1.25)] + 0.5[\ln(0.8333)]$$
> $$= 0.0204.$$
>
> Taking the antilog of the expected log values gives
>
> $$e^{-0.0204} = 0.9798$$
>
> and
>
> $$e^{0.0204} = 1.0206.$$
>
> These antilogs are now reciprocals of each other, but although the symmetry between perspectives is preserved, neither transformed value (antilog of the resulting value) is equal to the expected exchange rate. The nonlinear nature of exchange rate reciprocals leads to an inconsistency between the expected values (arithmetic means) of exchange rates.

One of the suggestions sometimes made to deal with Siegel's paradox when working with percentage changes comes from the following analysis: The expected value of the sum of the rates of return from the two investors' perspectives, using Equation 1.2, is

$$E(r_c + r_f) = E\left(r_c - \frac{r_c}{1 + r_c}\right)$$

$$= E\left(\frac{r_c^2}{1 + r_c}\right). \quad (1.7)$$

By using a Taylor's series expansion, this expected value is approximately equal to

$$E\left(\frac{r_c^2}{1 + r_c}\right) \approx \frac{E(r_c^2)}{1 + E(r_c)}$$

$$= \frac{\mathrm{var}(r_c) + E(r_c)^2}{1 + E(r_c)}, \quad (1.8)$$

where $\text{var}(r_c)$ represents the variance of the currency return from the home investor's perspective.

A common argument is that in an efficient market, in which investors from each perspective share homogeneous expectations, $E(r_c)$ is close to zero. Based on this argument, the expression in Equation 1.8 can be approximated by

$$E(r_c + r_f) = E\left(\frac{r_c^2}{1+r_c}\right)$$

$$\approx \text{var}(r_c). \tag{1.9}$$

The discrepancy caused by Siegel's paradox is often split between the two perspectives so that, in the context of an efficient market, the long-run expected discrete returns are slightly positive from both perspectives:

$$E(r_f) = E(r_c)$$

$$= \frac{\text{var}(r_c)}{2}. \tag{1.10}$$

As noted earlier, however, the phenomenon disappears when one uses continuously compounded rates of return.

Implied Cross-Rates and Currency Returns

Because exchange rates express a relationship between two currencies, one can use the relationship of each separate currency to a common currency to imply a relationship between the two separate currencies. This implied exchange rate is referred to as the *implied cross-rate*. For example, if $_xS_y$ represents the spot exchange rate between currencies x and y from the perspective of currency x (that is, currency x/currency y) and $_xS_z$ represents the exchange rate between currencies x and z, the implied cross-rate between currencies y and z from the perspective of currency y would be

$$_yS_z = \frac{_xS_z}{_xS_y}. \tag{1.11}$$

Actual cross-rates for most currencies are typically very close to the implied cross-rates because any major discrepancies create opportunities for arbitrageurs to create riskless profits by pitting the actual cross-rate against the implied cross-rate.

The cross-rate relationship also has implications for currency returns. Using Equation 1.11 to express the relationship between currency returns gives

$$1 + {_yr_z} = \frac{1 + {_xr_z}}{1 + {_xr_y}}. \tag{1.12}$$

Solving for the discrete cross-rate return between currency y and currency z gives

$$_yr_z = \frac{{_xr_z} - {_xr_y}}{1 + {_xr_y}} \tag{1.13}$$

or, as a first approximation,

$$_yr_z \approx {_xr_z} - {_xr_y}, \tag{1.14}$$

indicating that the discrete currency return between currency y and currency z is approximately equal to the return between currency x and currency z minus the return between currency x and currency y.

A more exact relationship can be expressed with continuously compounded returns using the log transformation

$$\ln(1 + {_yr_z}) = \ln(1 + {_xr_z}) - \ln(1 + {_xr_y})$$

or

$$_yr_z^* = {_xr_z^*} - {_xr_y^*}, \tag{1.15}$$

where $_xr_y^*$ represents the continuously compounded return between currency x and currency y.

Currency Cross-Rates

For an example of the cross-rate relationship, consider the following exchange rates between the U.S. dollar and the Japanese yen and between the U.S. dollar and the British pound:

	Period 1	Period 2
Yen/USD	110.000	105.000
USD/BP	1.470	1.488
Implied yen/BP	161.700	156.240

The implied cross-rate in Period 1 between the British pound (£) and the Japanese yen (¥) is calculated as

$$_¥S_£ = {_¥S_{US\$}}({_{US\$}S_£})$$

$$= 110(1.470)$$

$$= 161.70;$$

the implied cross-rate in Period 2 would be

$$_¥S_£ = 105(1.488)$$

$$= 156.24.$$

The discrete and continuously compounded returns from Period 1 to Period 2 would be

	Discrete Return	Continuous Return
USD/yen	4.762%	4.652%
USD/BP	1.225	1.217
Implied yen/BP	−3.377	−3.435

Note that, to a first approximation, the discrete percentage cross-rate return would be 1.225 − 4.762 = −3.537 percent, compared with the actual discrete percentage return of −3.377 percent.

Hedged and Unhedged Asset Returns

The local return on a foreign asset in home currency units is a function of the local return on the foreign asset in foreign currency units and the currency return.[2] That is, the discrete return on a foreign asset translated into home currency units can be written as

$$1 + R = (1 + r_\ell)(1 + r_c) \tag{1.16}$$

where

R = the foreign local asset return expressed in home currency terms

r_ℓ = the foreign local asset return expressed in foreign currency terms (local asset return or asset return for the local investor)

r_c = currency return (percentage change in exchange rates using the home currency/foreign currency convention).

---

[2] The unhedged asset return expressed in home currency terms from the point of view of the U.S.-based investor is sometimes referred to as the *U.S.-dollar-based asset return* or the *asset return in* (translated to) *U.S. dollars*. It reflects the foreign local asset return expressed in home currency units (that is, unhedged).

Solving for the discrete percentage return gives

$$R = r_\ell + r_c + r_\ell r_c, \quad (1.17a)$$

which is approximately equal to

$$R \approx r_\ell + r_c. \quad (1.17b)$$

The cross-product term, $r_\ell r_c$, is typically small and is often ignored in the analysis of currency returns. When ignoring it simplifies the analysis without significant loss, we also will ignore it.

The purchase of a forward contract obligates the buyer to exchange the home currency into the foreign currency at the forward rate. The return from purchasing a forward contract and holding it to expiration depends on the forward premium at the time the contract is purchased and the currency return during the same time period. Because the purchase of the forward contract is an obligation to exchange the home currency for the foreign currency at the forward rate, the gain or loss from purchasing the forward contract will equal the spot exchange rate at expiration minus the initial forward rate. The percentage return from purchasing the forward contract relative to the spot exchange rate will equal the percentage change in the spot exchange rate minus the forward discount (or premium) embedded in the forward contract. That is, the return from purchasing a forward contract and holding it to expiration as a percentage of the home currency committed in the transaction is

$$\text{Forward contract return} = \frac{S - F}{S_o}$$

$$= r_c - f, \quad (1.18)$$

where r_c is the percentage change in the spot exchange rate and f is the forward premium (or discount) in the forward rate. This return on the forward contract is sometimes referred to as the *forward surprise* and represents the difference between the actual change in the spot exchange rate and the forward premium.

Combining investment positions in a foreign asset and a forward contract allows an examination of the composite returns on a hedged or unhedged foreign asset when translated into the home currency. Using the forward contract return with the unhedged asset return in Equation 1.16 provides a combined gross return of

$$1 + R = (1 + r_\ell)(1 + r_c) + h(r_c - f)$$

$$= 1 + r_\ell + r_c + r_\ell r_c + h(r_c - f), \quad (1.19)$$

where h is the fraction of the total asset exposure hedged—often called the *hedge ratio*. The hedge ratio is usually a negative number because forward contracts must be sold to create the hedge.

By disregarding the small cross-product, we can approximate the asset return as

$$R \approx (r_\ell + r_c) + h(r_c - f) \quad (1.20a)$$

$$\approx (r_\ell + f) + H(r_c - f), \quad (1.20b)$$

where $H = 1 + h$, the proportion of the total asset exposure left unhedged (that is, the currency exposure ratio).

Equation 1.20a indicates that the combined return is equal to the unhedged asset return plus the gain or loss from the currency hedge constructed by selling the forward contract. The perspective in Equation 1.20b is often useful, however, because it shows that the combined return also can be thought of as a fully hedged asset return plus the currency return from investing in a forward contract.

These relationships can be illustrated by examining the two polar cases. For an unhedged asset, the relationship between the asset return in home currency units and the local asset return can be seen by setting $h = 0$ (or $H = 1$). The *unhedged foreign asset return* is equal to the foreign asset return in local currency units plus the currency return. For a U.S. investor, the unhedged foreign asset return is often referred to as the *dollar-denominated return*:

$$R_{UH} \approx r_\ell + r_c. \quad (1.21)$$

Using continuously compounded rates of return produces

$$R^*_{UH} = \ln(1 + R_{UH})$$

$$= \ln(1 + r_\ell) + \ln(1 + r_c)$$

$$= r^*_\ell + r^*_c, \quad (1.22)$$

where the asterisk indicates a continuously compounded rate of return.

If the currency exposure in a foreign asset is hedged by selling a forward contract ($h = -1$ or $H = 0$), the *hedged return on the foreign asset* will be equal to the local asset return plus the forward premium (discount) in the forward contract. The forward premium (discount) is the price the hedger receives (pays) to hedge the currency risk in the foreign asset:

$$R_H \approx r_\ell + f. \quad (1.23)$$

Unfortunately, the fully hedged return has no continuously compounded return that can be easily decomposed like the unhedged asset return can because of the additive nature of the terms in Equation 1.19. Consequently, the returns based on discrete compounding are typically used instead of continuously compounded returns.

These interrelationships are pictured in Figure 1.1. Beginning with the foreign local asset return, the unhedged asset return is equal to the local asset return plus the currency return. The hedged asset return is equal to the local asset return plus the forward premium. Finally, the difference between the unhedged and hedged returns is equal to the difference between the currency return and the forward premium. This difference reflects the return on a forward contract used either to hedge or create the foreign currency exposure.

Figure 1.1. Relationship between Hedged and Unhedged Asset Returns

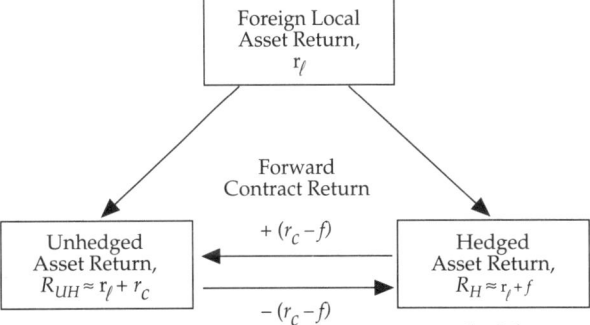

An important aspect to note is that the foreign local asset return is not available by itself to the domestic investor in terms of the investor's home currency. The foreign local asset return either carries with it the currency exposure or requires that its currency risk be hedged away at the cost of the forward discount or gain of the forward premium.

Hedged and Unhedged Asset Returns

For an illustration of the difference between a hedged and an unhedged foreign asset return, consider the following example:

$r_\ell = 5.2\%$

$r_c = -1.2$

$f = -0.4$.

If the currency exposure in the foreign asset is left unhedged, the approximate unhedged return to the domestic investor is

$R_{UH} \approx r_\ell + r_c$

$= 5.2 - 1.2$

$= 4.0\%$.

If the currency exposure is hedged, however, the approximate hedged return to the domestic investor is

$R_H \approx r_\ell + f$

$= 5.2 - 0.4$

$= 4.8\%$.

In this case, hedging has raised the return because the -1.2 percent currency return was less than the -0.4 percent cost of the hedge embedded in the forward discount.[3]

---

[3]Remember that we have disregarded the cross-product term between the foreign asset return and the currency return. In this example, the cross-product term would amount to $0.052(-0.012) = -0.06$ percent, a reduction in the approximate returns of only 6 basis points.

Table 1.1. Average Annualized Forward Premiums

Year	German Mark	British Pound	Japanese Yen	Australian Dollar	Canadian Dollar	French Franc	Swiss Franc
1980	4.74%	−2.68%	0.43%	0.95%	1.83%	2.17%	NA
1981	6.97	3.26	6.12	3.18	−1.84	−2.13	NA
1982	3.89	0.66	3.64	−1.76	−2.12	−7.71	NA
1983	4.68	−1.81	2.07	−1.56	−1.09	−6.50	NA
1984	5.78	0.79	4.33	−0.27	−0.59	−1.68	6.56
1985	3.62	−4.20	1.73	−7.05	−1.47	−2.48	3.74
1986	2.80	−4.13	3.28	−8.34	−2.53	−3.09	2.79
1987	2.96	−2.84	3.11	−9.38	−1.36	−1.54	3.29
1988	3.71	−2.14	4.55	−6.16	−1.43	−0.13	5.40
1989	2.44	−4.48	4.36	−8.69	−2.65	0.06	2.29
1990	0.00	−6.35	0.85	−6.91	−4.51	−1.62	0.94
1991	−3.07	−5.79	−1.52	−4.63	−3.10	−3.46	−2.19
1992	−5.96	−6.07	−0.80	−2.37	−3.01	−7.13	−4.28
1993	−4.97	−2.92	0.10	−2.51	−1.84	−5.90	−2.07

Note: Calculations of average annualized forward premiums are based on an average of one-month forward premiums multiplied by 12. Exchange rates are quoted in units of USD/FX.
NA = not available.

It is the forward premium (or discount) that contributes to the cost of currency hedging. Hedging foreign assets when foreign interest rates are high relative to domestic interest rates will reduce the foreign local asset return (because the forward rate is priced at a discount). Hedging when foreign interest rates are low relative to domestic interest rates will increase the foreign local asset return. Consequently, the "cost" of hedging can be either positive or negative, depending on the interest rate environments in the two countries.

Table 1.1 shows the average annualized forward premiums for various currencies year by year since 1980. Note that in recent years, from a U.S. investor's perspective, hedging foreign investments has often reduced returns because of the forward discount caused by higher foreign interest rates. Germany, Japan, and Switzerland have been exceptions until recently.

Equation 1.23 suggests that a complete hedge can eliminate all of the currency risk from holding the foreign asset, but when the asset return is uncertain, the hedge does not have this capability because the size of the full currency exposure is unknown when the hedge is put in place. Remember, the small cross-product term $r_\ell r_c$ is often disregarded in Equation 1.19, so the cross-product term representing the currency exposure of the return on the asset itself always creates some noise in the hedging relationship; it cannot be hedged exactly if the asset return is uncertain. The exposure is typically small relative to the currency exposure in the principal amount, however, and the size of the hedge can be adjusted periodically to adjust for the slippage.[4]

Hedging and Cash Flows

The cash flow consequences of hedging are important to understand because returns from hedging may be realized at a different time from the currency translation gains or losses from the underlying assets. The returns from currency hedging are usually realized and settled in cash, whereas the currency translation gains or losses associated with holding foreign assets are usu-

---

[4]Sometimes, the expected slippage created by the cross-product term is dealt with by setting $h = -[1 + E(r_\ell)]$, where $E(r_\ell)$ is the expected local return on the foreign asset. In this case, the *ex post* return realized from the hedge will be $R_H = r_\ell + f + fE(r_\ell) + r_c[r_\ell - E(r_\ell)]$. The last two terms are typically an order of magnitude smaller than the first two because they represent the product of two returns. In the event the actual return on the asset turns out to equal its expected return, the realized hedged return will be independent of the currency return, giving $R_H = r_\ell + f + fr_\ell$. For any other realized local asset return, the hedged return will always depend to some extent on the actual currency return.

Figure 1.2. Currency Hedging and Cash Flows

	Foreign Currency Appreciates	Foreign Currency Depreciates
Foreign Assets	Unrealized Translation Gains until Assets Repatriated	Unrealized Translation Losses until Assets Repatriated
Currency Hedge	Realized FX Losses Settled in Cash	Realized FX Gains Settled in Cash
Short-Run Impact on Portfolio Cash Flow	Cash Outflows	Cash Inflows

ally not realized until the assets are sold and the proceeds repatriated.

This asymmetry between the realization of gains and losses can present challenges for the management of cash flows in the portfolio. For example, suppose a U.S. investor hedges the British pound exposure in a portfolio of U.K. stocks. If the pound appreciates relative to the U.S. dollar, the U.K. stock portfolio will have a gain from currency translation, but no cash will be realized from the appreciation of the pound until the stocks are sold and the proceeds converted into U.S. dollars. On the other hand, the currency hedge will have generated a loss, which is realized at the maturity of the forward contracts used to hedge (or realized on a daily basis if futures contracts are used). The realized losses will drain cash from the portfolio until the unrealized gains can be liquidated to cover the realized losses. Depreciation of the foreign currency produces the opposite effect. The realized gains from the currency hedge generate cash in the portfolio to offset the unrealized translation losses on the underlying assets. Figure 1.2 summarizes the cash flow implications of currency hedging in a portfolio.

Some investors are reluctant to become involved in hedging currency risk because of the cash flow issues. It is not uncommon for a portfolio manager to leave the international part of a portfolio unhedged because doing so avoids having to deal with the cash shortfall if the currency appreciates while the hedge is in place.

Other investors have become alarmed over the results of a hedging program when they have had to supply cash to a portfolio as the dollar depreciated and the hedge generated a loss. They have often failed to realize that the assets have unrealized gains that offset the realized losses from the hedge. Failure to see the complete picture often leads to a misinterpretation of the results and poor decision making when it comes to currency hedging.

Cash Flow Implications of Currency Hedging

The cash flow implications of currency hedging can be illustrated with a simple example. Suppose a £100 million portfolio of U.K. stocks (UK) has the following characteristics over a three-month period (percents):

$r_{UK} = 3.0$

$r_£ = 2.0$

$f = -0.4.$

The unhedged portfolio will appreciate approximately 5.0 percent in U.S. dollar terms:

$$R_{UH} \approx r_{UK} + r_£$$
$$= 3.0 + 2.0$$
$$= 5.0\%.$$

The unrealized gain on the stock portfolio in U.S. dollars is

$$0.05(£100,000,000) = US\$5,000,000,$$

composed of a gain of US$3,000,000 from the stocks and US$2,000,000 from currency appreciation.

The hedged return on the portfolio is approximately

$$R_H \approx r_{UK} + f$$
$$= 3.0 - 0.4$$
$$= 2.6\%,$$

resulting in a dollar gain of

$$0.026(£100,000,000) = US\$2,600,000,$$

composed of US$3,000,000 from the stocks minus US$400,000 from the discount on the forward contract.

The difference between the unrealized gain on the underlying stock portfolio and the return on the hedged portfolio is equal to the realized loss on the currency hedge from the short forward contract.

$$\text{Currency hedge} = -(r_£ - f)(£100,000,000)$$
$$= -(2.0 + 0.4)(£100,000,000)$$
$$= -US\$2,400,000,$$

composed of a loss of US$2,000,000 from the currency appreciation and a loss of US$400,000 from the forward discount. The hedged portfolio would have an unrealized gain of US$5,000,000 but a cash loss of US$2,400,000, giving a net gain of US$2,600,000:

Unrealized gain on stocks	US$5,000,000	5.0%
Realized loss on currency hedge	−2,400,000	−2.4
Net gain	US$2,600,000	2.6%

Covered Interest Arbitrage and the Forward Premium

By using Equation 1.19, we can show what happens to the return of a fully hedged, riskless, foreign asset. If the number of forward contracts is set properly, all of the currency risk can be removed (even the effect of the small cross-product term, because the riskless return is not uncertain). With the currency risk hedged away, the combination of the riskless foreign asset and the currency hedge should yield the riskless rate in the base currency to avoid arbitrage profits. Setting the hedge ratio h equal to $[-(1 + i_f t)]$ in Equation 1.19 in order to hedge the currency risk of the principal as well as the interest earned until expiration produces

$$1 + R_H = (1 + i_\ell t)(1 + r_c) - (1 + i_\ell t)(r_c - f)$$
$$= (1 + i_\ell t) - (1 + f)$$
$$= (1 + i_d t), \quad (1.24)$$

where i_ℓ is the foreign riskless interest rate (annualized), i_d is the domestic riskless interest rate (annualized), and t is time to expiration of the forward contract (fraction of a year).

Rearranging Equation 1.24 to solve for the forward premium shows that it is related to the relative riskless interest rates between the two countries with maturities equal to the maturity of the forward contract.[5] This relationship is called covered interest arbitrage or *covered interest parity*:

$$\frac{F}{S_o} = 1 + f$$
$$= \frac{1 + i_d t}{1 + i_\ell t} \quad (1.25a)$$

or

$$f \approx (i_d - i_\ell)t, \quad (1.25b)$$

where F is the current forward foreign exchange rate with maturity t and S_o is the current spot foreign exchange rate.

The arbitrage relationship can also be expressed using continuously compounded interest rates:[6]

$$F = S_o e^{(i_d^* - i_\ell^*)t}. \quad (1.26)$$

In practice, the covered interest arbitrage relationship is usually quite accurate for liquid currencies. Any substantial deviation from covered interest arbitrage is usually quickly closed by active arbitrage traders.

Covered interest arbitrage implies that one

---

[5]The forward premium or discount is often quoted on an annualized basis similar to the way simple interest rates are quoted. If this convention is used, f can be conveniently replaced in each formula by $f_a t$, where f_a represents the annualized forward premium or discount. The annualized forward premium can then be approximated by $f_a \approx i_d - i_\ell$.

[6]A continuous-rate analog to the discrete forward premium also exists; it is defined as $f^* = \ln(1 + f) = \ln(1 + i_d t) - \ln(1 + i_\ell t) = (i_d^* - i_\ell^*)t$. The annualized form of the continuously compounded forward premium would be $f_a^* = f^*/t = i_d^* - i_\ell^*$.

Table 1.2. Covered Interest Arbitrage: Example Scenarios

	Pound Declines 10% to 1.3500	Pound Increases 10% to 1.6500
Interest cost	$ −50,000	$ −50,000
Interest earned	90,000	110,000
P/L[a] on principal currency translation	−100,000	100,000
P/L on hedge	60,000	−160,000
Net P/L	$ 0	$ 0

[a]Profit or loss.

cannot profit by borrowing in a low-interest-rate country, converting to the currency of a high-interest-rate country, lending in that country, and hedging away the currency risk. The interest rate advantage is exactly offset by the cost of hedging.

For example, suppose that the spot rate to exchange dollars for pounds is 1.5000 and that the one-year interest rate is 5 percent in the United States and 10 percent in the United Kingdom. The one-year forward rate must equal 1.43182 (that is, 1.5[1.05/1.10]). Table 1.2 shows the flows that would occur in two scenarios for an investor borrowing US$1 million in the United States, lending it in the United Kingdom, and hedging away the currency risk. One scenario assumes that the pound depreciates 10 percent versus the dollar; the other scenario assumes that the pound appreciates 10 percent.

First, consider the scenario in which the pound depreciates 10 percent. The interest cost is US$50,000 (5 percent of US$1,000,000). The investor converts the US$1,000,000 to £666,666.67 (that is, US$1,000,000/1.5000), and lends this amount at a rate of 10 percent. This transaction yields interest equal to £66,666.67, which is converted to US$90,000 at the end of the period (£66,666.67[1.3500]). The £666,666.67 of principal are converted back to US$900,000, resulting in a US$100,000 loss. The investor also hedges the loan by selling £733,333.34 forward at an exchange rate of 1.43182, which is the amount necessary to hedge both the principal and the interest (£666,666.67 + £66,666.67). This hedge position results in a gain of US$60,000 because the

£733,333.34 that were sold at 1.43182 are repurchased at 1.3500, producing a gain of £733,333.34 × (1.43182 − 1.3500) = US$60,000. The net result of all these transactions is a return of zero.

In the scenario in which the pound increases 10 percent, the investor also incurs an interest cost of US$50,000, but the loan generates interest income equal to US$110,000 and a profit on the principal exposure of US$100,000. The hedge position generates a loss of US$160,000 because the forward contract that was sold at 1.43182 is repurchased at 1.65000. So, again, the net result is neither a gain nor a loss. Indeed, as long as the hedge is implemented precisely, the result will be no gain and no loss at the end of the period regardless of the level of the spot exchange rate.

If the forward contract in this example had been priced above 1.43182—at, say, 1.4500—arbitrageurs would have earned a profit from the transactions. With a 10 percent decline in the pound, the hedge position would generate a US$73,333.33 gain and a net profit of US$13,333.33. With a 10 percent rise in the pound, the hedge position would produce a loss of US$146,666.67 and a net profit of US$13,333.33. If the forward contract had been priced below 1.43182, arbitrageurs could have profited by reversing the preceding transactions. Clearly, such transactions would quickly drive the forward price to its fair value.

Forward Points and the Forward Premium

The forward rate derived from the covered interest arbitrage relationship is a function of the current spot rate, the differential interest rates between the two countries, and the maturity of the forward contract. Suppose the following data represent the relationship between the U.S. dollar and the German mark:

S_o = 0.6000 USD/DM
i_{US} = 5.1%
i_{GER} = 7.8%
t = 180 days (using a 360-day year).

The forward rate for 180 days would be

$$F = S_o \left(\frac{1 + i_{US}t}{1 + i_{GER}t} \right)$$

$$= \frac{0.60[1 + 0.051(180/360)]}{1 + 0.078(180/360)}$$

$$= 0.5922 \text{ USD/DM}.$$

This forward rate could be quoted in forward points as

$$\text{Forward points} = F - S_o$$

$$= 0.5922 - 0.6000$$

$$= -0.0078 \text{ USD/DM}.$$

The forward premium would be negative and equal to

$$f = \frac{\text{Forward points}}{S_o}$$

$$= \frac{-0.0078}{0.6000}$$

$$= -1.30\%,$$

or, by approximation, using the relative interest rates,

$$f \approx (i_{US} - i_{GER})t$$
$$= (0.051 - 0.078)(180/360)$$
$$= -1.35\%.$$

The annualized equivalent would be

$$f_a = \frac{f}{t}$$
$$= \frac{-1.30}{180/360}$$
$$= -2.60\%.$$

The continuously compounded annualized interest rates would be

$$i^*_{US} = \frac{\ln(1 + i_{US}t)}{t}$$
$$= \frac{\ln[1 + 0.051(180/360)]}{180/360}$$
$$= 5.04\%$$

and

$$i^*_{GER} = \frac{\ln(1 + i_{GER}t)}{t}$$
$$= \frac{\ln[1 + 0.078(180/360)]}{180/360}$$
$$= 7.65\%,$$

giving an annualized continuously compounded forward premium of

$$f^*_a = i^*_{US} - i^*_{GER}$$
$$= 5.04 - 7.65$$
$$= -2.61\%.$$

Using these continuously compounded rates in the covered interest arbitrage relationship gives

$$F = S_o e^{(i^*_{US} - i^*_{GER})t}$$
$$= 0.60 e^{(0.0504 - 0.0765)(180/360)}$$
$$= 0.5922 \text{ USD/DM},$$

which results in the same forward rate as using the discrete formulation.

> ### Hedged Foreign Asset Returns
>
> Investors sometimes structure portfolios to take advantage of steeper yield curves in foreign markets than in the domestic market. When attempting to capture the larger yield differential between short-term and long-term foreign interest rates, the investor can hedge away much of the short-term currency risk, as can be seen in the hedged return from such a strategy given in Equation 1.26.
>
> Suppose three-month Eurodollar rates are 4 percent while Euroyen rates are 2 percent. Furthermore, suppose that long-term U.S. rates are 7 percent while long-term Japanese rates are 6 percent. If the expected return in each bond market is equal to its yield, the annualized expected return from a hedged Japanese bond portfolio over the next three months would be
>
> $$E(R_H) \approx E(r_\ell) + f_a$$
> $$= 6.0 + 2.0$$
> $$= 8.0\%,$$
>
> where the annualized forward premium is equal to the short-term interest rate differential: $f_a \approx i_d - i_\ell = 4.0 - 2.0 = 2.0$ percent.
>
> The 8 percent annualized expected return compares favorably with the 7 percent expected return in the U.S. bond market. The incremental expected return of 1.0 percent occurs because of the 1.0 percent difference in the yield curve between the two countries. The investor has substituted Japanese for U.S. interest rate risk, however, and will have to decide if the difference in expected return is worth the difference in risk.

Looking at the hedged asset return from another point of view gives an interesting perspective. We have seen that the forward premium is related to the short-term interest rate differential between the two countries. When the hedged asset return in Equation 1.23 is used with the forward premium in Equation 1.25b, the hedged asset return can be approximated as

$$R_H \approx r_\ell + f$$
$$= i_d t + (r_\ell - i_\ell t). \qquad (1.27)$$

As a result, the hedged asset return can be thought of as being equal to the domestic riskless interest rate plus the risk premium on the foreign risky asset.[7] It is the forward premium in the hedging relationship that adjusts for the difference in interest rates between the two countries. Hedging a foreign asset allows the foreign asset to pass along its local risk premium but then adjusts the total return to reflect the level of interest rates in the investor's home currency.

It is interesting to examine the return that results from investing funds in short-term domestic cash reserves and purchasing a forward contract of the appropriate size. If a contract equal to $(1 + i_\ell t)$ per unit of home currency is purchased, this strategy is equivalent to exchanging the home currency for the foreign currency and subsequently investing the foreign funds at the foreign short-term interest rate. Using the covered interest arbitrage relationship of Equation 1.25a gives the return to the home currency investor as

$$R = i_d t + (1 + i_\ell t)(r_c - f)$$
$$= (1 + i_\ell t)(1 + r_c) - 1$$
$$\approx i_\ell t + r_c. \qquad (1.28)$$

The first line in Equation 1.28 represents the return from investing cash domestically plus the return from purchasing the forward contract; rearranging terms gives the second line, which

---

[7] The exact relationship using all of the cross-product terms from Equation 1.24 is $R_H = i_d t + (r_\ell - i_\ell t) + r_\ell r_c - [i_\ell t(i_d t - i_\ell t)]/(1 + i_\ell t)$.

> **Foreign Cash Reserves versus Forward Contracts**
>
> Investors in low-interest-rate countries often pursue increased yield by investing in foreign high-interest-rate cash reserves. Equation 1.27 showed that this strategy is equivalent to leaving funds in cash reserves in the investor's home currency while buying foreign currency futures or a forward contract of the same maturity. In each case, the investor's return will be equal to the foreign interest rate plus the currency return.
>
> For an illustration of this equivalence, consider a U.S. investor with an opportunity to invest in three-month Eurodollar deposits yielding 4 percent versus Euromark deposits yielding 6 percent. Because of the covered interest arbitrage relationship, the annualized forward exchange premium should be
>
> $$f_a \approx 4.0 - 6.0$$
> $$= -2.0\%.$$
>
> If the German mark depreciates by 1 percent during the next three months, the investor's return from holding Eurodollars and buying the forward contract will be
>
> $$R = i_d t + (1 + i_\ell t)(r_c - f_a t)$$
> $$= 4.0(3/12) + [1 + 0.06(3/12)][-1.0 + 2.0(3/12)]$$
> $$= 0.5\%.$$
>
> The investor's return from investing in Euromark deposits will be approximately
>
> $$R \approx i_\ell t + r_c$$
> $$= 6.0(3/12) - 1.0$$
> $$= 0.5\%.$$
>
> The equivalence comes from the fact that the forward premium or discount keeps the hedged foreign interest rate equivalent to the domestic interest rate.

represents the return from investing unhedged funds at the foreign short-term interest rate. These two strategies are equivalent ways of achieving the same return because of the arbitrage relationship embedded in the forward premium.

Note in Equation 1.25a that the forward exchange rate is a function of the current spot exchange rate and the relationship between interest rates in the two countries. The forward exchange rate does not have to be an unbiased predictor of the future spot exchange rate; that is, $F \neq E(S)$. The idea that the forward rate is an unbiased predictor of the future spot rate is sometimes referred to as *uncovered interest parity*, and empirical evidence shows that it generally has not held in the past (see Froot and Thaler 1990). Current forward exchange rates do not seem to be unbiased predictors of future spot rates because forward exchange rates are driven by the potential arbitrage of interest rate levels between countries. Those differences in interest rates often do not maintain a tight relationship with expected future exchange rates. Much of the empirical evidence suggests that current spot exchange rates are better predictors of future spot rates than are forward exchange rates. This evidence is examined in more detail in Chapter 2.

Statistical Relationships: Expected Returns and Risk

The analysis of risk and expected returns associated with asset and currency positions in a portfolio requires a discussion of some statistical relationships. In an effort to keep the algebra as simple as possible in this section, we will examine the risk and expected return for a simple portfolio composed of a domestic asset and a foreign asset. A little generalization allows the substitution of a portfolio of domestic and foreign assets for the individual assets without changing the framework. For the broadest application, the framework can be expanded to a general portfolio of many different domestic and foreign assets, each with a separate currency exposure.

Expected Returns. The discrete percentage return on a foreign asset translated into home currency units was given in Equation 1.20b. If a domestic asset and a foreign asset are combined in a simple portfolio, that relationship can be used to examine the expected portfolio return.

Disregarding the cross-product term between the foreign local asset return and the currency return allows the expected portfolio return to be expressed as

$$E(R) = w_d E(r_d) + w_\ell [E(r_\ell) + f] + H[E(r_c) - f], \quad (1.29)$$

where

- w_d = the portfolio proportion held in the domestic asset
- $w_\ell = 1 - w_d$, the portfolio proportion held in the foreign asset
- H = the proportion of the total portfolio with foreign currency exposure.

Sometimes, comparing the expected return on a portfolio with a benchmark portfolio return is useful. Isolating this difference is particularly important when the investor has a specific benchmark portfolio as a neutral position and wants to see how the actual portfolio is performing relative to that neutral position. (To isolate the difference resulting from asset allocation and currency hedging, we are assuming here no active management in the underlying portfolio segments, so each portfolio segment performs like its respective benchmark segment.) The expected return relative to a benchmark is given by

$$E(\Delta R) = \Delta w_d E(r_d) + \Delta w_\ell [E(r_\ell) + f] + \Delta H [E(r_c) - f] \quad (1.30)$$

where

- Δw_d = the difference between the portfolio and the benchmark domestic asset exposure
- Δw_ℓ = the difference between the portfolio and the benchmark foreign asset exposure
- ΔH = the difference between the portfolio and the benchmark foreign currency exposure.

Figure 1.3. Risk Relationships in a Portfolio

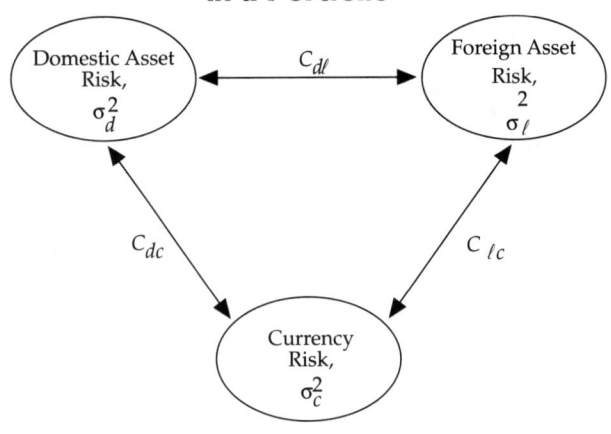

Risk Measures: Variance and Covariance. The variance of the return on a portfolio that contains both a domestic and a foreign asset can be found by taking the variance of the total portfolio return. The variance is a function of the individual asset and currency variances plus the interactions between them, as shown in Figure 1.3:

$$\sigma_R^2 = w_d^2 \sigma_d^2 + w_\ell^2 \sigma_\ell^2 + H^2 \sigma_c^2 + 2 w_d w_\ell C_{d\ell} + 2H(w_d C_{dc} + w_\ell C_{\ell c}) \quad (1.31)$$

where

σ_d^2 = the variance of domestic asset returns

σ_ℓ^2 = the variance of foreign local asset returns
σ_c^2 = the variance of currency returns
$C_{d\ell}$ = the covariance of domestic asset returns with foreign local asset returns
$C_{\ell c}$ = the covariance of foreign local asset returns with currency returns
C_{dc} = the covariance of domestic asset returns with currency returns.

The covariance between two returns can be expressed as a function of their own variances and a correlation coefficient that ranges between plus and minus 1.0. For example, the covariances between asset returns and between asset and currency returns can be expressed as:

$$C_{d\ell} = \rho_{d\ell}\sigma_d\sigma_\ell,$$
$$C_{dc} = \rho_{dc}\sigma_d\sigma_c,$$

and

$$C_{\ell c} = \rho_{\ell c}\sigma_\ell\sigma_c,$$

where

$\rho_{d\ell}$ = the correlation between domestic asset returns and foreign local asset returns
ρ_{dc} = the correlation between domestic asset returns and currency returns
$\rho_{\ell c}$ = the correlation between foreign local asset returns and currency returns.

Note the variance of a portfolio at the extremes, where the currency is either unhedged or fully hedged. For the fully hedged portfolio ($H = 0$), the variance is

$$\sigma_R^2(\text{Fully hedged}) = w_d^2\sigma_d^2 + w_\ell^2\sigma_\ell^2 + 2w_dw_\ell C_{d\ell}. \quad (1.32)$$

Hedging out the currency risk leaves the variance of the portfolio as a function of the individual asset variances and the covariance between asset returns.

For an unhedged portfolio ($H = w_\ell$), the variance is

$$\sigma_R^2(\text{Unhedged}) = w_d^2\sigma_d^2 + w_\ell^2\sigma_\ell^2 + w_\ell^2\sigma_c^2$$
$$+ 2w_dw_\ell C_{d\ell}$$
$$+ 2w_\ell(w_d C_{dc} + w_\ell C_{\ell c}). \quad (1.33)$$

The variance of the unhedged portfolio will be greater than the variance of the hedged portfolio if

$$\sigma_R^2(\text{Unhedged}) - \sigma_R^2(\text{Hedged}) = w_\ell^2\sigma_c^2$$
$$+ 2w_\ell(w_d C_{dc} + w_\ell C_{\ell c}) > 0. \quad (1.34)$$

Positive correlations between asset returns and currency returns assure that the variance of an unhedged portfolio will be greater than the variance of a fully hedged portfolio. If the asset covariances with currency returns are sufficiently negative, however, hedging the currency exposure could actually increase the variance of the portfolio. Sufficiently negative correlations would allow positive currency exposure to reduce the risk of the asset positions naturally, leaving the variance of the unhedged portfolio less than that of a hedged portfolio.

The tables of Chapter 2 indicate that the average correlations between currency returns and bonds for most countries from a U.S. perspective have been positive whereas the correlations between currency returns and stocks have sometimes been slightly negative. These correlations suggest that unhedged foreign bond returns have had higher volatility than hedged foreign bond returns.

Leaving foreign equity exposure unhedged may have some chance of reducing portfolio variance. As a rough approximation of how negative the correlation must be for currency exposure to lower portfolio variance, consider a simple example in which domestic and foreign asset variances are equal and domestic and foreign local asset correlations with currency returns are also equal. In this case, Equation 1.34 reduces to

$$\rho_{\ell c} < \frac{-w_\ell\sigma_c}{2\sigma_\ell}. \quad (1.35)$$

If the correlation between asset and currency returns is less than minus one half the ratio of currency to asset volatility times the exposure to foreign assets, the unhedged portfolio will have a lower variance than the hedged portfolio.

Table 1.3 shows the threshold correlations for various proportions of foreign asset exposure needed for unhedged asset positions to lower portfolio volatility. For example, if the portfolio contains 10 percent foreign asset exposure and the currency is as volatile as the assets, the correlation between currency returns and both foreign and domestic asset returns would need

Currency Management: Concepts and Practices

Table 1.3. Threshold Correlation below Which the Unhedged Portfolio Has a Lower Variance

Percent Allocation to Foreign Assets	\multicolumn{8}{c}{Ratio of Currency Volatility to Asset Volatility}
	0.5	0.6	0.7	0.8	0.9	1.0	1.1	1.2
0	0.00	0.00	0.00	0.00	0.00	0.00	0.00	0.00
10	−0.03	−0.03	−0.03	−0.04	−0.05	−0.05	−0.06	−0.06
20	−0.05	−0.06	−0.07	−0.08	−0.09	−0.10	−0.11	−0.12
30	−0.08	−0.09	0.11	−0.12	−0.14	−0.15	−0.17	−0.18
40	−0.10	−0.12	−0.14	−0.16	−0.18	−0.20	−0.22	−0.24
50	−0.13	−0.15	−0.18	−0.20	−0.23	−0.25	−0.28	−0.30
60	−0.15	−0.18	−0.21	−0.24	−0.27	−0.30	−0.33	−0.36
70	−0.18	−0.21	−0.24	−0.28	−0.32	−0.35	−0.39	−0.42
80	−0.20	−0.24	−0.28	−0.32	−0.36	−0.40	−0.44	−0.48
90	−0.23	−0.27	−0.32	−0.36	−0.41	−0.45	−0.50	−0.54
100	−0.25	−0.30	−0.35	−0.40	−0.45	−0.50	−0.55	−0.60

Note: The correlations between currency returns and asset returns are assumed to be the same for both foreign and domestic assets.

to be less than only −0.05 for the unhedged portfolio to have a lower volatility than the hedged portfolio. The negative correlation threshold can be quite modest for a small amount of foreign asset exposure because the currency correlation with both domestic and foreign assets is assumed to be the same, which magnifies its diversifying capability. Zero correlation between currency returns and domestic asset returns forces the correlation with foreign assets to be much more negative before risk will be decreased by leaving the portfolio unhedged.[8]

Note also that if currency returns are less volatile than asset returns, the negative correlation can be somewhat closer to zero for a given level of foreign asset exposure. Higher currency volatility than asset volatility requires a more negative correlation before the volatility of an unhedged portfolio will decline. Historically, from a U.S. perspective, only a few equity correlations have reached a sufficiently negative value for any extended time period, and only occasionally; foreign bonds rarely do. As a result, most unhedged portfolios of either foreign stocks or bonds are unlikely to have lower volatility than a hedged portfolio for any extended period of time.

Another way to examine this relationship is to compare the unhedged portfolio's volatility with that of a hedged portfolio for various levels of foreign asset exposure and currency correlations. Table 1.4 shows the ratio of standard deviations between the unhedged and hedged portfolios when asset and currency variances are assumed equal and assets are uncorrelated with each other.

Notice that unless correlations are negative between assets and currencies, the unhedged portfolio volatility will always be at least as great as that of the hedged portfolio. If correlations are sufficiently negative, however, the unhedged portfolio volatility will be less than that of the hedged portfolio. The reason is that if currencies are negatively correlated with both domestic and foreign local asset returns, hedging the currency exposure reduces the natural diversification that currency exposure provides. Lower foreign asset exposure in the portfolio means less currency exposure to provide diversification, which requires that the currency be more negatively correlated to provide the same level of risk reduction.

The final consideration is the variance of the portfolio return relative to a benchmark (the tracking error). This relative variance can be found by taking the variance of the relative return in Equation 1.30, which gives

---

[8]Working with Equation 1.34 under the assumption that domestic assets are uncorrelated with currency returns forces the threshold correlation to be more negative before hedging increases the risk of the portfolio; that is, $\rho_{\ell c} < (-\sigma_c/2\sigma_\ell)$.

1. Terminology, Conventions, and Basic Relationships

$$\sigma_{\Delta R}^2 = \Delta w_d^2 \sigma_d^2 + \Delta w_\ell^2 \sigma_\ell^2$$
$$+ 2\Delta w_d \Delta w_\ell C_{d\ell}$$
$$+ \Delta H^2 \sigma_c^2 + 2\Delta H(\Delta w_d C_{dc} + \Delta w_\ell C_{\ell c}). \quad (1.36)$$

The variance relationships in Equations 1.31 and 1.36 are used in subsequent chapters to derive the optimal combination of assets and currencies in a portfolio.

Table 1.4. Ratio of Unhedged to Hedged Portfolio Variance

Percent Allocation to Foreign Assets	\multicolumn{9}{c}{Correlations between Asset and Currency Returns}
	−0.4	−0.3	−0.2	−0.1	0.0	0.1	0.2	0.3	0.4
0	1.00	1.00	1.00	1.00	1.00	1.00	1.00	1.00	1.00
10	0.97	0.98	0.99	0.99	1.00	1.01	1.02	1.03	1.03
20	0.93	0.95	0.97	0.99	1.01	1.03	1.05	1.07	1.08
30	0.89	0.93	0.96	1.00	1.03	1.06	1.09	1.13	1.15
40	0.85	0.91	0.96	1.01	1.06	1.11	1.15	1.19	1.24
50	0.83	0.91	0.97	1.04	1.10	1.16	1.21	1.26	1.31
60	0.83	0.92	1.00	1.07	1.14	1.20	1.26	1.32	1.37
70	0.85	0.94	1.02	1.09	1.16	1.23	1.29	1.35	1.41
80	0.89	0.97	1.04	1.11	1.18	1.24	1.30	1.36	1.42
90	0.92	0.99	1.06	1.13	1.19	1.25	1.30	1.36	1.41
100	0.95	1.02	1.08	1.14	1.19	1.24	1.30	1.34	1.39

Note: Asset volatilities are assumed to be 17 percent; the currency volatility is 11 percent. Domestic and foreign asset correlations with currency returns are assumed to be the same. Domestic and foreign asset returns are assumed to be uncorrelated with each other.

Expected Portfolio Returns and Risk

For an illustration of the statistical relationships, consider a simple portfolio of 80 percent U.S. stocks and 20 percent Japanese stocks, with the following expected annualized local returns and risk characteristics from the perspective of a U.S. investor (percents):

U.S. stocks	$E(r_{US}) = 15.6$	$\sigma_{US} = 13.9$
Japanese stocks	$E(r_{JP}) = 12.0$	$\sigma_{JP} = 17.3$
Currency	$E(r_¥) = -2.4$	$\sigma_¥ = 10.4$
	$f = 1.2$	

Table 1.5 contains the correlation and covariance matrixes for this example.

The expected return on the portfolio from the perspective of the U.S. investor with full foreign asset exposure to the yen ($H_¥ = 0.2$) would be

$$E(R_{UH}^{US}) = w_{US}E(r_{US}) + w_{JP}[E(r_{JP}) + f] + H_¥[E(r_¥) - f]$$
$$= 0.8(15.6) + 0.2(12.0 + 1.2) + 0.2(-2.4 - 1.2)$$
$$= 14.4\%.$$

If the currency exposure to the yen were fully hedged ($H_¥ = 0$), the expected return would be

$$E(R_H^{US}) = w_{US}E(r_{US}) + w_{JP}[E(r_{JP}) + f]$$
$$= 0.8(15.6) + 0.2(12.0 + 1.2)$$
$$= 15.1\%.$$

The variance of the unhedged portfolio from the perspective of the U.S. investor would be

$$\sigma_R^2(\text{Unhedged}) = w_d^2\sigma_d^2 + w_\ell^2\sigma_\ell^2 + w_\ell^2\sigma_c^2 + 2w_dw_\ell C_{d\ell} + 2w_\ell(w_d C_{dc} + w_\ell C_{\ell c})$$

$$= (0.8)^2(0.139)^2 + (0.2)^2(0.173)^2 + (0.2)^2(0.104)^2$$
$$+ 2(0.8)(0.2)(0.0072) + 2(0.2)[0.8(-0.0015) + 0.2(0.0036)]$$
$$= 0.01611;$$

so,

$$\sigma_R(\text{Unhedged}) = 12.79\%.$$

The variance of a fully hedged portfolio would be

$$\sigma_R^2(\text{Hedged}) = w_d^2\sigma_d^2 + w_\ell^2\sigma_\ell^2 + 2w_dw_\ell C_{d\ell}$$
$$= (0.8)^2(0.139)^2 + (0.2)^2(0.173)^2 + 2(0.8)(0.2)(0.0072)$$
$$= 0.0159;$$

so,

$$\sigma_R(\text{Hedged}) = 12.6\%.$$

Note that because the expected return on a yen forward contract is negative, hedging the Japanese stock exposure increases the expected return. The impact on risk of hedging the yen exposure is not large because of the small proportional allocation to Japanese stocks and because the negative covariance of the yen with U.S. stock returns works to reduce the currency risk somewhat if it is left unhedged.

The impact of a change in currency perspective on a portfolio's parameters can be seen by looking at the portfolio from the point of view of the yen-based investor. The expected return on the same portfolio from the perspective of the yen-based investor with full exposure to the dollar ($H_{USD} = 0.8$) would be

$$E(R_{UH}^{JP}) = 0.8(15.6 - 1.2) + 0.2(12.0) + 0.8(2.4 + 1.2)$$
$$= 16.8\%.$$

If the currency exposure to the U.S. dollar were fully hedged ($H_{USD} = 0$), the expected return would be

$$E(R_H^{JP}) = 0.8(15.6 - 1.2) + 0.2(12.0)$$
$$= 13.9\%.$$

The variance of the unhedged portfolio would be

$$\sigma_R^2(\text{Unhedged}) = (0.8)^2(0.139)^2 + (0.2)^2(0.173)^2 + (0.8)^2(0.104)^2$$
$$+ 2(0.8)(0.2)(0.0072) + 2(0.8)[0.8(0.00151) + 0.2(-0.0036)]$$
$$= 0.0236;$$

so,

$$\sigma_R(\text{Unhedged}) = 15.3\%.$$

The results can be summarized as follows:

	USD Perspective	Yen Perspective
Expected return		
Unhedged	14.4%	16.8%
Hedged	15.1	13.9
Standard deviation		
Unhedged	12.7	15.3
Hedged	12.6	12.6

Simple algebra shows that the difference in return between the hedged and unhedged perspectives depends on the allocation to the foreign currency times the expected return on the foreign currency forward contract. The difference in returns between the unhedged portfolios from the two perspectives depends on the expected currency return. Finally, the difference in return between the two hedged portfolios depends on the forward premium between the two currencies.

The risk of the two hedged portfolios depends only on the risk of the underlying assets. This risk is the same for both investors. The difference in risk between the two unhedged portfolios depends not only on the risk of the underlying assets but also on the risk of the currency and on how much currency exposure the portfolio has. In this example, the yen-based investor has larger foreign currency exposure than the U.S.-dollar-based investor, with little diversifying effect; so, the yen-based investor's risk increases.

Table 1.5. Correlation and Covariance Matrixes: Example

	U.S. Stocks	Japanese Stocks	Yen
Correlation matrix			
U.S. stocks	1.0	0.3	−0.1
Japanese stocks		1.0	0.2
Yen			1.0
Covariance matrix			
U.S. stocks	0.0193	0.0072	−0.0015
Japanese stocks		0.0299	0.0036
Yen			0.0108

Note: Correlations are calculated from the perspective of a U.S. investor.

The Effect of Currency Perspective on Covariance. The covariance between local asset returns in two different countries is not affected by the currency perspective of the investor doing the analysis. The covariance between the returns of a currency and a local asset, however, or the covariance between two currency returns is affected by the currency perspective of the analyst. As a result, the covariance matrix used in optimization problems varies with respect to the home currency of the analyst. Any covariance terms involving a currency will change as the home currency perspective changes.

For illustration of this phenomenon, suppose an investor in country x is measuring the covariance between the local return on asset A and the currency return of country z (from the country x perspective). This covariance is expressed as

$$C_{Az}^x = \text{cov}(r_A, {}_xr_z). \tag{1.37}$$

Suppose now that an investor in country y is also measuring the covariance between asset A and the currency return of country z (from the country y perspective). In this case,

$$C_{Az}^y = \text{cov}(r_A, {}_yr_z). \tag{1.38}$$

Currency Management: Concepts and Practices

The reciprocal relationship between exchange rates allows the cross-currency returns between countries to be expressed as

$$1 + {}_y r_z = \frac{1 + {}_x r_z}{1 + {}_x r_y} \qquad (1.39)$$

or, by approximation,

$${}_y r_z \approx {}_x r_z - {}_x r_y. \qquad (1.40)$$

Expression 1.40 indicates that the currency return of country z for a country y investor is approximately equal to the currency return of country z minus the currency return of country y for a country x investor. Using Equation 1.40 in Equation 1.38 gives

$$\begin{aligned} C^y_{Az} &= \operatorname{cov}(r_A, {}_x r_z) - \operatorname{cov}(r_A, {}_x r_y) \\ &= C^x_{Az} - C^x_{Ay}. \end{aligned} \qquad (1.41)$$

Consequently, the covariance between asset A and currency z will not be the same from the perspective of investor x and investor y unless the covariance between the local asset return and currency y is zero from the perspective of country x.

Covariance versus Investor Perspective

Suppose a U.S. investor is measuring the covariance between the return on Japanese bonds (JPB) and the return on the British pound. Furthermore, suppose that, from a U.S. perspective, the risk and correlations between markets are

$$\begin{aligned} \sigma_£ &= 11.7\% \\ \sigma_{JPB} &= 8.1\% \\ \sigma_¥ &= 11.8\% \\ \rho_{¥, JPB} &= 0.37 \\ \rho_{£, JPB} &= 0.22. \end{aligned}$$

The covariance between Japanese bonds and the British pound from a U.S. perspective would be

$$\begin{aligned} C^{US}_{£, JPB} &= \sigma_£ \sigma_{JPB} \rho_{£, JPB} \\ &= (0.117)(0.081)(0.22), \\ &= 0.0021, \end{aligned}$$

but the covariance between Japanese bonds and the British pound from a Japanese investor's point of view would be

$$\begin{aligned} C^{JP}_{£, JPB} &= C^{US}_{£, JPB} - C^{US}_{¥, JPB} \\ &= 0.0021 - 0.0035 \\ &= -0.0014 \end{aligned}$$

because the covariance between Japanese bonds and the yen from a U.S. perspective is

$$\begin{aligned} C^{US}_{¥, JPB} &= \sigma_¥ \sigma_{JPB} \rho_{¥, JPB} \\ &= (0.118)(0.081)(0.37) \\ &= 0.0035. \end{aligned}$$

Note that the covariance from the Japanese point of view is negative whereas from the U.S. viewpoint, the covariance is positive. The difference arises when returns must be translated into different home currencies. That translation inserts a separate covariance term related to the cross-currency risk into the equation, which can change the relative risk based on the investor's home currency perspective.

Summary

- Direct quotation of the exchange rate (that is, home currency/foreign currency) provides currency returns that match the investor's intuition: Investors in the foreign currency make money when the return is positive.
- A "strong" foreign currency or a "weak" home currency when a direct quotation convention is used implies that foreign currency returns are positive.
- A "weak" foreign currency or a "strong" home currency when a direct quotation convention is used implies that foreign currency returns are negative.
- The forward premium between currencies equalizes the short-term interest rate differential between two countries (the covered interest parity relationship). When a direct quotation convention is used, the forward premium is negative for a high-interest-rate currency:

$$f \approx (i_d - i_\ell)t.$$

- The percentage return from purchasing a forward contract (forward surprise) can be thought of as the percentage change in the spot rate (currency return) minus the forward premium:

$$\text{Forward surprise} = r_c - f.$$

- Unhedged local asset returns are approximately equal to the local foreign asset return plus the currency return:

$$R_{UH} \approx r_\ell + r_c.$$

- Hedged local asset returns are approximately equal to the local foreign asset return plus the forward premium:

$$R_H \approx r_\ell + f.$$

- Hedging currency exposure decreases the volatility of a portfolio of foreign assets if the local asset returns are positively correlated with currency returns.
- Hedging currency exposure increases the volatility of a portfolio of foreign assets only if local asset returns are substantially negatively correlated with currency returns—that is, to the extent that the correlation overcomes the variance of the currencies themselves.
- The covariance of currency returns with local asset returns or with other currency returns depends on the investor's home currency perspective. It is not invariant with respect to the currency of residence.

2. Historical Perspective on Foreign Exchange Risk

Although the future is not likely to repeat the past precisely, past events may provide valuable lessons that will improve our understanding of how foreign exchange markets will function in the future.

Major Historical Events in the Foreign Exchange Markets

Foreign exchange management is motivated by the need to conduct international trade and manage international capital investments. In the postbarter era, international trade and investing have been conducted under a variety of foreign exchange regimes. This section briefly describes these regimes, beginning with the gold standard in 1870.

The Gold Standard. From 1870 through the beginning of World War II, most of the world was on the gold standard. The United States joined this arrangement in 1879. Under the gold standard, each country committed to exchange its currency for a specific quantity of gold, which effectively fixed exchange rates for extended periods of time. Commitment to the gold standard required countries to maintain gold reserves. It also meant that central banks had to deflate their currencies during periods of trade deficits and inflate their currencies during periods of trade surpluses. These adjustments were required to discourage investors from exchanging their currency holdings for gold and thus depleting a country's gold reserve.

Between the Wars. World War I temporarily halted use of the gold standard as international trade declined sharply and gold shipments were suspended. In the aftermath of the war, countries experienced vastly different rates of inflation; a return to the prewar fixed exchange rates was impossible because the nominal prices of goods between countries had changed so much. Fluctuation in exchange rates contributed to a decline in international trade, which was exacerbated by the Great Depression.

In an attempt to promote international trade and economic growth, some of the major countries returned to the gold standard. They failed to achieve stable parity values, however, partly because of variation in economic policies, which generated different rates of inflation. The lack of economic coordination strained many countries' balance of payments and domestic economies and led most of them, once again, to abandon the gold standard.

Some countries, most notably France, remained on the gold standard and imposed import quotas to address balance-of-payments deficits. As a result, the French franc became significantly overvalued. France negotiated an arrangement with the United States and England to devalue its currency without retaliatory devaluations, but this cooperation in exchange rate management ended with the outbreak of World War II.

The Bretton Woods Agreement. In July 1944, as World War II drew to a close, 44 countries met in Bretton Woods, New Hampshire, to discuss the future of the international monetary system. The two major participants were the United Kingdom, represented by John Maynard Keynes, and the United States, represented by Harry Dexter White. The participants took the following major actions:

- The International Monetary Fund was established with the authority to lend foreign exchange to member countries on the condition that they pursue sound economic policies. These funds were to be used to stabilize exchange rates.
- The U.S. dollar and the pound sterling were established as reserve currencies.
- Exchange rates were fixed within a 1 percent band relative to the dollar, and the dollar was fixed relative to gold at a rate of $35 an ounce. The United States committed to convert dollars into gold.
- After a transition period, currencies were to become convertible into gold.

IMF member countries were required to make a payment of gold and currency to fund the IMF's lending activities, and their voting privileges were proportional to their financial contributions.

By the late 1950s, the West European countries were discussing banding together to promote trade and financial cooperation among the countries. On March 25, 1957, France, West Germany, Belgium, the Netherlands, Luxembourg, and Italy signed the Treaty of Rome, which created the European Economic Community (the Common Market). At the same time, the United States was encouraging European countries to increase their exports to the United States in order to build up their dollar reserves. The Europeans succeeded to the point that by 1960, their dollar claims on the United States exceeded its gold supply.

This U.S. balance-of-payments deficit motivated Presidents John F. Kennedy and Lyndon B. Johnson to impose credit and capital controls, which spurred the development of the Eurodollar market. Eurodollars are dollar-denominated deposits in banks outside the United States that are not subject to U.S.-imposed credit controls.

The United Kingdom also ran a deficit in the mid-1960s, which led to a 14 percent devaluation of the pound in 1967. This devaluation, in turn, heightened fears that the dollar would be devalued, especially in light of continuing U.S. balance-of-payments deficits.

The fear of a dollar devaluation produced a run on gold that forced the creation in 1968 of a two-tiered system for trading gold. Under this system, central banks could trade gold at a fixed official price whereas private investors could trade gold only at fluctuating market prices. Also, in December 1969, the IMF issued Special Drawing Rights to augment gold and the dollar as international reserves.

By the late 1960s, the Japanese yen and the German mark had become significantly undervalued relative to the dollar, partly because of rising U.S. inflation induced by the Vietnam War and President Johnson's Great Society social welfare programs. In 1971, in an attempt to support the dollar's exchange rate, West Germany bought a massive amount of dollars, which caused Germany's money supply to expand by more than 20 percent. This strategy for supporting the dollar was not sustainable.

To remedy the U.S. balance-of-payments problem, the United States wanted West Germany and Japan to revalue their currencies upward. For their part, Germany and Japan wanted the United States to curb the growth in its money supply, tighten its credit, and cut its spending. Finally, in May 1971, Germany halted its intervention in the foreign exchange markets, thereby allowing the mark to float upward and effectively ending the Bretton Woods Agreement.

The Smithsonian Agreement and the Aftermath. In 1971, the United States suspended the dollar's convertibility into gold and allowed the dollar to float freely. This decision was motivated by a large trade deficit that almost depleted the United States' gold supply. The dollar was devalued, and in an arrangement

2. Historical Perspective on Foreign Exchange Risk

known as the Smithsonian Agreement, exchange rates were allowed to fluctuate within a 4.5 percent band. The official gold price was raised to US$38/ounce, but convertibility was not resumed. By 1973, most currencies were floating against the dollar, which caused a fall in the dollar's value.

During the next 20 years, a variety of events had an impact on foreign exchange rates. These events are summarized briefly in this section, and their effects on the German mark/U.S. dollar exchange rate are depicted in Figure 2.1.

■ *The Jamaica Accord.* In 1976, at a meeting in Jamaica, the IMF officially agreed to floating exchange rates. Also, the countries forming the European Monetary Union established parities with narrow margins for their mutual exchange rates and agreed to let their currencies continue to float in a wide band with respect to the dollar. This arrangement was known as "the snake in the tunnel."

In 1979, the European Monetary System was created and the Exchange Rate Mechanism (ERM) was put in place. Under the ERM, the member countries, with the exception of Italy and the United Kingdom, pledged to maintain their exchange rates within a band of ±2.5 percent around parity, which was referenced to the European Currency Unit. Italy and the United Kingdom observed a band of ±6 percent. During the next ten years, numerous realignments of the parity relationships took place.

■ *The Plaza and Louvre Accords.* In 1985, the dollar reached an all-time high relative to the

Figure 2.1. German Mark/U.S. Dollar Exchange Rate: June 1973–December 1993

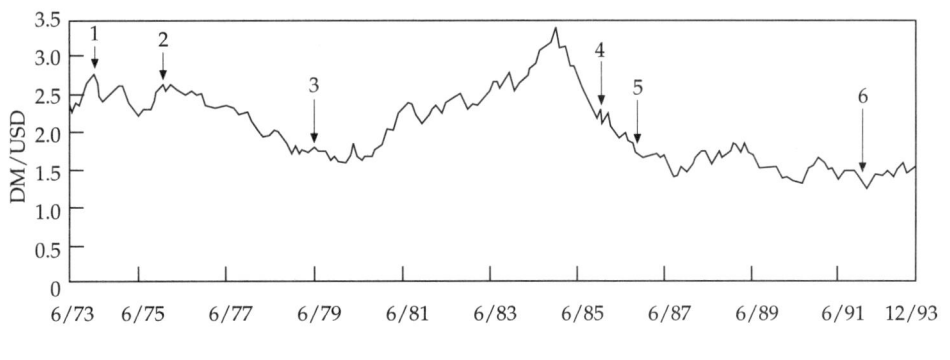

July 22, 1944	The creation of the IMF, the World Bank, and a system of fixed exchange rates tied to gold results from a conference in Bretton Woods, NH.
March 25, 1957	The Treaty of Rome, creating the European Economic Community, is agreed to by France, West Germany, Belgium, the Netherlands, Luxembourg, and Italy.
August 15, 1971	The convertibility of the dollar into gold is suspended by President Richard M. Nixon as part of his New Economic Policy.
December 17–18, 1971	A new system of fixed exchange rates is created and major currencies are revalued as a result of a meeting at the Smithsonian Institution in Washington, DC.
1. November 12, 1973	The dollar is allowed to float, and central bank governors, meeting in Basel, Switzerland, terminate the gold agreement.
2. November 15, 1975	The first economic summit is held at the Château de Rambouillet, southwest of Paris, France.
3. March 13, 1979	The European Monetary System is formally initiated.
4. September 22, 1985	The Plaza Accord is agreed to by the Group of Five finance ministers.
5. February 21–22, 1987	The major industrial nations agree to the Louvre Accord.
6. September 16, 1992	Britain and Italy opt out of the ERM.

major currencies and the United States experienced a high deficit. In September of that year, in an agreement known as the Plaza Accord, the Group of Five (France, West Germany, Japan, the United Kingdom, and the United States) coordinated their economic policies to drive down the price of the dollar. The Plaza Accord inaugurated a plan for the "orderly appreciation" of other currencies against the U.S. dollar. These efforts resulted in a 30 percent decline in the dollar's value during the next two years.

To cope with the possibility that the dollar might overshoot its "natural level," the major industrial nations met again in February 1987 and reached a new agreement known as the Louvre Accord. Declaring that the U.S. dollar had fallen far enough, the signers pledged to cooperate in stabilizing it and agreed to try as far as possible to maintain the then-current exchange rate levels.

■ *The Maastricht Accord.* In 1991, the European countries met in Maastricht and set a timetable and rules to establish a single European currency. They conditioned membership in this currency union on the maintenance of narrow bands around parity exchange rates.

When the reunification of Germany motivated the Bundesbank in 1992 to pursue a tight monetary policy to forestall the onset of inflation, the narrow exchange rate bands forced other European countries to raise their interest rates at a time when their economies were mired in recession. This circumstance led speculators to sell the weak European currencies in anticipation of devaluation. Sweden, in an ill-fated attempt to defend the parity relationship of the krona, raised interest rates to 500 percent. The Bank of England unsuccessfully spent billions of pounds defending its exchange rate. The United Kingdom and Italy withdrew from the Maastricht Accord in September 1992, and several other European currencies were devalued shortly thereafter. A general realignment occurred in August 1993; bands were ±15 percent around the new parity exchange rates. The Maastricht Accord was ratified in September 1993, but with considerably less enthusiasm for a unified European currency in the foreseeable future.

Over the years, exchange rate policies among nations have varied according to two major dimensions—cooperation versus noncooperation and rules-based intervention versus discretionary intervention. Figure 2.2 indicates the place of the major agreements discussed here along those two dimensions. The current

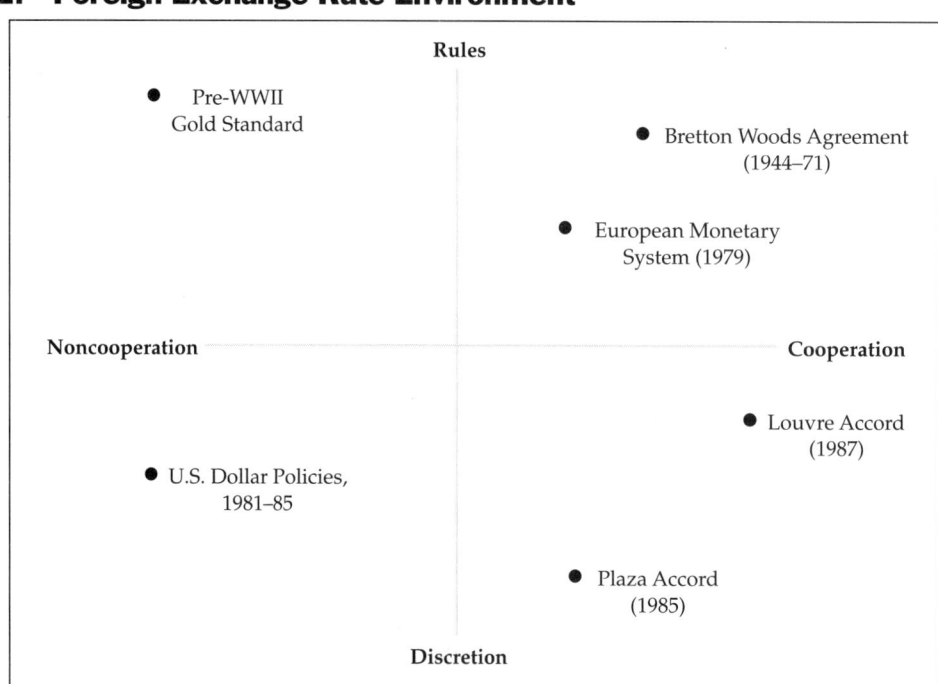

Figure 2.2. Foreign Exchange Rate Environment

Source: The Economist (May 21 and May 28, 1988).

Table 2.1. Historical Currency Returns Relative to the U.S. Dollar

Year	British Pound	German Mark	French Franc	Swiss Franc	Japanese Yen	Australian Dollar	Canadian Dollar
A. Annual Returns							
1974	1.13%	12.27%	5.80%	28.01%	−6.89%	NA	NA
1975	−13.90	−8.09	−0.71	−3.16	−1.38	−5.25%	−2.47%
1976	−15.86	11.02	−9.90	6.94	4.06	−13.19	0.73
1977	12.10	11.92	5.33	21.30	22.05	4.50	−7.78
1978	6.80	15.60	12.82	24.63	23.44	1.05	−7.76
1979	9.25	5.71	3.85	1.53	−18.80	−3.85	1.56
1980	7.10	−11.94	−11.41	−9.65	18.26	6.85	−2.19
1981	−19.90	−12.74	−20.67	−1.72	−7.78	−4.52	0.69
1982	−15.24	−5.65	−15.10	−10.15	−6.46	−13.12	−3.54
1983	−10.35	−12.56	−19.07	−8.21	1.43	−8.52	−1.19
1984	−20.17	−13.69	−13.55	−16.24	−7.80	−7.98	−5.84
1985	24.74	28.94	26.97	26.34	25.45	−17.36	−5.49
1986	2.46	25.50	17.79	27.84	26.33	−2.42	1.27
1987	26.94	24.14	20.92	26.58	30.89	8.52	6.21
1988	−3.75	−11.56	−12.06	−15.16	−3.09	18.21	9.00
1989	−10.81	4.95	4.45	−2.68	−13.21	−7.52	3.01
1990	19.87	13.56	14.08	21.62	6.37	−2.19	−0.22
1991	−3.38	−1.81	−2.48	−6.56	8.45	−1.64	0.41
1992	−19.16	−6.33	−6.25	−7.44	−0.04	−9.26	−9.09
1993	−2.09	−6.74	−6.14	−1.31	11.87	−1.55	−4.08
Annualized compound return	−2.23%	2.24%	−1.15%	3.99%	4.71%	3.46%	−1.51%
B. Rolling Five-Year Annualized Returns							
1978	−2.59%	8.19%	2.38%	14.92%	7.56%	NA	NA
1979	−1.07	6.89	2.00	9.71	4.65	−3.54%	−3.22%
1980	3.34	5.98	−0.30	8.20	8.53	−1.19	−3.17
1981	2.33	1.00	−2.80	6.39	5.94	0.71	−3.17
1982	−3.23	−2.39	−6.91	0.19	0.45	−2.95	−2.30
1983	−6.56	−7.69	−12.89	−5.75	−3.42	−4.86	−0.94
1984	−12.24	−11.36	−16.03	−9.31	−0.94	−5.69	−2.43
1985	−9.53	−4.34	−9.76	−3.02	0.24	−10.41	−3.10
1986	−4.96	2.87	−2.34	2.21	6.75	−10.02	−2.99
1987	3.03	8.68	4.82	9.47	14.17	−5.93	−1.11
1988	4.51	8.92	6.57	7.76	13.13	−0.98	0.85
1989	6.85	13.27	10.68	11.04	11.77	−0.88	2.68
1990	6.00	10.43	8.34	10.20	8.15	2.52	3.80
1991	4.77	5.14	4.32	3.50	4.90	2.68	3.62
1992	−4.28	−0.62	−0.85	−2.78	−0.61	−0.93	0.45
1993	−3.95	0.44	0.45	0.20	2.29	−4.49	−2.09

NA = not available.

environment for most major currencies is characterized by government cooperation but with intervention at the discretion of the major central banks.

Historical Returns, Volatility, and Correlations. Table 2.1 contains the historical returns of several major currencies relative to the U.S. dollar during the modern floating-rate era; annual returns are in Part A, and rolling five-year annualized returns are in Part B. Note that these currencies have experienced enormously wide swings in performance for periods as long as five years and that even the entire floating-rate period offers little evidence that currency returns cancel out. With the exception of the British pound, the Canadian dollar, and the French franc, average currency returns relative to the U.S. dollar have been positive since 1974, which reflects the depreciation of the dollar. The broad average masks several periods of dollar strength in the late 1970s and the mid-1980s, however, as illustrated in Figure 2.3. Dollar strength against the pound, the mark, and the yen was substantial during these subperiods.

Pure currency returns affect the value of unhedged foreign investments, but hedging currency exposure involves a cost embodied in the forward premium. Table 2.2 shows the average *forward surprise* year by year for a U.S.-based investor for each of the major currencies. The forward surprise is the difference between the currency return and the forward premium $(r_c - f)$. It is the return an investor in a forward contract would earn or, equivalently, the return a hedger would have to net out against the underlying unhedged asset return in a portfolio. When currency returns are adjusted by the forward premium, the average forward surprise is closer to zero for most currencies than is the currency return by itself.

Table 2.3 shows the historical volatility of currency returns relative to the U.S. dollar. Currency volatility has been relatively stable for rolling five-year horizons. Historically, currencies have had volatilities close to those of long-term bonds and substantially less than stock volatilities, as shown by the average risk and return data in Table 2.4 for investors with a variety of currency bases. The one exception is that of the Canadian dollar relative to the U.S. dollar. The Canadian economy is so closely linked to that of the United States that its currency volatility has been more muted than that of other countries relative to the U.S. dollar. Note that from a U.S. investor's perspective (Part A), during the 1980–93 period, unhedged asset returns have been more volatile than hedged returns whereas hedged returns have had virtually identical volatility to local asset returns. During this period, currency exposure would not have diversified asset risk, but it would have increased the volatility of international asset returns.

Figures 2.4 and 2.5 show the relative volatilities of stocks (Figure 2.4) and bonds (Figure 2.5) with and without the currency exposure hedged. In both asset classes, hedging would have decreased the volatility from a U.S. investor's perspective, but the reduction in volatility would have been more substantial for international bonds than for stocks. As with most market-determined prices, the volatility of exchange rates is generally considered to be higher than the volatility of the underlying economic fundamentals that influence exchange rates (see Shiller 1981). The difference is assumed to be caused by shifts in investor sentiment and psychology that add volatility to the underlying economic forces.

Table 2.5, containing the historical correlations of currency returns with each other, reveals that the major European currencies have generally become increasingly correlated during the floating-rate period and that the correlation of the Australian and Canadian dollars has declined. The higher correlations between European currencies have developed as Europe has worked toward establishing a single European currency.

Recall from Chapter 1 that the risk of a foreign asset portfolio is related to the variance of currency returns and the covariance of the local asset returns with currencies. The risk of a simple portfolio with a domestic and a foreign asset is expressed as

$$\sigma_R^2 = w_d^2\sigma_d^2 + w_\ell^2\sigma_\ell^2 + 2w_d w_\ell C_{d\ell} + H^2\sigma_c^2$$
$$+ 2H(w_d C_{dc} + w_\ell C_{\ell c}). \qquad (2.1)$$

The last two terms capture the impact of currency exposure on the risk of the portfolio. Positive currency exposure in the portfolio will add to the risk of the total portfolio if

$$H^2\sigma_c^2 + 2H(w_d C_{dc} + w_\ell C_{\ell c}) > 0. \qquad (2.2)$$

Unless the covariances (correlations) of currency returns with domestic and foreign local asset returns are sufficiently negative to overcome the volatility of the currency itself, the addition of currency exposure will add risk to the portfolio. Because most correlations have not been that negative, hedging at least some of the currency exposure that accompanies foreign asset exposure has reduced overall portfolio risk.

Table 2.6 shows correlation matrixes for local asset returns and currencies for selected markets since 1980 for investors based in a variety of currencies. Correlations between local asset returns themselves are invariant with respect to the currency perspective.

From the relationship between hedged asset returns and currency returns, the correlations can be written as

$$\rho_{dc} = \frac{C_{dc}}{\sigma_d \sigma_c}$$

and

$$\rho_{\ell c} = \frac{C_{\ell c}}{\sigma_\ell \sigma_c}.$$

Notice from Table 2.6, Part A, that from a U.S. perspective, some currency returns have been slightly negatively correlated with local equity returns over time but have generally been positively correlated with bond returns and with other currencies. As a result, at least some hedging of currency risk would have reduced the volatility of global portfolio returns in the past 14 years for a U.S. investor.

The higher correlation of currency returns with bond returns is driven by the fact that interest rates are so much a part of currency relationships. Stocks also respond to changes in interest rates, as is evident from the generally positive correlation between stock and bond returns, but currency movements seem to be more anchored in monetary phenomena than are stock movements.

One implication of the greater correlation between currencies and bonds than between currencies and equities is that global bond portfolios will have much more of their volatility influenced by currency risk than will global equity portfolios. Consequently, global bond managers typically pay more attention to currency risk than do global equity managers and explicitly factor the currency decision into the asset decision.

Table 2.7 shows the correlation for the same time period as in Table 2.6 for unhedged asset returns for investors based in a variety of currencies. Note that the addition of currency risk sometimes increases and sometimes decreases the correlations between asset returns. The change in correlation is a function of the correlation of local asset returns with currency returns and the size of the currency volatility itself. For example, by using the relationship between unhedged (UH) asset returns and currency returns, one can write the correlation between a domestic asset and an unhedged foreign asset as

$$\rho_{d,UH} = \frac{\rho_{d\ell}\sigma_\ell + \rho_{dc}\sigma_c}{(\sigma_\ell^2 + \sigma_c^2 + 2\rho_{\ell c}\sigma_\ell \sigma_c)^{1/2}}. \quad (2.3)$$

If the correlation between domestic and foreign local asset returns is represented as $\rho_{d\ell}$, the correlation between the domestic asset and the unhedged foreign asset will increase or decrease in accord with the size of the correlations between currency returns and local asset returns as well as with the currency volatility itself. If currency returns are not sufficiently negatively correlated with local asset returns, the unhedged correlation will be higher than the correlation between local asset returns.

The pattern of correlations between asset and currency returns often varies from one year to the next. For example, Table 2.8 shows the rolling five-year correlations of U.S. stocks and bonds with selected currencies. Correlations tended to be positive in the early 1980s but have been smaller, and sometimes negative, in the early 1990s. Even the years of negative correlation have usually not been negative enough to overcome the contribution to risk from the currency volatility itself, however, so the net volatility of an unhedged portfolio from a U.S. perspective has generally been greater than that of a hedged portfolio.

Figure 2.3. U.S. Dollar Exchange Rates with Major Currencies, Selected Periods

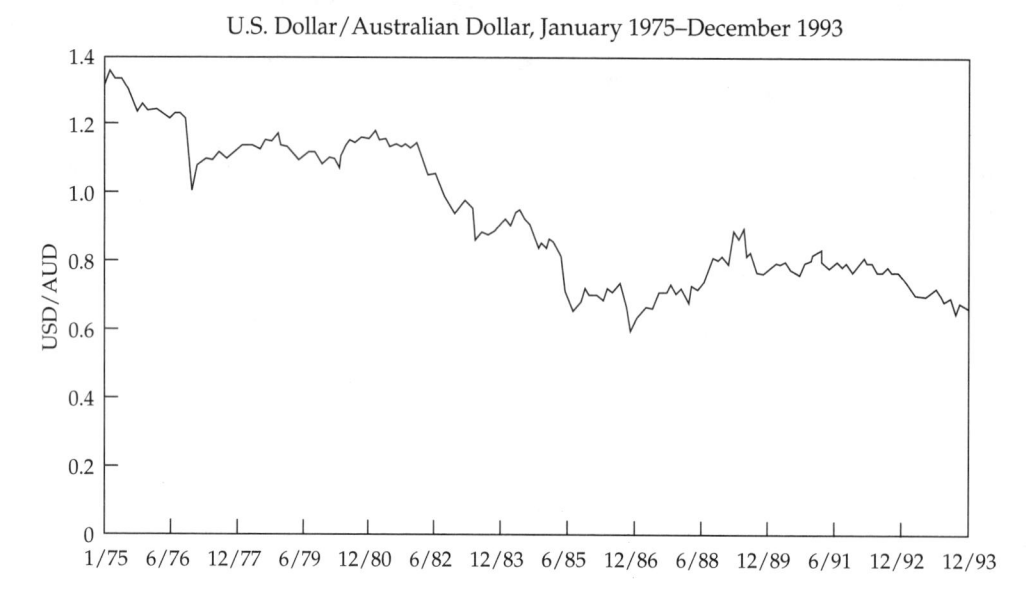

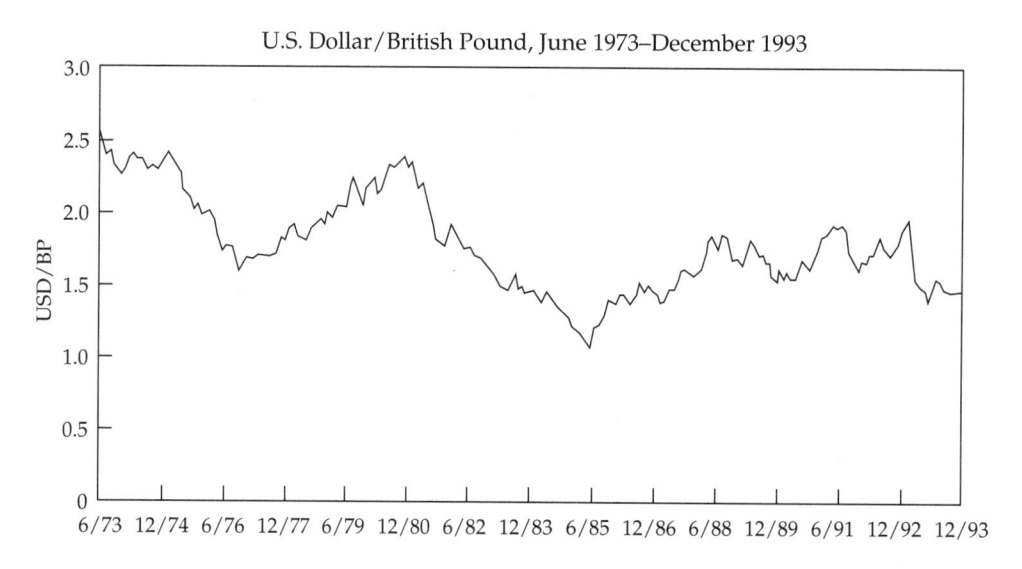

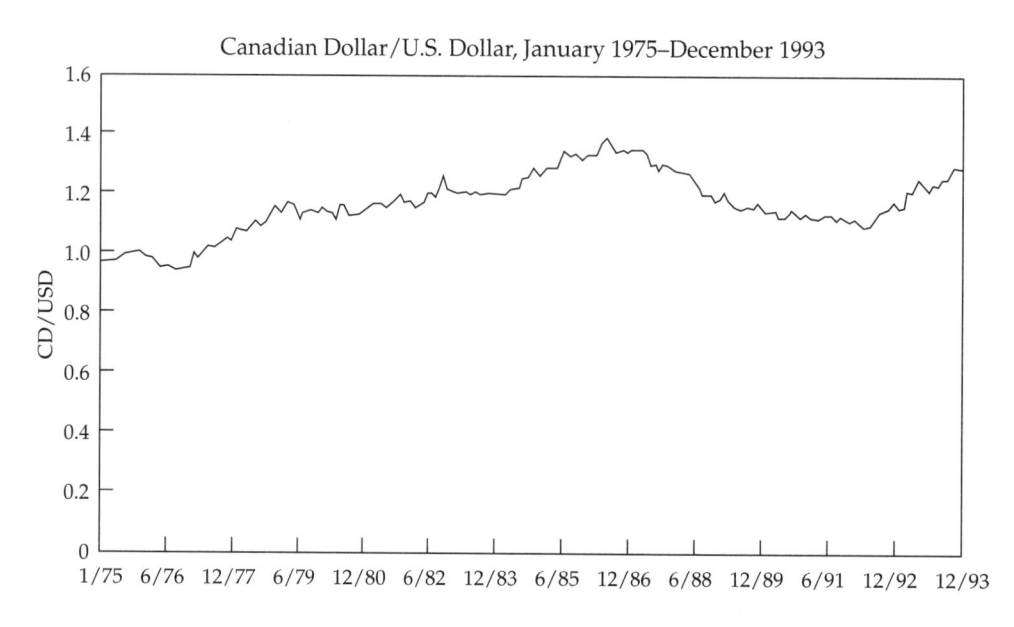

U.S. Dollar/Australian Dollar, January 1975–December 1993

U.S. Dollar/British Pound, June 1973–December 1993

Canadian Dollar/U.S. Dollar, January 1975–December 1993

Japanese Yen/U.S. Dollar, June 1973–December 1993

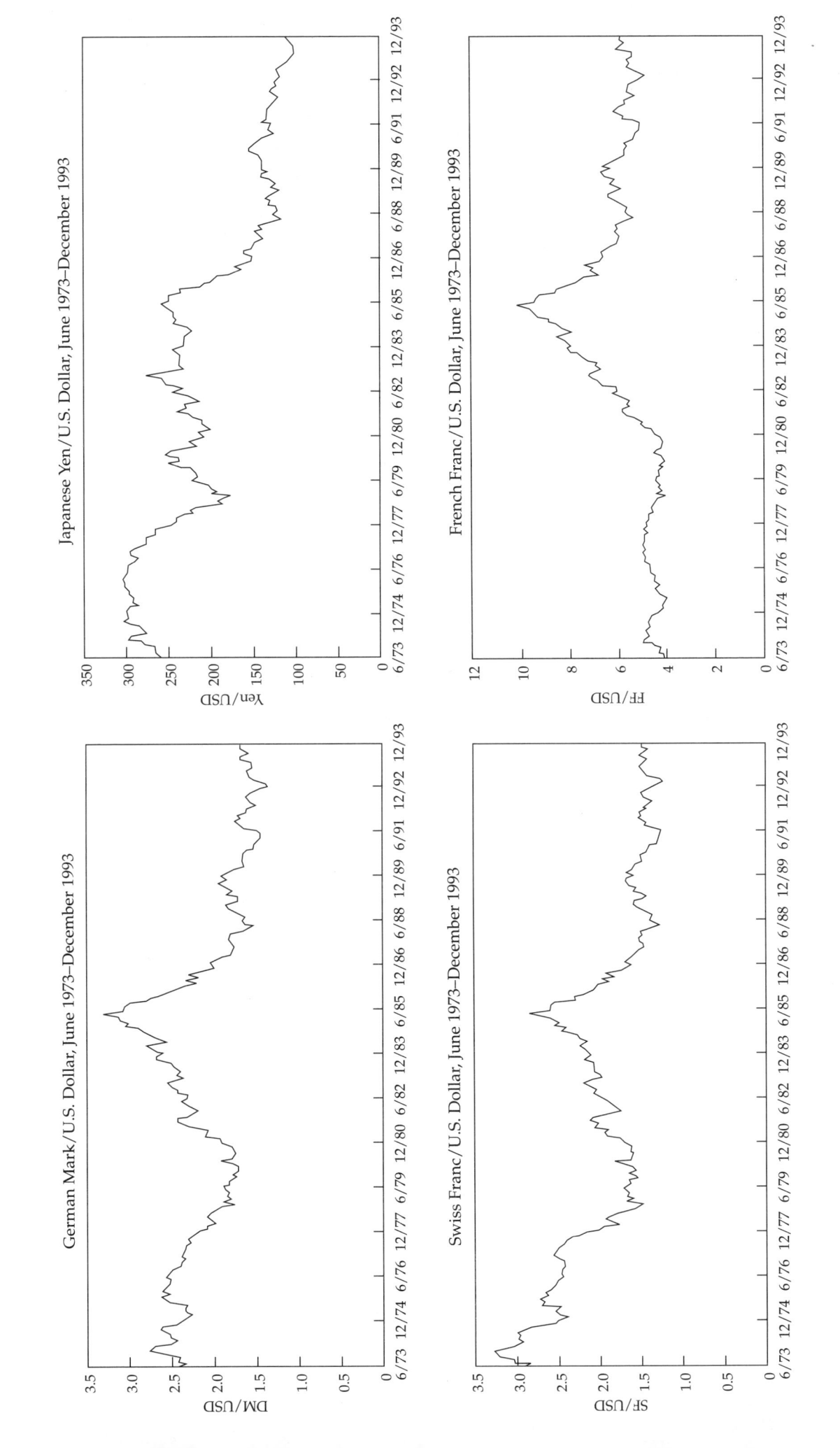

German Mark/U.S. Dollar, June 1973–December 1993

French Franc/U.S. Dollar, June 1973–December 1993

Swiss Franc/U.S. Dollar, June 1973–December 1993

Table 2.2. Average Annual Forward Surprise

Year	British Pound	German Mark	French Franc	Swiss Franc	Japanese Yen	Australian Dollar	Canadian Dollar
1976	−8.92%	9.05%	−6.24%	NA	2.71%	NA	NA
1977	14.12	9.68	10.19	NA	18.44	7.69%	−6.45%
1978	7.74	9.13	13.37	NA	16.33	2.36	−8.21
1979	12.08	−0.08	2.45	NA	−26.80	−5.00	1.52
1980	8.38	−17.54	−11.64	NA	11.38	5.81	−3.49
1981	−24.55	−18.65	−21.35	NA	−14.66	−7.71	2.74
1982	−16.86	−9.82	−12.62	NA	−14.17	−12.01	−2.13
1983	−10.78	−17.65	−16.97	−16.81	0.12	−7.09	−1.30
1984	−22.72	−19.27	−12.53	−23.72	−11.62	−8.19	−5.51
1985	24.50	22.36	27.61	21.06	19.66	−12.18	−4.45
1986	6.12	21.86	18.17	23.28	20.78	6.18	3.46
1987	27.99	16.86	20.51	21.12	26.14	13.81	7.11
1988	−1.44	−15.37	−11.71	−20.98	−6.36	20.80	10.07
1989	−6.99	2.61	5.57	−4.12	−17.84	−0.24	5.53
1990	24.24	12.47	15.01	18.91	5.43	3.62	4.25
1991	2.47	1.87	1.82	−3.61	9.79	2.52	3.03
1992	−15.52	−0.87	0.67	−2.07	0.94	−7.58	−6.45
1993	0.36	−2.74	−1.68	1.28	11.00	0.51	−2.76
Annualized average	0.45%	−0.49%	1.01%	3.12%	2.48%	0.19%	−0.18%

Note: Returns are annualized by multiplying the monthly average by 12. The forward surprise is equal to the monthly currency return minus the one-month forward premium from a U.S. investor's perspective. The forward surprise is equivalent to the return from investing in rolling one-month forward contracts.
NA = not available.

Table 2.3. Rolling Five-Year Annualized Currency Standard Deviations Relative to the U.S. Dollar

Five Years Ending in	British Pound	German Mark	Swiss Franc	French Franc	Japanese Yen	Australian Dollar	Canadian Dollar
1978	9.56%	9.97%	13.30%	10.40%	10.66%	NA	NA
1979	10.40	9.52	13.58	9.55	10.92	9.48%	4.83%
1980	10.38	10.14	14.30	9.70	12.21	9.60	5.28
1981	11.08	11.61	16.15	11.05	13.48	4.43	4.69
1982	10.95	11.89	16.33	12.33	15.15	5.37	5.07
1983	10.36	10.48	12.66	10.55	12.75	6.63	4.76
1984	10.07	11.05	12.27	10.94	12.08	7.62	4.55
1985	12.57	11.81	12.96	12.29	11.83	10.46	4.41
1986	12.12	12.76	13.14	12.71	12.22	12.53	4.12
1987	12.83	12.98	13.30	12.05	11.29	13.11	3.80
1988	13.41	13.56	14.36	12.34	12.42	13.41	4.46
1989	13.63	13.53	14.63	12.35	13.46	13.95	4.31
1990	11.90	12.34	12.97	11.11	13.56	11.93	3.99
1991	12.35	12.12	12.38	11.48	12.57	10.00	3.98
1992	13.94	12.59	13.16	12.08	11.20	9.33	4.49
1993	13.28	12.29	12.67	11.95	10.47	8.57	4.17
Average	11.84%	11.83%	13.14%	11.55%	11.74%	10.07%	4.58%

Note: Standard deviations of monthly returns are annualized by multiplying by $\sqrt{12}$.
NA = not available.

Empirical Tendencies of Exchange Rates

Although it is reasonable to expect currency hedging to reduce a portfolio's risk, the extent by which risk is reduced and the cost of achieving that effect are not obvious. The effect of currency hedging is complicated by certain peculiar tendencies of currency returns that have been empirically evident. Specifically, the forward exchange rate has been a biased estimate of changes in the spot exchange rate, and currency returns have not conformed to the random walk model; instead, they have been positively serially correlated.

Unless these tendencies are but a single pass through history, they have important consequences for the estimation of expected return and risk from currency-hedging instruments.

The Forward Rate Bias. Covered interest arbitrage drives the relationship between the spot rate and the forward rate. As noted in Chapter 1, the forward rate is related to the current spot exchange rate by the interest rate differential between two countries:

$$F = \frac{S_o(1 + i_d t)}{1 + i_\ell t}. \qquad (2.4)$$

Therefore, an investor cannot profit by borrowing funds in a low-interest-rate country, converting those funds into the currency of a high-interest-rate country, lending in the high-interest-rate country, and hedging away the currency risk. The interest rate advantage is exactly offset by the cost of hedging.

In contrast, the theory of uncovered interest parity holds that an investor should not expect to profit from interest rate differentials even if the currency exposure is not hedged. According to this theory, the forward exchange rate is an unbiased estimate of the future spot rate. The theory assumes that the forward rate sometimes overestimates changes in the spot rate and sometimes underestimates changes in the spot rate but that, on average, the errors cancel out. If uncovered interest parity holds, therefore, a forward contract's expected return should equal zero.

If, instead, the prevailing spot exchange rate is a less biased estimate of the future spot rate than is the forward rate, the investor should expect to profit, on average, by borrowing in low-interest-rate countries and lending in high-interest-rate countries, while bearing the currency risk. In this case, independent of other considerations, the investor should be more inclined to hedge when forward contracts sell at a premium than when they sell at a discount.

In order to evaluate empirically whether or not the forward rate is biased, one must first distinguish between a conditional and an unconditional test of bias. An *unconditional* test addresses whether or not the forward rate systematically over- or underpredicts the level of the future spot rate irrespective of whether it predicts the spot rate to increase or decrease. A *conditional* test addresses whether or not the forward rate systematically over- or underpredicts the average level of the future spot rate *conditioned* on whether the forward rate is predicting an increase or a decrease. That is, an unconditional test determines whether or not the forward rate is a biased predictor of the level of the future spot rate, whereas a conditional test determines whether or not the forward rate is a biased predictor of the change in the future spot rate.

Consider, for example, the following hypothetical spot and forward exchange rates:

Period	Spot Rate	Forward Rate
1	1.00	1.10
2	1.00	0.90
3	1.00	—

The forward rate in Period 1 overpredicted the future (Period 2) spot rate by 0.10, and the forward rate in Period 2 underpredicted the future (Period 3) spot rate by 0.10. Thus, on average, the forward rate was an unbiased predictor of the average *level* of the future spot rate. When the expected spot rate is conditioned on the *direction* of the forward rate, however, the forward rate can be seen to have incorrectly predicted the change in the spot rate in both periods.

The empirical record reveals an actual pattern that is the same as in this example. Table 2.9 shows the rates of return that one would have achieved by selling one-month forward currency contracts during the modern floating-rate era. During the months when the

Table 2.4. Average Annualized Risk and Return from International Stocks and Bonds, 1980–93

Asset/Country	Local Asset Return	Hedged Asset Return	Unhedged Asset Return	Local Asset Risk	Hedged Asset Risk	Unhedged Asset Risk
A. Perspective of a U.S.-Based Investor						
Stocks						
United States	15.7%	na	na	21.1%	na	na
United Kingdom	20.4	17.6%	18.3%	21.9	21.9%	23.5%
Germany	20.9	22.9	21.7	23.4	23.3	25.0
France	19.2	16.3	17.2	25.2	25.2	26.6
Japan	11.1	13.4	17.3	23.7	23.8	26.6
Australia	17.8	13.8	14.8	24.9	24.9	27.6
Canada	11.3	9.5	10.5	22.1	22.1	23.4
Bonds						
United States	12.6%	na	na	19.0%	na	na
United Kingdom	15.5	12.7%	13.4%	17.1	17.1%	22.4%
Germany	12.9	14.9	13.7	13.2	13.3	21.2
France	13.2	10.2	11.1	13.7	13.4	20.0
Japan	9.4	11.7	15.6	13.8	13.8	21.4
Australia	21.3	17.3	18.4	16.8	16.6	21.6
Canada	13.0	11.2	12.2	17.3	17.3	19.2
B. Perspective of an Australia-Based Investor						
Stocks						
United States	15.7%	19.7%	19.8%	21.1%	21.2%	23.1%
United Kingdom	20.4	21.6	21.9	21.9	21.8	23.8
Germany	20.9	26.9	25.5	23.4	23.4	25.9
France	11.1	20.3	21.0	23.7	25.2	27.1
Japan	19.2	17.4	21.1	25.2	23.8	27.4
Australia	17.8	na	na	24.9	na	na
Canada	11.3	13.5	14.5	22.1	22.1	23.7
Bonds						
United States	12.6%	16.6%	20.7%	19.0%	19.1%	21.7%
United Kingdom	15.5	16.7	17.0	17.1	17.0	22.9
Germany	12.9	18.9	17.5	13.2	13.4	22.6
France	13.2	14.2	15.0	13.7	13.6	21.6
Japan	9.4	15.7	19.4	13.8	13.9	22.3
Australia	21.3	na	na	16.8	na	na
Canada	13.0	15.2	16.2	17.3	17.4	20.7
C. Perspective of a Canada-Based Investor						
Stocks						
United States	15.7%	17.5%	16.7%	21.1%	21.1%	21.1%
United Kingdom	20.4	19.4	19.1	21.9	21.9	23.5
Germany	20.9	24.7	22.6	23.4	23.4	25.1
France	11.1	18.1	18.2	23.7	25.2	26.5
Japan	19.2	15.3	18.2	25.2	23.8	26.6
Australia	17.8	15.7	15.1	24.9	24.9	27.4
Canada	11.3	na	na	22.1	na	na
Bonds						
United States	12.6%	14.5%	15.5%	19.0%	19.0%	19.3%
United Kingdom	15.5	14.5	14.2	17.1	17.1	22.1
Germany	12.9	16.7	14.6	13.2	13.3	21.1
France	13.2	12.1	12.1	13.7	13.5	20.0
Japan	9.4	13.6	16.5	13.8	13.8	21.1
Australia	21.3	19.2	19.3	16.8	16.7	21.5
Canada	13.0	na	na	17.3	na	na

Table 2.4. (continued)

Asset/Country	Local Asset Return	Hedged Asset Return	Unhedged Asset Return	Local Asset Risk	Hedged Asset Risk	Unhedged Asset Risk
D. Perspective of a Germany-Based Investor						
Stocks						
United States	15.7%	13.7%	16.5%	21.1%	21.2%	23.9%
United Kingdom	20.4	15.6	17.9	21.9	21.9	24.1
Germany	20.9	na	na	23.4	na	na
France	11.1	14.3	17.2	23.7	25.1	26.6
Japan	19.2	11.5	17.3	25.2	23.7	26.5
Australia	17.8	14.9	15.5	24.9	24.9	28.9
Canada	11.3	7.5	10.5	22.1	22.1	23.4
Bonds						
United States	12.6%	10.7%	11.5%	19.0%	19.1%	21.0%
United Kingdom	15.5	10.7	13.1	17.1	17.1	20.7
Germany	12.9	na	na	13.2	na	na
France	13.2	8.3	10.5	13.7	13.5	14.0
Japan	9.4	9.8	15.6	13.8	13.8	19.7
Australia	21.3	15.4	19.0	16.8	16.8	23.3
Canada	13.0	9.2	12.9	17.3	17.4	20.9
E. Perspective of a U.K.-Based Investor						
Stocks						
United States	15.7%	18.5%	19.5%	21.1%	21.2%	23.9%
United Kingdom	20.4	na	na	21.9	na	na
Germany	20.9	25.7	24.4	23.4	23.4	25.1
France	11.1	19.1	19.9	23.7	25.2	26.4
Japan	19.2	16.2	20.3	25.2	23.7	26.1
Australia	17.8	16.6	18.2	24.9	25.0	27.8
Canada	11.3	12.3	14.1	22.1	22.1	24.3
Bonds						
United States	12.6%	15.4%	19.2%	19.0%	19.0%	21.4%
United Kingdom	15.5	na	na	17.1	na	na
Germany	12.9	17.7	16.3	13.2	13.2	19.2
France	13.2	13.0	13.8	13.7	13.5	18.5
Japan	9.4	14.5	18.6	13.8	13.8	20.3
Australia	21.3	20.1	21.7	16.8	16.7	22.7
Canada	13.0	14.0	15.8	17.3	17.3	20.8
F. Perspective of a Japan-Based Investor						
Stocks						
United States	15.7%	13.4%	10.9%	21.1%	21.2%	23.9%
United Kingdom	20.4	15.3	12.6	21.9	21.9	23.8
Germany	20.9	20.6	16.1	23.3	23.4	25.6
Japan	11.1	na	na	23.7	na	na
France	19.2	14.0	11.7	25.2	25.1	26.2
Australia	17.8	11.5	9.8	24.9	25.0	27.9
Canada	11.3	7.2	5.7	22.1	22.1	24.4
Bonds						
United States	12.6%	10.3%	5.6%	19.0%	19.0%	21.6%
United Kingdom	15.5	10.4	7.8	17.1	17.1	21.4
Germany	12.9	12.6	8.1	13.2	13.3	19.8
France	13.2	7.9	5.6	13.7	13.5	18.8
Japan	9.4	na	na	13.8	na	na
Australia	21.3	15.0	13.4	16.8	16.7	23.0
Canada	13.0	8.9	7.4	17.3	17.3	20.3

na = not applicable.

Figure 2.4. International Stocks: Hedged versus Unhedged Annualized Risk, 1980–93

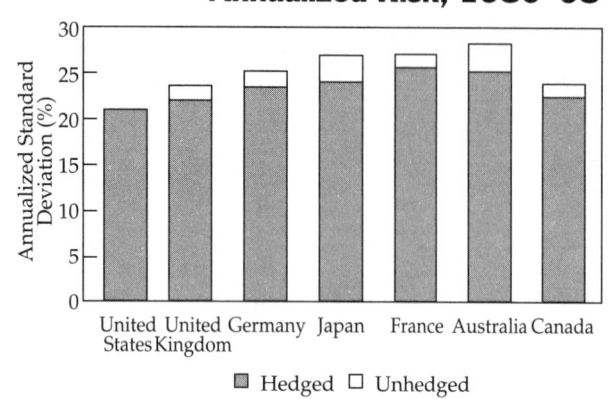

[Bar chart showing annualized standard deviation (%) for United States, United Kingdom, Germany, Japan, France, Australia, Canada, with Hedged and Unhedged bars]

Figure 2.5. International Bonds: Hedged versus Unhedged Annualized Risk, 1980–93

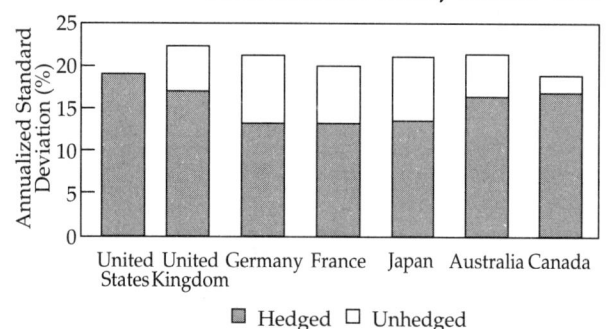

[Bar chart showing annualized standard deviation (%) for United States, United Kingdom, Germany, France, Japan, Australia, Canada, with Hedged and Unhedged bars]

forward rate (FR) was priced at a discount to the spot rate (foreign interest rates exceeded domestic interest rates), the spot rate did not depreciate to the level predicted by the forward rate. Hence, the forward contracts generated a positive return, on average, which resulted in a negative return to hedging.

In contrast, during the months when the forward rate was priced at a premium to the spot rate, the spot rate failed to rise to the level predicted by the forward rate, resulting in a negative return from the forward contracts and a positive return to hedging. The reason such a strategy has worked historically can be seen by looking at the average annualized returns on forward contracts conditioned on whether the forward rate was at a discount or a premium.

Table 2.10 uses the data in Table 2.2 for 1976 through 1993 to show the average forward surprise for each of the major currencies conditioned on the sign of the forward rate. For example, the period contained 161 months in which the forward rate on the pound was priced at a discount to the spot rate. The average annualized forward surprise during those months was −3.90 percent. In contrast, the forward rate on the pound was priced at a premium to the spot rate in 40 months. In these months, the annualized forward surprise was 5.11 percent. Because the conditional returns nearly cancel out, the unconditional forward surprise for the period was 0.45 percent.

The relevant point is that to the extent the forward exchange rate overpredicts changes in the spot rate, the cost of hedging will be higher when foreign interest rates exceed domestic rates and will be lower, even negative, when domestic interest rates exceed foreign rates.

Serial Dependence. The term "serial dependence" refers to the notion that returns are correlated with their prior values. If returns revert to an average value, for example, they are said to revert to the mean. Another variation of serial dependence is known as trending. A trending pattern is one in which a positive return is more likely to be followed by another positive return than by a reversal and, similarly, a negative return is more likely to be succeeded by another negative return instead of a positive return.[1]

Serial dependence is relevant to the issue of hedging because to the extent that returns are nonrandom, their variance will depend on the interval used to measure the returns. For example, if returns are positively serially correlated (that is, they trend), then the variance estimated from quarterly returns will be more than 3 times the variance of monthly returns and the variance of annual returns will be more than 12 times the variance of monthly returns. For example, if returns are random and the measured standard deviation of monthly yen returns is 3.39 percent, the annualized standard deviation will be $\sqrt{12}(3.39) = 11.74$ percent. If the measured annual standard deviation is greater than 11.74 percent, then monthly yen returns will have had a tendency to trend. If the measured annual

---

[1] See Levich (1993) for a review of the literature on random walks and trends.

Table 2.5. Rolling Five-Year Currency Correlations: US$-Based Returns

Five Years Ending in	£ and DM	£ and FF	£ and SF	£ and ¥	£ and A$	£ and C$	DM and SF	DM and FF	DM and ¥	DM and A$	DM and C$	SF and FF	SF and ¥	SF and A$	SF and C$	FF and ¥	FF and A$	FF and C$	¥ and A$	¥ and C$	A$ and C$
1978	0.58	0.58	0.55	0.55	NA	NA	0.81	0.73	0.55	NA	NA	0.63	0.49	NA	NA	0.62	NA	NA	NA	NA	NA
1979	0.53	0.59	0.51	0.42	0.23	−0.01	0.83	0.82	0.47	0.35	0.10	0.68	0.51	0.29	0.02	0.58	0.33	0.04	0.37	−0.11	0.53
1980	0.52	0.63	0.51	0.42	0.25	0.12	0.85	0.85	0.40	0.32	0.23	0.73	0.46	0.27	0.10	0.53	0.32	0.19	0.38	−0.04	0.56
1981	0.61	0.63	0.58	0.54	0.71	0.34	0.88	0.91	0.44	0.63	0.25	0.76	0.48	0.61	0.18	0.55	0.70	0.25	0.77	0.09	0.29
1982	0.59	0.59	0.55	0.47	0.62	0.43	0.87	0.91	0.51	0.64	0.31	0.76	0.52	0.61	0.22	0.61	0.71	0.35	0.79	0.20	0.29
1983	0.45	0.48	0.41	0.38	0.47	0.51	0.88	0.91	0.45	0.39	0.43	0.80	0.48	0.45	0.39	0.49	0.56	0.47	0.58	0.28	0.28
1984	0.52	0.53	0.45	0.44	0.48	0.50	0.87	0.92	0.51	0.41	0.41	0.79	0.55	0.46	0.39	0.56	0.56	0.45	0.54	0.37	0.31
1985	0.66	0.66	0.63	0.45	0.36	0.43	0.88	0.94	0.65	0.42	0.37	0.83	0.66	0.48	0.42	0.67	0.48	0.40	0.42	0.37	0.37
1986	0.69	0.68	0.69	0.42	0.32	0.40	0.91	0.94	0.75	0.29	0.32	0.88	0.79	0.28	0.35	0.73	0.36	0.35	0.23	0.23	0.27
1987	0.72	0.74	0.75	0.55	0.33	0.38	0.93	0.95	0.75	0.23	0.32	0.90	0.82	0.24	0.33	0.72	0.32	0.31	0.16	0.20	0.36
1988	0.79	0.80	0.79	0.64	0.35	0.30	0.95	0.97	0.77	0.24	0.01	0.94	0.83	0.23	0.21	0.76	0.29	0.18	0.18	0.11	0.35
1989	0.77	0.79	0.78	0.71	0.28	0.26	0.96	0.97	0.81	0.13	0.13	0.94	0.83	0.10	0.13	0.79	0.17	0.14	0.10	0.08	0.38
1990	0.74	0.75	0.74	0.76	0.20	0.11	0.94	0.97	0.77	−0.04	0.05	0.91	0.80	−0.08	−0.01	0.75	0.01	0.04	0.03	0.00	0.26
1991	0.85	0.86	0.84	0.80	0.22	0.00	0.93	0.99	0.73	0.04	0.03	0.92	0.75	0.07	−0.04	0.72	0.09	0.04	0.17	−0.01	0.34
1992	0.83	0.84	0.79	0.68	0.19	0.18	0.94	0.99	0.68	0.03	0.05	0.93	0.67	0.03	−0.02	0.69	0.05	0.05	0.10	−0.08	0.31
1993	0.80	0.81	0.78	0.54	0.07	0.12	0.92	0.98	0.54	−0.09	0.05	0.92	0.55	−0.09	−0.07	0.52	−0.08	0.04	−0.04	−0.09	0.39
Average	0.69	0.69	0.65	0.53	0.27	0.22	0.90	0.92	0.60	0.20	0.18	0.83	0.60	0.20	0.13	0.61	0.24	0.18	0.25	0.09	0.39

Note: Correlations are calculated using monthly returns.

Key:
£ = British pound
DM = German mark
FF = French franc
SF = Swiss franc
¥ = Japanese yen
A$ = Australian dollar
C$ = Canadian dollar

NA = not available.

Table 2.6. Correlations of Local Asset and Currency Returns, 1980–93

	Stocks							Bonds							Currency					
Asset/Country	U.S.	Ger.	U.K.	Jap.	Aus.	Can.	Fra.	U.S.	Ger.	U.K.	Jap.	Aus.	Can.	Fra.	Ger.	U.K.	Jap.	Aus.	Can.	Fra.
Stocks																				
United States	1.00																			
Germany	0.43	1.00																		
United Kingdom	0.63	0.49	1.00																	
Japan	0.35	0.31	0.37	1.00																
Australia	0.50	0.37	0.47	0.28	1.00															
Canada	0.77	0.40	0.55	0.34	0.60	1.00														
France	0.49	0.55	0.49	0.36	0.39	0.42	1.00													
Bonds																				
United States	0.35	0.15	0.06	0.09	−0.03	0.23	0.07	1.00												
Germany	0.20	0.25	0.10	0.14	0.06	0.19	0.20	0.49	1.00											
United Kingdom	0.25	0.16	0.35	0.14	0.07	0.27	0.18	0.36	0.45	1.00										
Japan	0.17	0.04	0.06	0.22	−0.08	0.13	0.15	0.45	0.59	0.45	1.00									
Australia	0.25	0.16	0.20	0.07	0.39	0.24	0.03	0.20	0.08	0.13	0.08	1.00								
Canada	0.29	0.15	0.03	0.08	0.05	0.32	0.12	0.76	0.46	0.41	0.39	0.17	1.00							
France	0.26	0.25	0.18	0.20	0.08	0.20	0.45	0.32	0.52	0.35	0.40	0.08	0.32	1.00						

A. Currency Correlations from the Perspective of a U.S.-Based Investor

Germany	0.00	−0.10	−0.23	0.02	−0.05	0.00	−0.07	0.26	0.31	0.06	0.31	0.10	0.19	0.05	1.00					
United Kingdom	−0.02	−0.10	−0.16	0.09	0.13	0.10	−0.05	0.18	0.17	0.18	0.22	0.12	0.19	−0.03	0.72	1.00				
Japan	−0.05	−0.10	−0.13	0.17	0.08	0.02	0.01	0.18	0.26	0.14	0.39	0.06	0.24	0.11	0.63	0.56	1.00			
Australia	0.06	0.04	0.08	0.01	0.29	0.17	0.06	0.02	0.06	0.05	0.08	0.29	0.08	−0.02	0.17	0.28	0.21	1.00		
Canada	0.21	0.07	0.07	0.10	0.23	0.38	0.11	0.23	0.20	0.16	0.18	0.24	0.39	0.13	0.21	0.29	0.16	0.34	1.00	
France	0.00	−0.11	−0.20	0.00	−0.02	0.02	−0.06	0.23	0.29	0.03	0.28	0.12	0.16	0.00	0.96	0.73	0.63	0.22	0.23	1.00

Table 2.6. (continued)

	Stocks							Bonds							Currency					
Asset/Country	U.S.	Ger.	U.K.	Jap.	Aus.	Can.	Fra.	U.S.	Ger.	U.K.	Jap.	Aus.	Can.	Fra.	Ger.	U.K.	Jap.	Aus.	Can.	Fra.

B. Currency Correlations from the Perspective of an Australia-Based Investor

Germany	−0.03	−0.09	−0.24	0.02	−0.25	−0.10	−0.07	0.20	0.21	0.03	0.20	−0.12	0.10	0.07	1.00					
United Kingdom	−0.02	−0.14	−0.19	0.10	−0.11	0.00	−0.09	0.13	0.08	0.12	0.15	−0.12	0.11	−0.01	0.78	1.00				
Japan	−0.08	−0.15	−0.13	0.16	−0.14	−0.08	−0.01	0.06	0.12	0.04	0.23	−0.21	0.10	0.09	0.70	0.66	1.00			
Australia	−0.05	−0.03	−0.08	0.00	−0.27	−0.14	−0.04	−0.03	−0.06	−0.04	−0.08	−0.29	−0.09	0.04	0.58	0.52	0.60	1.00		
Canada	−0.01	−0.03	−0.07	0.02	−0.23	−0.06	−0.01	−0.01	−0.02	0.00	−0.05	−0.26	−0.03	0.05	0.58	0.53	0.59	0.95	1.00	
France	−0.04	−0.10	−0.23	0.00	−0.22	−0.09	−0.08	0.17	0.19	0.00	0.18	−0.12	0.07	0.03	0.97	0.78	0.71	0.57	0.57	1.00

C. Currency Correlations from the Perspective of a Canada-Based Investor

Germany	−0.03	−0.09	−0.23	0.00	−0.10	−0.07	−0.08	0.25	0.28	0.04	0.29	0.07	0.14	0.04	1.00					
United Kingdom	−0.02	−0.13	−0.15	0.09	0.09	0.05	−0.09	0.16	0.10	0.13	0.22	0.09	0.14	−0.05	0.69	1.00				
Japan	−0.08	−0.16	−0.10	0.17	0.05	−0.04	0.00	0.08	0.17	0.05	0.32	−0.02	0.15	0.07	0.56	0.53	1.00			
Australia	0.00	0.02	0.06	−0.02	0.23	0.05	0.02	0.01	0.02	0.00	0.05	0.25	0.02	−0.05	0.17	0.28	0.22	1.00		
Canada	−0.12	−0.01	−0.01	−0.06	−0.13	−0.25	−0.07	−0.05	−0.12	−0.12	−0.08	−0.11	−0.19	−0.04	0.15	0.13	0.19	0.20	1.00	
France	−0.04	−0.10	−0.20	−0.01	−0.06	−0.06	−0.08	0.22	0.25	0.00	0.26	0.08	0.11	−0.01	0.96	0.70	0.58	0.22	0.13	1.00

D. Currency Correlations from the Perspective of a Germany-Based Investor

Germany	−0.01	0.08	0.23	−0.02	0.05	0.00	0.05	−0.26	−0.31	−0.07	−0.31	−0.11	−0.19	−0.05	1.00					
United Kingdom	0.01	−0.06	−0.11	0.11	0.23	0.15	−0.01	−0.12	−0.23	0.12	−0.10	0.01	0.00	−0.12	0.41	1.00				
Japan	−0.06	−0.07	0.15	0.16	0.15	0.03	0.08	−0.19	−0.13	0.01	0.02	−0.11	0.00	0.03	0.53	0.42	1.00			
Australia	0.02	0.08	0.24	−0.01	0.24	0.09	0.07	−0.20	−0.22	−0.03	−0.20	0.11	−0.10	−0.07	0.73	0.44	0.47	1.00		
Canada	0.03	0.08	0.23	0.00	0.09	0.07	0.07	−0.24	−0.28	−0.03	−0.28	−0.08	−0.14	−0.04	0.96	0.42	0.52	0.72	1.00	
France	−0.03	−0.04	0.12	−0.07	0.15	0.06	0.00	−0.15	−0.14	−0.14	−0.13	0.02	−0.14	−0.18	0.23	0.27	0.30	0.31	0.25	1.00

E. Currency Correlations from the Perspective of a U.K.-Based Investor

Germany	−0.02	0.06	−0.10	−0.11	−0.23	−0.15	0.02	0.11	0.23	−0.12	0.10	−0.02	0.00	0.11	1.00					
United Kingdom	−0.01	0.13	0.15	−0.11	−0.12	−0.12	0.07	−0.17	−0.13	−0.16	−0.23	−0.12	−0.19	0.04	0.39	1.00				
Japan	−0.07	−0.02	0.06	0.07	−0.05	−0.10	0.09	−0.09	0.06	−0.09	0.10	−0.12	0.00	0.13	0.45	0.53	1.00			
Australia	0.02	0.13	0.19	−0.09	0.09	−0.01	0.09	−0.13	−0.07	−0.12	−0.15	0.11	−0.11	0.01	0.25	0.69	0.42	1.00		
Canada	0.02	0.13	0.15	−0.09	−0.09	−0.05	0.09	−0.15	−0.10	−0.13	−0.21	−0.09	−0.14	0.06	0.39	0.96	0.51	0.68	1.00	
France	−0.02	0.05	−0.06	−0.14	−0.19	−0.14	0.02	0.07	0.19	−0.17	0.06	−0.01	−0.05	0.06	0.94	0.41	0.49	0.31	0.41	1.00

F. Currency Correlations from the Perspective of a Japan-Based Investor

Germany	0.06	0.07	−0.15	−0.17	−0.15	−0.03	−0.08	0.19	0.14	−0.01	−0.01	0.10	0.00	−0.02	1.00					
United Kingdom	0.07	0.02	−0.06	−0.07	0.04	0.10	−0.09	0.09	−0.06	0.09	−0.10	0.12	0.00	−0.12	0.64	1.00				
Japan	0.06	0.16	0.10	−0.19	−0.09	−0.03	−0.02	−0.09	−0.20	−0.09	−0.35	−0.01	−0.21	−0.08	0.41	0.42	1.00			
Australia	0.07	0.15	0.14	−0.15	0.13	0.08	0.02	−0.06	−0.13	−0.05	−0.23	0.21	−0.11	−0.09	0.32	0.42	0.68	1.00		
Canada	0.09	0.17	0.10	−0.14	−0.04	0.07	0.02	−0.07	−0.16	−0.06	−0.33	0.04	−0.14	−0.06	0.38	0.40	0.93	0.67	1.00	
France	0.05	0.06	−0.12	−0.20	−0.11	−0.01	−0.09	0.15	0.10	−0.06	−0.05	0.12	−0.04	−0.08	0.95	0.65	0.41	0.37	0.40	1.00

Note: Correlations are calculated using monthly returns.

Table 2.7. Correlations of Unhedged Asset Returns, 1980–93

	Stocks							Bonds						
Asset/Country	U.S.	Ger.	U.K.	Jap.	Aus.	Can.	Fra.	U.S.	Ger.	U.K.	Jap.	Aus.	Can.	Fra.
A. U.S. Dollar Perspective														
Stocks														
United States	1.00													
Germany	0.37	1.00												
United Kingdom	0.53	0.47	1.00											
Japan	0.26	0.36	0.43	1.00										
Australia	0.43	0.29	0.50	0.26	1.00									
Canada	0.73	0.36	0.54	0.29	0.56	1.00								
France	0.44	0.63	0.51	0.42	0.34	0.39	1.00							
Bonds														
United States	0.35	0.28	0.17	0.15	0.00	0.27	0.19	1.00						
Germany	0.08	0.56	0.30	0.35	0.05	0.13	0.46	0.40	1.00					
United Kingdom	0.13	0.34	0.61	0.36	0.19	0.27	0.33	0.34	0.60	1.00				
Japan	0.03	0.31	0.27	0.63	0.10	0.11	0.36	0.33	0.67	0.54	1.00			
Australia	0.19	0.20	0.31	0.12	0.67	0.32	0.16	0.13	0.17	0.25	0.17	1.00		
Canada	0.31	0.26	0.21	0.19	0.18	0.52	0.23	0.69	0.36	0.41	0.35	0.25	1.00	
France	0.12	0.53	0.33	0.37	0.10	0.16	0.58	0.36	0.90	0.57	0.65	0.21	0.33	1.00
B. Australian Dollar Perspective														
Stocks														
United States	1.00													
Germany	0.49	1.00												
United Kingdom	0.62	0.49	1.00											
Japan	0.38	0.40	0.49	1.00										
Australia	0.26	0.13	0.32	0.13	1.00									
Canada	0.79	0.43	0.58	0.37	0.40	1.00								
France	0.51	0.67	0.52	0.46	0.21	0.45	1.00							
Bonds														
United States	0.57	0.44	0.33	0.29	−0.19	0.42	0.33	1.00						
Germany	0.32	0.63	0.35	0.42	−0.20	0.26	0.53	0.60	1.00					
United Kingdom	0.33	0.39	0.63	0.41	−0.04	0.36	0.37	0.50	0.64	1.00				
Japan	0.28	0.35	0.36	0.68	−0.15	0.25	0.43	0.49	0.70	0.59	1.00			
Australia	0.04	0.04	0.08	−0.07	0.39	0.07	−0.05	−0.02	−0.08	−0.02	−0.15	1.00		
Canada	0.54	0.40	0.30	0.34	−0.13	0.56	0.34	0.82	0.54	0.52	0.52	−0.07	1.00	
France	0.37	0.61	0.39	0.45	−0.17	0.30	0.63	0.58	0.92	0.62	0.70	−0.08	0.53	1.00

Table 2.7. (continued)

	Stocks							Bonds						
	U.S.	Ger.	U.K.	Jap.	Aus.	Can.	Fra.	U.S.	Ger.	U.K.	Jap.	Aus.	Can.	Fra.

C. Canadian Dollar Perspective

Stocks

United States	1.00													
Germany	0.37	1.00												
United Kingdom	0.55	0.44	1.00											
Japan	0.24	0.31	0.43	1.00										
Australia	0.41	0.26	0.48	0.24	1.00									
Canada	0.71	0.31	0.52	0.25	0.53	1.00								
France	0.43	0.63	0.48	0.40	0.32	.36	1.00							

Bonds

United States	0.36	0.29	0.18	0.11	−0.02	0.16	0.18	10.00						
Germany	0.07	0.56	0.26	0.31	0.01	0.02	0.46	0.41	1.00					
United Kingdom	0.14	0.30	0.60	0.33	0.17	0.20	0.30	0.34	0.56	1.00				
Japan	0.03	0.23	0.28	0.62	0.08	0.03	0.35	0.29	0.61	0.51	1.00			
Australia	0.17	0.18	0.30	0.09	0.65	0.19	0.12	0.15	0.15	0.22	0.14	1.00		
Canada	0.25	0.22	0.12	0.14	0.06	0.33	0.18	0.69	0.30	0.36	0.30	0.13	1.00	
France	0.12	0.53	0.31	0.33	0.06	0.05	0.57	0.37	0.90	0.54	0.61	0.18	0.26	1.00

D. German Mark Perspective

Stocks

United States	1.00													
Germany	0.38	1.00												
United Kingdom	0.66	0.37	1.00											
Japan	0.34	0.22	0.45	1.00										
Australia	0.56	0.31	0.59	0.33	1.00									
Canada	0.53	0.37	0.49	0.26	0.49	1.00								
France	0.43	0.54	0.43	0.34	0.37	0.41	1.00							

Bonds

United States	0.60	0.18	0.32	0.17	0.25	0.17	0.11	1.00						
Germany	−0.05	0.26	−0.03	0.06	−0.06	0.22	0.19	0.14	1.00					
United Kingdom	0.28	0.07	0.61	0.28	0.29	0.29	0.13	0.33	0.16	1.00				
Japan	0.22	−0.04	0.29	0.62	0.23	0.08	0.17	0.31	0.17	0.37	1.00			
Australia	0.45	0.15	0.42	0.18	0.73	0.22	0.12	0.40	−0.13	0.28	0.23	1.00		
Canada	0.60	0.16	0.35	0.25	0.36	0.30	0.17	0.80	0.08	0.40	0.40	0.46	1.00	
France	0.23	0.22	0.21	0.21	0.17	0.24	0.48	0.25	0.43	0.20	0.31	0.13	0.24	1.00

Table 2.7. (continued)

	Stocks							Bonds						
	U.S.	Ger.	U.K.	Jap.	Aus.	Can.	Fra.	U.S.	Ger.	U.K.	Jap.	Aus.	Can.	Fra.

E. British Pound Perspective

Stocks

United States	1.00													
Germany	0.47	1.00												
United Kingdom	0.59	0.38	1.00											
Japan	0.31	0.28	0.34	1.00										
Australia	0.49	0.29	0.48	0.24	1.00									
Canada	0.81	0.40	0.56	0.30	0.58	1.00								
France	0.49	0.63	0.43	0.37	0.33	.43	1.00							

Bonds

United States	0.61	0.36	0.18	0.16	0.14	0.45	0.25	1.00						
Germany	0.22	0.55	−0.03	0.19	−0.04	0.13	0.43	0.44	1.00					
United Kingdom	0.10	0.08	0.34	0.08	0.00	0.15	0.10	0.17	0.12	1.00				
Japan	0.23	0.20	0.08	0.58	0.09	0.19	0.31	0.37	0.49	0.15	1.00			
Australia	0.42	0.24	0.26	0.11	0.67	0.40	0.17	0.38	0.14	−0.01	0.19	1.00		
Canada	0.59	0.33	0.15	0.20	0.23	0.59	0.27	0.81	0.36	0.19	0.41	0.41	1.00	
France	0.32	0.52	0.05	0.24	0.05	0.22	0.57	0.46	0.85	0.06	0.52	0.22	0.39	1.00

F. Japanese Yen Perspective

Stocks

United States	1.00													
Germany	0.50	1.00												
United Kingdom	0.64	0.48	1.00											
Japan	0.16	0.18	0.28	1.00										
Australia	0.50	0.32	0.52	0.15	1.00									
Canada	0.82	0.44	0.62	0.18	0.59	1.00								
France	0.48	0.63	0.47	0.25	0.34	0.43	1.00							

Bonds

United States	0.61	0.41	0.32	−0.07	0.16	0.48	0.23	1.00						
Germany	0.25	0.60	0.22	−0.07	0.02	0.20	0.41	0.47	1.00					
United Kingdom	0.31	0.32	0.60	0.04	0.20	0.35	0.24	0.41	0.48	1.00				
Japan	−0.08	0.03	−0.01	0.22	−0.18	−0.07	0.12	0.11	0.26	0.22	1.00			
Australia	0.44	0.31	0.40	−0.07	0.68	0.44	0.18	0.41	0.22	0.30	−0.12	1.00		
Canada	0.59	0.37	0.29	−0.08	0.24	0.61	0.24	0.81	0.37	0.41	0.03	0.43	1.00	
France	0.34	0.58	0.29	−0.06	0.09	0.27	0.54	0.47	0.86	0.46	0.18	0.28	0.38	1.00

Note: Correlations are calculated using monthly returns.

Table 2.8. Rolling Five-Year Correlations between Currencies and U.S. Assets: Perspective of U.S. Investor

Five Years Ended	£/$ Stock	£/$ Bond	DM/$ Stock	DM/$ Bond	SF/$ Stock	SF/$ Bond	FF/$ Stock	FF/$ Bond	¥/$ Stock	¥/$ Bond	A$/$ Stock	A$/$ Bond	C$/$ Stock	C$/$ Bond
1978	−0.09	−0.09	0.12	0.11	0.00	0.08	0.08	0.07	0.02	−0.14	NA	NA	NA	NA
1979	−0.01	0.12	0.12	0.20	0.05	0.17	0.16	0.07	−0.05	0.02	0.12	−0.02	0.23	0.07
1980	0.03	0.18	0.08	0.39	0.03	0.34	0.06	0.28	−0.11	0.20	0.10	0.07	0.35	0.11
1981	0.11	0.38	0.12	0.35	0.10	0.40	0.10	0.28	−0.06	0.30	0.08	0.36	0.28	0.24
1982	0.15	0.36	0.15	0.33	0.09	0.34	0.14	0.25	0.03	0.23	0.12	0.19	0.30	0.32
1983	0.29	0.44	0.34	0.47	0.27	0.50	0.29	0.41	0.11	0.35	0.12	0.21	0.38	0.36
1984	0.19	0.32	0.25	0.36	0.26	0.42	0.21	0.32	−0.15	0.29	0.10	0.14	0.36	0.38
1985	0.09	0.31	0.12	0.22	0.11	0.21	0.09	0.21	0.16	0.20	0.03	0.13	0.21	0.42
1986	0.01	0.19	−0.03	0.18	−0.05	0.12	0.00	0.23	0.01	0.10	0.06	0.06	0.21	0.38
1987	−0.13	0.17	−0.14	0.23	−0.15	0.17	−0.09	0.25	−0.12	0.16	0.10	0.02	0.19	0.20
1988	−0.18	0.03	−0.16	0.10	−0.17	0.09	−0.11	0.10	−0.14	0.02	0.09	−0.08	0.18	0.13
1989	−0.17	0.07	−0.21	0.16	−0.25	0.14	−0.15	0.16	−0.20	0.02	0.09	−0.07	0.18	0.09
1990	−0.20	0.01	−0.21	0.13	−0.26	0.11	−0.18	0.12	−0.17	0.06	0.11	−0.14	0.28	0.11
1991	−0.17	−0.06	−0.14	0.12	−0.21	0.07	−0.12	0.07	−0.12	0.00	0.04	−0.19	0.26	0.06
1992	−0.04	0.04	−0.08	0.18	−0.14	0.17	−0.10	0.15	−0.12	0.03	0.08	−0.12	0.13	0.10
1993	0.02	0.14	−0.02	0.26	−0.12	0.21	−0.06	0.21	−0.08	0.20	0.01	0.05	0.10	0.10
Average	−0.01	0.17	0.03	0.24	−0.03	0.23	0.03	0.22	−0.03	0.16	0.08	0.01	0.22	0.20

Note: Correlations are calculated using monthly returns.

Key: £ = British pound
DM = German mark
FF = French franc
SF = Swiss franc
¥ = Japanese yen
A$ = Australian dollar
C$ = Canadian dollar
$ = U.S. dollar

NA = not available.

Table 2.9. Annualized Hedging Returns

	Pound	Mark	French Franc	Swiss Franc	Yen	Australian Dollar	Canadian Dollar
Unconditional hedged return	−0.98%	−0.11%	−2.55%	−0.12%	−2.42%	1.13%	0.08%
Number of months FR was at a premium	37	192	40	189	167	45	35
Hedged return	19.84%	0.97%	20.97%	1.41%	0.85%	6.59%	8.05%
Number of months FR was at a discount	200	48	198	51	65	158	166
Hedged return	−4.67%	−4.32%	−6.66%	−5.58%	−10.28%	−3.38%	−1.81%

Note: Returns for 1974 through 1993 except for Australian and Canadian dollars, for which the period is 1977 through 1993.

Table 2.10. Average Annualized Forward Surprise Conditional on the Forward Premium: Perspective of U.S. Investor

	Pound	Mark	French Franc	Swiss Franc	Yen	Australian Dollar	Canadian Dollar
Unconditional average	0.45%	−0.49%	1.01%	3.12%	2.48%	0.19%	−0.18%
Conditional average							
$f > 0$	−3.90	−0.61	−2.61	1.15	−0.38	−1.30	−1.27
$f < 0$	5.11	0.27	4.16	1.64	2.50	1.49	1.19
Number of observations, $f > 0$	40	161	42	75	151	46	35
Number of observations, $f < 0$	161	41	161	47	43	158	167
Total observations	201	202	203	122	194	204	202

Note: Returns are annualized by multiplying the monthly average by 12. The forward surprise is equal to the monthly currency return minus the one-month forward premium from a U.S. investor's perspective. The Swiss franc is measured for the 1983–93 period, and the Australian and Canadian dollars, for 1977–93; all other currencies are measured for 1976–93.

standard deviation is less than 11.74, yen returns will have had a tendency to be mean reverting.

One approach to measuring serial dependence is called a *variance ratio* test. If a sequence of returns is random and several estimates of the variance are computed based on different return intervals, the estimates should be linearly related to one another. Specifically, the variance estimated from two-day returns should be twice as large as the variance estimated from daily returns, and the variance estimated from quarterly returns should be three times as large as the variance estimated from monthly returns.

The statistic called the variance ratio (*VR*) is computed by dividing the variance of returns estimated from the longer interval by the variance estimated from the shorter interval and then normalizing this value to 1 by dividing it by the ratio of the longer interval to the shorter interval, as shown in the following equation:

$$VR = \frac{\sigma_L^2/\sigma_S^2}{L/S}, \qquad (2.5)$$

where

σ_L^2 = variance estimated from longer-interval returns
σ_S^2 = variance estimated from shorter-interval returns
L = number of periods in longer interval
S = number of periods in shorter interval.

A variance ratio of less than 1 suggests that the shorter-interval returns tend toward mean reversion within the duration of the longer interval. On the other hand, a variance ratio that exceeds 1 suggests that the shorter-interval returns trend within the duration of the longer interval. The historical record, shown in Table 2.11, suggests that currency returns trend, but this trending is statistically significant only for the French franc and the Canadian dollar. For example, the one-year variance ratio for the Japanese yen using monthly return data for the shorter interval is $(193.03/11.49)/(12/1) = 1.40$.

This serial dependence has important consequences for hedging. If variances change proportionally with time, the investment horizon does not affect the decision to hedge. If the variances increase at an increasing rate with time, however, investors might choose to hedge a different fraction of their currency exposure when they are dealing with a longer horizon than they would if hedging for a shorter horizon.

Serial dependence also has important implications for option pricing. The value of an option is conditioned on five factors: the price of the underlying asset, the strike price, the riskless rate of interest, the time remaining to expiration, and the volatility of the underlying asset. If all factors are constant except volatility, the value of an option will increase with the volatility of the underlying asset because uncertainty increases the expected payoff if the option ends up in the money.

If the returns of the underlying asset are positively serially correlated within a quarter, then the variance of quarterly returns will exceed three times the variance of monthly returns. Therefore, if the volatility of the underlying asset is estimated from monthly or higher-frequency data and then extrapolated, according to the Black–Scholes assumption that variance changes linearly with time, the value of the three-month option will be underestimated.

The annualized variance estimated from shorter intervals can be extrapolated simply by multiplying it by the appropriate variance ratio. Similarly, the annualized standard deviation can be extrapolated by multiplying it by the square root of the appropriate variance ratio. For example, suppose the aim is to estimate the value of an option that expires in three months and the estimate of standard deviation is based on daily returns. If the variance ratio of three-month returns to one-month returns equals 1.21, to value the three-month option, the approach is simply to multiply the annualized standard deviation of daily returns by 1.1, the square root of the variance ratio, 1.21.

Kurtosis. Another empirical tendency is for daily returns to be *leptokurtic*. A leptokurtic distribution has wide tails and a tall narrow peak. It has a higher kurtosis ratio than a normal distribution, which has a kurtosis ratio equal to 3. Table 2.12 shows the kurtosis of daily and monthly currency returns for the 20-year period beginning January 1, 1974, and ending December 31, 1993.

Although monthly currency returns are only slightly leptokurtic, daily currency returns are significantly leptokurtic. The cause might be price jumps that occur in response to the accumulated information that is released during nontrading hours, especially on weekends. As the measurement interval increases, these price jumps cancel out, which explains why monthly

Table 2.11. Variance Ratio Tests for Serial Dependence, July 1973–December 1993

Currency	One Year	Two Years	Three Years
Pound	1.93	1.33	1.54
	(1.36)	(1.30)	(1.24)
Mark	1.28	1.50	1.60
	(1.17)	(1.41)	(1.37)
French franc	1.53	1.90	2.27
	(2.18)*	(2.55)*	(2.90)*
Swiss franc	1.27	1.36	1.39
	(1.11)	(1.02)	(0.90)
Yen	1.40	1.41	1.42
	(1.66)	(1.17)	(0.96)
Australian dollar	1.03	1.37	1.55
	(0.11)	(0.95)	(1.16)
Canadian dollar	1.54	2.32	2.56
	(2.07)*	(3.45)*	(3.28)*

Note: Variances in the denominators are estimated from monthly returns. Numbers in parenthesis are *t*-statistics.

*Indicates the variance ratio is significantly different from 1 at the 5 percent level of significance. The Lo and MacKinlay (1988) approach is used to adjust significance levels for overlapping periods.

Table 2.12. Kurtosis of Monthly and Daily Currency Returns, January 1, 1974, to December 31, 1993

Currency	Monthly	Daily
Pound	4.20	7.03
Mark	3.23	23.80
French franc	3.67	16.43
Swiss franc	3.40	31.82
Yen	3.46	106.91

Note: Normally distributed returns have a kurtosis measure of 3. Kurtosis greater than 3 implies the return distribution has wider tails and a narrower peak than normal.

returns are typically less leptokurtic than daily returns.

The leptokurtic nature of short-interval currency returns has important implications for dynamic hedging strategies, discussed in Chapter 3. These strategies, which generate option-like payoffs, require continual adjustments to the hedge ratios. A leptokurtic distribution implies that the exchange rate may jump significantly before the hedger has time to adjust the hedge ratio, with the consequence that either the hedging strategy will fail to provide the anticipated protection or it will cost more than initially expected.

Chapter 4 describes strategies that can be used to profit from the forward rate bias and serial dependence if those phenomena persist in the future.

Summary

- Through the years, nations' exchange rate policies have varied along two major dimensions—cooperation versus noncooperation and rules-based intervention versus discretionary intervention. The current policy for most countries is cooperative but with discretionary intervention.
- Since currencies began to float in 1973, most currencies have had extended periods of nonzero returns, with volatility somewhere between that of stocks and that of bonds.
- Correlations between most major currencies from a U.S. perspective have been positive since 1973, with the occasional exception of the Canadian dollar.
- Correlations between currencies have not always been stable and have tended to drift somewhat over time.
- Local equity and bond returns have generally been positively correlated with each other. From a U.S. investor's perspective, currency returns have been more positively correlated with local bond returns than with local equity returns.
- Currency returns have generally exhibited a forward rate bias. High-interest-rate currencies have generally depreciated less than the forward discount, yielding a positive forward surprise to investors in the currency and negative returns to hedgers. Low-interest-rate currencies have generally appreciated less than the forward premium, yielding a negative forward surprise to investors and positive returns to hedgers. Barring other considerations, a hedger's best strategy is to hedge more of low-interest-rate currency exposure and less of high-interest-rate currency exposure.
- Currencies have tended to exhibit persistent monthly trends (serial correlation) within longer time periods. A common supposition is that the serial dependence is introduced by central bank interventions intended to smooth currency fluctuations. Investors can profit from these trends by hedging less of their currency exposure when positive foreign currency trends exist.
- Daily currency returns tend to exhibit a greater frequency of large moves than is characteristic of a normal distribution. These larger moves make smooth dynamic hedge adjustments difficult.

3. Hedging Currency Risk

The investor can react to foreign exchange risk in one of two ways. One alternative is to do nothing. In this case, the investor is left with the foreign exchange risk and retains either the gains or the losses from the currency exposure. The alternative is to hedge the risk in some way by shifting some of the risk to others. The decisions about whether to hedge or not and, if so, how much to hedge and when can be complex. The choices depend on how much volatility the investor is exposed to, how much the volatility can be reduced, how much it costs to hedge, what expectations the investor has for foreign exchange movements, and what trade-off the investor is willing to make between the reduction in volatility and the cost of the hedge.

For the investor who has decided to hedge some part of foreign exchange exposure, Figure 3.1 shows three typical hedge alternatives. The first is a symmetrical hedge using forward or futures contracts to minimize both currency gains and losses. A *matched hedge* uses the same currency to hedge as the investor is exposed to. A *currency-basket hedge* uses a portfolio of currencies to hedge the investor's exposure; the portfolio is configured in such a way as to reduce the expected hedging cost while minimizing the tracking error of the hedge.

The asymmetrical hedge uses options. The asymmetry of options is designed to preserve some gains from currency exposure while protecting against losses. The two most common option strategies are the protective put and the range forward or collar. The *protective put* is generally the most expensive protection, but it preserves the majority of the gains from favorable currency exposure. The *range forward (collar)* is a somewhat less expensive alternative; it lowers the cost by capturing the gains from favorable currency exposure only up to a certain level.

The final hedging alternative consists of *active management of the hedge*. In this strategy, currency exposure is left unhedged when currency returns are expected to be favorable and hedged when currency returns are expected to be unfavorable. The goal of active hedge management is to capture the benefits of hedging while paying as little as possible for the protection. One might think of it as trying to create the same results as a protective put while minimizing the cost of the put option. Effective active hedge management requires a systematic, ongoing evaluation of potential changes in foreign exchange rates. Chapter 5 discusses a framework for making a conscious trade-off between risk minimization and return enhancement.

Constructing Symmetrical Hedges

The matched hedge uses the same currency to construct a hedge as the currency to which the investor is exposed. The currency-basket hedge

Currency Management: Concepts and Practices

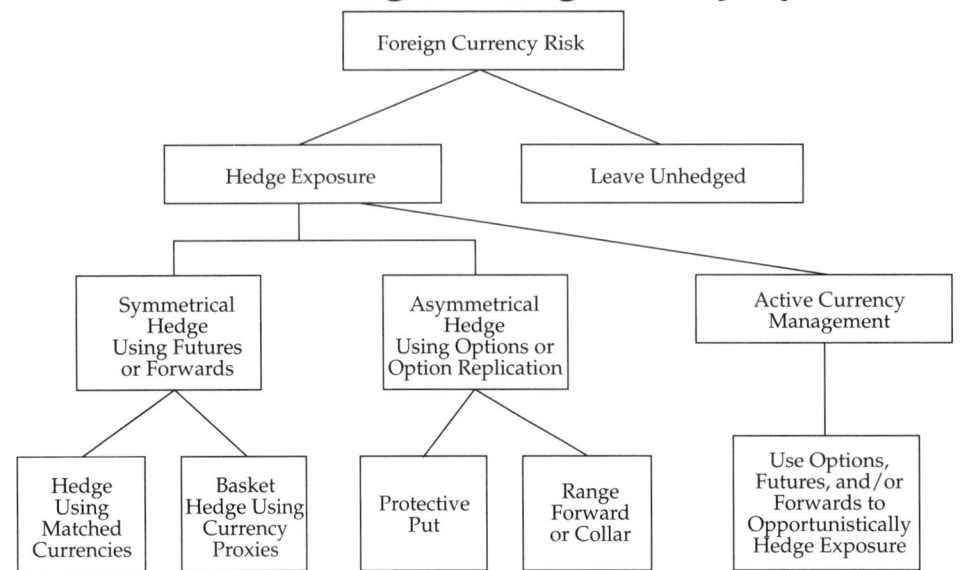

Figure 3.1. Alternatives for Dealing with Foreign Currency Exposure

uses a portfolio of currencies as a proxy to hedge the investor's exposure.

Matched Hedge. In a matched hedge, the investor uses the same currency to which the asset in the portfolio is exposed to hedge the foreign exchange exposure. For example, if the investor holds German stocks, a matched hedge of the currency exposure would involve selling German marks forward using futures or forward contracts. A three-month hedge would be constructed by selling contracts with three months to expiration. Using contracts with longer or shorter maturities exposes the hedge to some tracking error when longer-term contracts are terminated early or when the hedge has to be extended by rolling shorter-term contracts to another maturity.

Chapter 1 gave the approximate return from a fully hedged asset, R_H, as

$$R_H \approx r_\ell + f, \tag{3.1}$$

where r_ℓ is the local asset return and f is the forward premium or discount.

Figure 3.2 compares conceptually the asset returns in the absence and presence of a symmetrical hedge. Notice that the hedged return on the fully hedged asset position mirrors the local asset return except for the cost of the hedge embodied in the forward premium or discount. Selling currency futures or forward contracts eliminates the currency risk, leaving the investor with the risk of the local asset position only. The effects of the hedge are symmetrical because both upside and downside currency movements are affected to the same extent.

Figure 3.2. Symmetrical Hedged and Unhedged Asset Returns

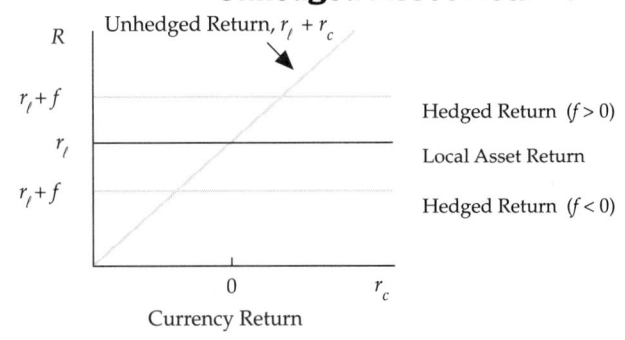

Fully Hedged Asset Exposure

Suppose a U.S. investor holds German stocks valued at DM10,000,000. A fully matched hedge for six months would require selling DM10,000,000 forward for that period. Assume that the current exchange rate is 0.6000 USD/DM with a six-month forward rate of 0.5922, resulting in a forward discount of −1.3 percent. The effect of the currency hedge if the mark appreciates or depreciates by 5 percent during the next six months while the equity portfolio appreciates by 10 percent would be

	USD/DM Exchange Rate	Portfolio Value (DM thousands)	Percent Change in DM	Unhedged Portfolio Value (US$ thousands)	Percent Change in USD
Current	0.6000	10,000	na	6,000	na
After six months	0.6300	11,000	10.0%	6,930	15.5%
After six months	0.5700	11,000	10.0	6,270	4.5

na = not applicable.

If the mark appreciates, the sale of DM10,000,000 forward at a forward rate of 0.5922 will generate a loss in U.S. dollar terms of

$$10,000,000(0.5922 - 0.6300) = -US\$378,000.$$

The U.S. dollar value of the hedged portfolio would be

$$6,930,000 - 378,000 = US\$6,552,000,$$

for a net appreciation of

$$\frac{6,552,000 - 6,000,000}{6,000,000} = 9.2\%.$$

The formula for the hedged return on a foreign asset would result in the following return:

$$R_H = r_\ell + f + r_\ell r_c$$
$$= 0.10 - 0.013 + (0.10 \times 0.05)$$
$$= 9.2\%,$$

or, by approximation (when the cross-product term is disregarded),

$$R_H \approx r_\ell + f$$
$$= 0.10 - 0.013$$
$$= 8.7\%.$$

If the German mark were to depreciate, the sale of DM10,000,000 forward would generate a gain in U.S. dollar terms of

$$10,000,000(0.5922 - 0.5700) = US\$222,000.$$

The dollar value of the hedged portfolio would be

$$6,270,000 + 222,000 = US\$6,492,000,$$

for a net appreciation of

$$\frac{6{,}492{,}000 - 6{,}000{,}000}{6{,}000{,}000} = 8.2\%,$$

which is equivalent to the return from the hedged-return algebra of

$$R_H = r_\ell + f + r_\ell r_c$$
$$= 0.10 - 0.013 + (0.10 \times -0.05)$$
$$= 8.2\%.$$

The approximate return for the fully hedged position of 8.7 percent falls between the two actual returns, depending on the appreciation or depreciation of the currency. The 0.5 percent discrepancy is not trivial because both the asset return and the currency return are not small. This tracking error in the hedge occurs because the return on the underlying stocks is unknown at the time the currency hedge is put in place. The currency risk in the invested principal amount can be hedged, but the currency risk in the asset return cannot be readily hedged with a standard forward or futures contract because the asset return is uncertain.

■ *Minimum-variance hedge for a single foreign asset.* Even though a fully matched hedge removes the risk of currency fluctuations, such a hedge may not be desirable if the currency return is correlated with the return on the asset. The conditions under which currency exposure increases the risk of a foreign asset can be seen by examining the components of the variance:

$$\sigma_R^2 = \sigma_\ell^2 + \sigma_c^2 + 2C_{\ell c}; \tag{3.2}$$

that is, the variance of the return on an unhedged foreign asset is equal to the variance of the underlying asset and the variance of the currency exposure plus twice the covariance between the two.

The impact of currency exposure on risk beyond the asset variance itself will be positive if

$$\sigma_R^2 - \sigma_\ell^2 = \sigma_c^2 + 2C_{\ell c} > 0. \tag{3.3}$$

Expressed in terms of the correlation coefficient instead of the covariance, the inequality becomes[1]

$$\rho_{\ell c} > \frac{-\sigma_c}{2\sigma_\ell}. \tag{3.4}$$

Consequently, if the correlation between the currency return and the local asset return is greater than $-\tfrac{1}{2}$ times the ratio of their respective standard deviations, the risk of the unhedged asset return will be greater than that of the local asset return itself. Sufficiently large negative correlation, however, will cause the combined asset and unhedged currency exposure actually to reduce the volatility of the unhedged asset.

The minimum volatility that can be achieved by hedging the currency exposure of the foreign asset can be found by choosing H to minimize the variance of the portfolio return in

$$\sigma_R^2 = \sigma_\ell^2 + H^2 \sigma_c^2 + 2H C_{\ell c}. \tag{3.5}$$

From the optimality condition generated by taking the derivative of Equation 3.5 with respect to H, the minimum-variance currency exposure is achieved when

$$H = \frac{-C_{\ell c}}{\sigma_c^2}$$
$$= \frac{-\rho_{\ell c}\sigma_\ell}{\sigma_c} \tag{3.6a}$$

or, equivalently, when the hedge ratio is

$$h = H - 1$$
$$= \frac{-(C_{\ell c} + \sigma_c^2)}{\sigma_c^2}. \tag{3.6b}$$

Setting the currency exposure equal to its minimum-variance level results in a minimized variance for the hedged asset of

---

[1] Equation 3.4 can also be written in terms of the currency beta as $\beta_\ell = [\rho_{\ell c}\sigma_\ell/\sigma_c] > -(1/2)$, where β_ℓ is estimated from the regression of the local asset return on the currency return.

$$\sigma_R^2 = \sigma_\ell^2(1 - \rho_{\ell c}^2). \tag{3.7}$$

Note that as long as the foreign asset return and the currency return are correlated, a minimum-variance position can be constructed to have a lower variance than the variance of the local asset return by itself.

Equation 3.6a indicates that zero correlation between the asset return and the currency (a zero currency beta) gives the minimum-variance currency exposure equal to zero (a fully hedged foreign asset), which leaves the portfolio risk equal to the underlying asset risk. If the correlation (or currency beta) is negative, the minimum-variance currency exposure will be greater than zero, implying at least a partial hedge. If the correlation (or currency beta) is positive, however, the minimum-variance currency exposure will be less than zero (more than fully hedged). If portfolio policy does not allow a net short position in the currency, the best the investor can do is fully hedge the currency exposure to reduce the variance as much as possible.

Note also in Equation 3.6a that the minimum-variance currency exposure can be estimated as the negative of the asset currency beta found by regressing the local asset return on the currency return:

$$H = \frac{-\rho_{\ell c}\sigma_\ell}{\sigma_c} = -\beta_\ell \tag{3.8a}$$

or

$$h = -(\beta_\ell + 1). \tag{3.8b}$$

Minimum-Variance Currency Hedge Ratio Using Regression Analysis

The minimum-variance currency exposure can be calculated by using regression analysis. For example, consider the regression relationship between the following monthly returns from the Japanese yen and Japanese stocks (JP) during 1992 and 1993 from the perspective of a U.S. investor:

Month End	Japanese Stocks (r_{JP})	Yen ($r_¥$)
1992		
January	−4.81%	−0.56%
February	−4.62	−2.78
March	−8.67	−2.79
April	−7.12	−0.32
May	4.47	4.33
June	−10.18	1.51
July	−1.37	−1.14
August	13.64	3.40
September	−5.41	2.47
October	−2.42	−2.42
November	3.47	1.08
December	−1.19	−0.34
1993		
January	−0.67	−0.12
February	−1.13	5.80
March	11.50	2.83
April	13.19	3.28
May	0.98	4.04
June	−3.44	0.45
July	5.04	1.49
August	2.00	0.22
September	−3.95	−1.32
October	0.27	−2.15
November	−15.73	−0.46
December	4.75	−2.45

The regression relationship results in

$$r_{JP} = 0.01 + 1.2 r_¥$$
$$(-0.78) \quad (2.15)$$

with an adjusted R^2 of 0.14 (the numbers in parenthesis represent the *t*-statistics for each coefficient).

With the use of the slope coefficient, the minimum-variance currency exposure can be represented as

$$H = -\beta_{JP}$$
$$= -1.2$$

or the minimum-variance hedge ratio can be represented as

$$h = H - 1$$
$$= -2.2.$$

The positive beta coefficient for Japanese stocks indicates that stock returns and yen returns are positively correlated. Consequently, positive exposure to the yen would tend to increase the volatility of Japanese stock returns.

The regression analysis indicates that the minimum-variance currency exposure would be −120 percent, or a hedge ratio of −220 percent. If the minimum currency position is constrained to be nonnegative, the best the investor can do is reduce the currency exposure to zero by hedging all of the Japanese stock exposure ($H = 0$ or $h = -1$).

Figure 3.3 shows the variance of the hedged and unhedged foreign asset position depending on the correlation between the foreign asset return and the currency return. Full currency exposure will yield the minimum-variance position if the correlation is sufficiently negative in proportion to the relative risk of the assets and currency ($\rho_{\ell c} = -\sigma_c/\sigma_\ell$). Zero currency exposure will yield the minimum-variance position if the currency is uncorrelated with asset returns. Correlations outside this range will require minimum-variance currency exposure either to be negative or to be greater than 100 percent. In general, negative correlation will imply a minimum-variance currency exposure greater than zero (in which case, exposure should be unhedged or partially hedged); positive correlation dictates a minimum-variance currency exposure less than zero (more than fully hedged).

Many investors will not be able to take short currency positions beyond the fully hedged position. In this case, the most that the variance can be reduced is to the level of the foreign asset itself. As the next subsection discusses, the inclusion of other assets in the portfolio will require adjustments to these simple relationships because the cross-correlations with other assets and currencies also influence the optimal currency exposure.

■ *Minimum-variance hedge for a portfolio with a domestic and a foreign asset.* Chapter 1 revealed that the variance of a simple portfolio composed of a domestic asset and a foreign asset is equal to

$$\sigma_R^2 = w_d^2 \sigma_d^2 + w_\ell^2 \sigma_\ell^2 + H^2 \sigma_c^2 + 2 w_d w_\ell C_{d\ell} + 2H[w_d C_{dc} + w_\ell C_{\ell c}], \quad (3.9)$$

where

w_d = the portfolio weight held in the domestic asset

$w_\ell = 1 - w_d$, the portfolio weight held in the foreign asset

H = the proportion of the portfolio with foreign currency exposure

σ_d^2 = the variance of domestic asset returns
σ_ℓ^2 = the variance of foreign local asset returns
σ_c^2 = the variance of currency returns
$C_{d\ell}$ = the covariance of domestic asset returns with foreign local asset returns
C_{dc} = the covariance of domestic asset returns with currency returns
$C_{\ell c}$ = the covariance of foreign local asset returns with currency returns.

Choosing H, as before, to minimize the variance gives the minimum-variance currency exposure as

$$H = -\left(\frac{w_d C_{dc} + w_\ell C_{\ell c}}{\sigma_c^2}\right) \quad (3.10a)$$

or, expressed as a hedge ratio,

$$h = H - 1$$
$$= -\left(\frac{\sigma_c^2 + w_d C_{dc} + w_\ell C_{\ell c}}{\sigma_c^2}\right). \quad (3.10b)$$

Note that the minimum-variance currency exposure is a function of the proportion held in domestic and foreign assets and the covariance between the local asset return and the currency return in addition to the volatility of the currency itself.

Equations 3.10a and 3.10b could also be written in terms of each asset's beta relative to the currency return:

$$H = -(w_d \beta_d + w_\ell \beta_\ell) \quad (3.11a)$$

or

$$h = -(1 + w_d \beta_d + w_\ell \beta_\ell). \quad (3.11b)$$

In general, the minimum-variance currency exposure is a function of all the assets in the portfolio, not the foreign asset alone. If w_d is equal to zero (that is, the portfolio contains only the foreign asset), Equation 3.10a reduces to the minimum-variance currency exposure for a single foreign asset, Equation 3.6, but if the portfolio contains other assets that are correlated with currency returns, the minimum-variance currency exposure will be affected by all of the asset and currency correlations. If no correlation exists between the asset and currency returns, the minimum-variance currency exposure is zero, which is a fully matched hedge.

Optimization relative to a benchmark can be carried out in a way that is similar to traditional variance minimization. Chapter 1 noted that the tracking error of a simple portfolio composed of a domestic asset and a foreign asset is equal to

$$\sigma_{\Delta R}^2 = \Delta w_d^2 \sigma_d^2 + \Delta w_\ell^2 \sigma_\ell^2 + 2\Delta w_d \Delta w_\ell C_{d\ell}$$
$$+ \Delta H^2 \sigma_c^2 + 2\Delta H [\Delta w_d C_{dc} + \Delta w_\ell C_{\ell c}], \quad (3.12)$$

where

Δw_d = the difference between the portfolio and the benchmark domestic asset exposure
Δw_ℓ = the difference between the portfolio and the benchmark foreign asset exposure
ΔH = the difference between the portfolio and the benchmark currency exposure.

Choosing ΔH to minimize the tracking error gives the optimal deviation from the benchmark currency exposure as

$$\Delta H = -\left(\frac{\Delta w_d C_{dc} + \Delta w_\ell C_{\ell c}}{\sigma_c^2}\right) \quad (3.13a)$$

or

$$\Delta H = -(\Delta w_d \beta_d + \Delta w_\ell \beta_\ell). \quad (3.13b)$$

The optimal relative currency exposure is a function of the asset deviations from their benchmark weights and the covariances (currency betas) between the asset and currency returns. If the assets are held at their benchmark weights or if the correlations between asset and currency returns are zero, the optimal currency exposure deviation will be zero and the currency exposure will be held at the benchmark weight. Equations 3.13a and 3.13b also give the optimal relative hedge ratio because $\Delta h = \Delta H$.

Currency Management: Concepts and Practices

Figure 3.3. Variance of Foreign Asset Exposure versus Asset–Currency Correlation (assuming $\sigma_\ell > \sigma_c$)

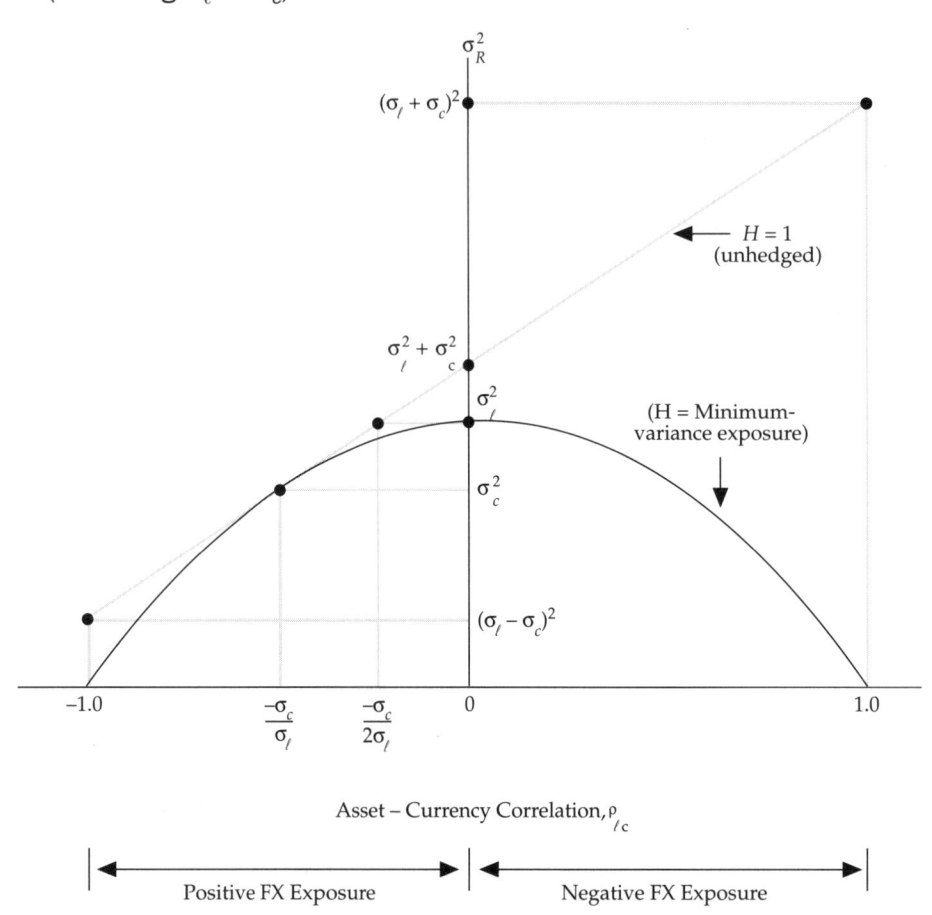

[Graph showing σ_R^2 on vertical axis vs Asset–Currency Correlation $\rho_{\ell c}$ on horizontal axis. Key points marked: $(\sigma_\ell + \sigma_c)^2$, $\sigma_\ell^2 + \sigma_c^2$, σ_ℓ^2, σ_c^2, $(\sigma_\ell - \sigma_c)^2$. Horizontal axis values: -1.0, $-\sigma_c/\sigma_\ell$, $-\sigma_c/2\sigma_\ell$, 0, 1.0. Lines labeled $H = 1$ (unhedged) and H = Minimum-variance exposure. Below axis: Positive FX Exposure (left of 0), Negative FX Exposure (right of 0).]

Minimum-Variance Currency Hedge Ratio for a Mixed Portfolio

Consider a portfolio composed of half U.S. stocks and half Japanese stocks, with the following annualized risk assumptions, from the perspective of a U.S. investor:

w_d = 50.0% $\quad\quad \rho_{d\ell}$ = 0.3
w_ℓ = 50.0% $\quad\quad \rho_{dc}$ = -0.1
σ_c = 10.0% $\quad\quad \rho_{\ell c}$ = 0.2
σ_d = 14.0% $\quad\quad C_{dc} = \rho_{dc}\sigma_d\sigma_c = -0.0014$
σ_ℓ = 18.0% $\quad\quad C_{\ell c} = \rho_{\ell c}\sigma_\ell\sigma_c = 0.0036$
$\quad\quad\quad\quad\quad\quad\quad\quad C_{d\ell} = \rho_{d\ell}\sigma_d\sigma_\ell = 0.0076.$

The currency exposure giving the minimum-variance risk position is

60

$$H = -\left(\frac{w_d C_{dc} + w_\ell C_{\ell c}}{\sigma_c^2}\right)$$

$$= -\left[\frac{(0.5 \times -0.0014) + (0.5 \times 0.0036)}{0.01}\right]$$

$$= -11.0\%.$$

Converting the currency exposure to a hedge ratio gives an h of -111 percent. In this case, the minimum-variance currency exposure would be negative, giving a hedge ratio greater than -100 percent.

The decline in volatility toward the minimum as the currency exposure declines is as follows:

H	$h = H - 1$	σ_R
1.00	0.00	17.0%
0.75	−0.25	15.5
0.50	−0.50	14.3
0.25	−0.75	13.4
0.00	−1.00	13.0
−0.11[a]	−1.11	12.9
−0.25	−1.25	13.0
−0.50	−1.50	13.5

[a]Minimum-variance exposure.

If portfolio policy does not allow the currency exposure to be negative, the investor is limited to setting the currency exposure to zero. In this example, most of the reduction in variance can be achieved with a full hedge.

If the benchmark asset exposures are 70 percent U.S. stocks and 30 percent Japanese stocks, the optimal currency exposure deviation from the benchmark of 30 percent Japanese yen that gives the minimum tracking error is

$$\Delta H = -\left[\frac{\Delta w_d C_{dc} + \Delta w_\ell C_{\ell c}}{\sigma_c^2}\right]$$

$$= \frac{-\{[(0.5 - 0.7)(-0.0014)] + [(0.5 - 0.3)(0.0036)]\}}{0.01}$$

$$= -10.0\%.$$

A portfolio position with the minimum tracking error would require underweighting the Japanese yen by 10 percent, resulting in a currency position of $30 - 10 = 20$ percent. The decline in tracking error can be seen as the incremental currency exposure approaches the minimum-tracking-error exposure:

ΔH	$H = H^B + \Delta H$	$\sigma_{\Delta R}$
20.0	50.0	7.4%
10.0	40.0	6.9
0.0	30.0	6.8
−10.0[a]	20.0	6.7
−20.0	10.0	6.8
−30.0	0.0	7.0

[a]Minimum-tracking-error exposure.

Basket Hedge. A basket hedge uses a portfolio of currency positions to create a symmetrical hedge similar to a matched hedge. The goal of the basket hedge is to use the natural correlations between specific currencies to construct a statistical proxy for the fully hedged position if it can be done at a cheaper cost than a full hedge. Expected cost savings can sometimes be achieved if lower-interest-rate currencies can be sold to create the hedge. The mix of currencies used in the basket hedge is usually decided by using an optimizer to minimize the expected cost subject to a penalty for how much risk is still left in the portfolio.

The disadvantage in using a basket hedge lies in the approximate nature of the hedge. The basket may perform differently from what is expected, leaving some uncertainty in the effectiveness of the hedge. An additional risk, in comparison with a fully matched hedge, is that *ex post* performance of the basket hedge depends on whether the estimated correlations are stable. Diversification is a powerful force, but its benefits can dissipate quickly if estimated correlations suddenly collapse in the face of unusual shocks to the market.[2]

For an illustration of a simple basket hedge, consider a portfolio using two currencies to create a proxy for a third currency that is the currency of the underlying foreign asset. The impact of the cost of the currency hedge in terms of its effect on the portfolio return would be

$$\text{Hedge impact} = -H_1 f_1 - H_2 f_2; \quad (3.14)$$

the variance of the portfolio return would be

$$\sigma_R^2 = w_d^2 \sigma_d^2 + w_\ell^2 \sigma_\ell^2 + H_c^2 \sigma_c^2 + H_1^2 \sigma_1^2 + H_2^2 \sigma_2^2$$
$$+ 2w_d w_\ell C_{d\ell} + 2w_d H_c C_{dc} + 2w_\ell H_c C_{\ell c}$$
$$+ 2H_1(w_d C_{d1} + w_\ell C_{\ell 1} + H_c C_{c1})$$
$$+ 2H_2(w_d C_{d2} + w_\ell C_{\ell 2} + H_c C_{c2})$$
$$+ 2H_1 H_2 C_{1,2}, \quad (3.15)$$

where the subscripts 1 and 2 represent the two currency proxies and σ^2, C, and H represent the appropriate variance, covariance, and currency exposures, respectively.

If λ represents the trade-off the investor is willing to make between the cost of hedging and the portfolio risk, the optimality conditions imply that the allocations to proxy currencies 1 and 2 are

$$H_1 = \frac{f_2 C_{1,2} - f_1 \sigma_2^2 - 2\lambda[(w_d C_{d1} + w_\ell C_{\ell 1} + H_c C_{c1})\sigma_2^2 - (w_d C_{d2} + w_\ell C_{\ell 2} + H_c C_{c2})C_{1,2}]}{2\lambda(\sigma_1^2 \sigma_2^2 - C_{1,2}^2)}$$
(3.16)

and

$$H_2 = \frac{f_1 C_{1,2} - f_2 \sigma_1^2 - 2\lambda[(w_d C_{d2} + w_\ell C_{\ell 2} + H_c C_{c2})\sigma_1^2 - (w_d C_{d1} + w_\ell C_{\ell 1} + H_c C_{c1})C_{1,2}]}{2\lambda(\sigma_1^2 \sigma_2^2 - C_{1,2}^2)}.$$
(3.17)

In addition to the investor's trade-off between risk and the cost of hedging, the optimal proportions in the currency basket depend in a complex way on the forward premiums, the currency variances, the cross-correlations between currencies, and the underlying asset returns.

Equations 3.16 and 3.17 give the optimal allocations for the unconstrained case. These allocations may change if the sizes of any of the positions are constrained, but the principles underlying the trade-off between cost and risk remain the same.

Two special cases are interesting to examine. The first case occurs when one of the proxy currencies is the same as that of the underlying asset. In this case, and using Currency 1 for the twin currency, the optimal currency basket weights become

$$H_1 = \frac{f_2 C_{1,2} - f_1 \sigma_2^2 - 2\lambda[(w_d C_{d1} + w_\ell C_{\ell 1})\sigma_2^2 - C_{1,2}(w_d C_{d2} + w_\ell C_{\ell 2})]}{2\lambda(\sigma_1^2 \sigma_2^2 - C_{1,2}^2)} - H_c$$
(3.18)

and

$$H_2 = \frac{f_1 C_{1,2} - f_2 \sigma_1^2 - 2\lambda[(w_d C_{d2} + w_\ell C_{\ell 2} + H_c C_{1,2})\sigma_1^2 - C_{1,2}(w_d C_{d1} + w_\ell C_{\ell 1} + H_c \sigma_1^2)]}{2\lambda(\sigma_1^2 \sigma_2^2 - C_{1,2}^2)}.$$
(3.19)

---

[2] Enhanced statistical techniques using GARCH (generalized autoregressive conditional heteroscedasticity) modeling have been applied with some success to the estimation of the covariance structure of currency baskets to improve the stability of their performance. See Sorensen, Mezrich, and Thadani (1992).

The consolidated weight in the underlying foreign asset currency would be $H_1 + H_c$.

If the currencies are uncorrelated with the asset returns, several terms drop out, giving

$$H_1 = \frac{f_2 C_{1,2} - f_1 \sigma_2^2}{2\lambda(\sigma_1^2 \sigma_2^2 - C_{1,2}^2)} - H_c \quad (3.20)$$

and

$$H_2 = \frac{f_1 C_{1,2} - f_2 \sigma_1^2}{2\lambda(\sigma_1^2 \sigma_2^2 - C_{1,2}^2)}. \quad (3.21)$$

The optimal currency weights depend importantly on the cost of the hedge embodied in the respective forward premiums and on the investor's preferred trade-off between cost and risk reduction.

The second special case results if the investor wants to minimize the variance of the portfolio without trying to balance out the relative cost of the hedge, which occurs by letting λ become so large that the penalty for taking on risk is great. The optimal currency allocations that create a minimum-variance basket hedge then converge to

$$H_1 = \frac{-[(w_d C_{d1} + w_\ell C_{\ell 1} + H_c C_{c1})\sigma_2^2 - (w_d C_{d2} + w_\ell C_{\ell 2} + H_c C_{c2})C_{1,2}]}{\sigma_1^2 \sigma_2^2 - C_{1,2}^2} \quad (3.22)$$

and

$$H_2 = \frac{-[(w_d C_{d2} + w_\ell C_{\ell 2} + H_c C_{c2})\sigma_1^2 - (w_d C_{d1} + w_\ell C_{\ell 1} + H_c C_{c1})C_{1,2}]}{\sigma_1^2 \sigma_2^2 - C_{1,2}^2}. \quad (3.23)$$

The optimal currency positions will likely be nonzero even in the absence of correlation with the underlying asset returns as long as the proxy currencies are correlated with the currency of the underlying asset. The reason can be seen by setting the currency correlations with assets equal to zero in Equations 3.22 and 3.23, giving

$$H_1 = \frac{-H_c(C_{c1}\sigma_2^2 - C_{c2}C_{1,2})}{\sigma_1^2 \sigma_2^2 - C_{1,2}^2}$$

$$= -H_c \beta_1 \quad (3.24)$$

and

$$H_2 = \frac{-H_c(C_{c2}\sigma_1^2 - C_{c1}C_{1,2})}{\sigma_1^2 \sigma_2^2 - C_{1,2}^2}$$

$$= -H_c \beta_2, \quad (3.25)$$

where β_1 and β_2 represent the beta coefficients from a regression in which the return from the asset-linked currency is regressed on the returns from the two proxy currencies in the following manner:

$$r_c = \alpha + \beta_1 r_c^1 + \beta_2 r_c^2 + e, \quad (3.26)$$

where r_c^1 and r_c^2 are the proxy currency returns, e is a random error term, and α is the intercept from the regression. The beta coefficients turn out to be identical to those in Equations 3.24 and 3.25 under the same risk and correlation assumptions reflected in the data used by the regression. The reason is that the multiple regression coefficients are calculated to minimize the variance of the errors in the proxy relationship.[3]

Finally, if one of the currencies is the same as that in which the underlying asset is denominated (Currency 1 in this example), the optimal weights become

$$H_1 = -\left[\frac{(w_d C_{d1} + w_\ell C_{\ell 1})\sigma_2^2 - C_{1,2}(w_d C_{d2} + w_\ell C_{\ell 2})}{\sigma_1^2 \sigma_2^2 - C_{1,2}^2}\right] - H_c \quad (3.27)$$

and

$$H_2 = -\left[\frac{(w_d C_{d2} + w_\ell C_{\ell 2})\sigma_1^2 - C_{1,2}(w_d C_{d1} + w_\ell C_{\ell 1})}{\sigma_1^2 \sigma_2^2 - C_{1,2}^2}\right]. \quad (3.28)$$

Now, if currency returns are uncorrelated with asset returns, the allocation to the first currency becomes $-H_c$ and the allocation to the second currency becomes zero. The position is now a fully matched hedge, and using the currency basket to create a minimum-variance hedge provides no advantage. The best hedge to use under these circumstances is the currency matched to the underlying asset.

---

[3] The regression estimates used in Equation 3.26 are limited to the case in which assets are assumed to be uncorrelated with currency returns. If assets are correlated with currency returns, the regression coefficients in Equation 3.26 will not provide accurate minimum-variance exposures.

Minimum-Variance Basket Hedge

Suppose a U.S. investor holds a position in French stocks and wants to create a proxy hedge for the French franc using the German mark and the British pound. Consider the construction of the optimal currency basket with the following annualized data:

$w_d = 0.0$ $\quad f_{DM} = -3.0\%$
$w_\ell = 1.0$ $\quad \sigma_{FF} = 10.5\%$
$H_{FF} = 1.0$ $\quad \sigma_\pounds = 11.7\%$
$f_{FF} = -4.0\%$ $\quad \sigma_{DM} = 11.6\%$
$f_\pounds = -3.5\%$ $\quad \sigma_\ell = 18.0\%$

The correlation matrix is

	French Stocks	French Franc	British Pound	German Mark
French stocks	1.0	−0.1	−0.1	−0.1
French franc		1.0	0.7	0.9
British pound			1.0	0.7
German mark				1.0

The covariance matrix is

	French Stocks	French Franc	British Pound	German Mark
French stocks	0.0324	−0.0019	−0.0021	−0.0021
French franc		0.0110	0.0086	0.0110
British pound			0.0137	0.0095
German mark				0.0135

Using Equations 3.16 and 3.17 to calculate the optimal portfolio allocations for the pound and the mark in the following table gives the trade-off between the impact of the cost of the hedge and the risk for various values of λ:

λ	$H_\pounds$	H_{DM}	H_{FF}	Hedge Impact on Return	σ_R
1	0.95	−0.22	1.0	2.68%	24.7%
2	0.46	−0.43	1.0	0.32	20.8
5	0.16	−0.55	1.0	−1.09	19.6
10	0.06	−0.59	1.0	−1.56	19.4
100	−0.03	−0.63	1.0	−2.00	19.4
Minimum-variance basket	−0.04	−0.64	1.0	−2.03	19.4
Fully matched hedge	0.00	0.00	0.0	−4.00	18.0
Unhedged	0.00	0.00	1.0	0.00	20.8

Varying λ allows the investor to choose what level of cost versus risk is most appealing. Notice that the more reduction the investor wants in risk, the lower the return received or the greater the cost of the hedge.

Basket hedges can also be constructed to make trade-offs between the incremental hedging cost and the tracking error relative to a benchmark currency position. For example, if a portfolio has incremental exposure in a currency because of its investment in an underlying asset position, the investor may be able to construct a basket of two other currencies to proxy for a hedged position at an impact on return that is somewhat reduced from the cost of the hedge.

The impact of the incremental cost of the basket hedge in terms of its effect on the portfolio return would be

$$\text{Hedge impact} = -\Delta H_1 f_1 - \Delta H_2 f_2; \quad (3.29)$$

the variance of the incremental currency exposures relative to the benchmark positions would be calculated as

$$\sigma^2_{\Delta R} = \Delta w_d^2 \sigma_d^2 + \Delta w_\ell^2 \sigma_\ell^2 + \Delta H_c^2 \sigma_c^2 + \Delta H_1^2 \sigma_1^2$$
$$+ \Delta H_2^2 \sigma_2^2 + 2\Delta H_1(\Delta w_d C_{d1} + \Delta w_\ell C_{\ell 1}$$
$$+ \Delta H_c C_{c1}) + 2\Delta H_2(\Delta w_d C_{d2} + \Delta w_\ell C_{\ell 2}$$
$$+ \Delta H_c C_{c2}) + 2\Delta H_1 \Delta H_2 C_{1,2}. \quad (3.30)$$

The subscripts c, 1, and 2 designate the asset currency and the proxy currencies, respectively. If γ represents the trade-off between the impact of the incremental hedge cost and the incremental risk of the basket hedge, the optimality conditions imply that the incremental allocations to proxy Currencies 1 and 2 are

$$\Delta H_1 = \frac{f_2 C_{1,2} - f_1 \sigma_2^2 - 2\gamma\sigma_2^2(\Delta w_d C_{d1} + \Delta w_\ell C_{\ell 1} + \Delta H_c C_{c1}) + 2\gamma C_{1,2}(\Delta w_d C_{d2} + \Delta w_\ell C_{\ell 2} + \Delta H_c C_{c2})}{2\gamma(\sigma_1^2 \sigma_2^2 - C_{1,2}^2)} \quad (3.31)$$

and

$$\Delta H_2 = \frac{f_1 C_{1,2} - f_2 \sigma_1^2 - 2\gamma\sigma_1^2(\Delta w_d C_{d2} + \Delta w_\ell C_{\ell 2} + \Delta H_c C_{c2}) + 2\gamma C_{1,2}(\Delta w_d C_{d1} + \Delta w_\ell C_{\ell 1} + \Delta H_c C_{c1})}{2\gamma(\sigma_1^2 \sigma_2^2 - C_{1,2}^2)}. \quad (3.32)$$

The optimal deviations from benchmark exposures for the currency proxies are a function of, in addition to the investor's trade-off between the impact of the incremental cost and risk, the forward premiums, the currency variances, and the cross-currency correlations.

Two special cases are also of interest in this discussion. First, if one of the currency proxies is equal to the currency for the underlying asset (Currency 1, in this example), the optimal currency deviations reduce to

$$\Delta H_1 = \frac{f_2 C_{1,2} - f_1 \sigma_2^2 - 2\gamma\sigma_2^2(\Delta w_d C_{d1} + \Delta w_\ell C_{\ell 1}) + 2\gamma C_{1,2}(\Delta w_d C_{d2} + \Delta w_\ell C_{\ell 2})}{2\gamma(\sigma_1^2 \sigma_2^2 - C_{1,2}^2)}$$
$$- \Delta H_c \quad (3.33)$$

and

$$\Delta H_2 = \frac{f_1 C_{1,2} - f_2 \sigma_1^2 - 2\gamma\sigma_1^2(\Delta w_d C_{d2} + \Delta w_\ell C_{\ell 2}) + 2\gamma C_{1,2}(\Delta w_d C_{d1} + \Delta w_\ell C_{\ell 1})}{2\gamma(\sigma_1^2 \sigma_2^2 - C_{1,2}^2)}. \quad (3.34)$$

Furthermore, if the proxy currencies are uncorrelated with the asset returns, several terms drop out, giving

$$\Delta H_1 = \frac{f_2 C_{1,2} - f_1 \sigma_2^2}{2\gamma(\sigma_1^2 \sigma_2^2 - C_{1,2}^2)} - \Delta H_c \quad (3.35)$$

and

$$\Delta H_2 = \frac{f_1 C_{1,2} - f_2 \sigma_1^2}{2\gamma(\sigma_1^2 \sigma_2^2 - C_{1,2}^2)}. \quad (3.36)$$

The second special case focuses on minimizing the tracking error for the basket; in this case, the allocations are

$$\Delta H_1 = \frac{-\sigma_2^2(\Delta w_d C_{d1} + \Delta w_\ell C_{\ell 1} + \Delta H_c C_{c1}) + C_{1,2}(\Delta w_d C_{d2} + \Delta w_\ell C_{\ell 2} + \Delta H_c C_{c2})}{\sigma_1^2 \sigma_2^2 - C_{1,2}^2} \quad (3.37)$$

and

$$\Delta H_2 = \frac{-\sigma_1^2(\Delta w_d C_{d2} + \Delta w_\ell C_{\ell 2} + \Delta H_c C_{c2}) + C_{1,2}(\Delta w_d C_{d1} + \Delta w_\ell C_{\ell 1} + \Delta H_c C_{c1})}{\sigma_1^2 \sigma_2^2 - C_{1,2}^2}. \quad (3.38)$$

If the proxy currencies are uncorrelated with the asset returns, Equations 3.37 and 3.38 reduce to

$$\Delta H_1 = \frac{-\Delta H_c(\sigma_2^2 C_{c1} - C_{1,2} C_{c2})}{\sigma_1^2 \sigma_2^2 - C_{1,2}^2}$$
$$= -\Delta H_c \beta_1 \quad (3.39)$$

and

$$\Delta H_2 = \frac{-\Delta H_c[\sigma_1^2 C_{c2} - C_{1,2} C_{c1}]}{\sigma_1^2 \sigma_2^2 - C_{1,2}^2}$$
$$= -\Delta H_c \beta_2, \quad (3.40)$$

where β_1 and β_2 are calculated from the regression in Equation 3.26. These equations take the same form as the minimum-variance allocations in Equations 3.24 and 3.25 except that the incremental allocations are measured relative to the incremental exposure in the desired currency (instead of the total exposure). Similarly, the allocations can be viewed as a function of the proxy currency regression coefficients β_1 and β_2 relative to the underlying currency.

Finally, if Currency 1 is the same as the underlying currency, the minimum-tracking-error allocations are

$$\Delta H_1 = \frac{-\sigma_2^2(\Delta w_d C_{d1} + \Delta w_\ell C_{\ell 1}) + C_{1,2}(\Delta w_d C_{d2} + \Delta w_\ell C_{\ell 2})}{\sigma_1^2 \sigma_2^2 - C_{1,2}^2} - \Delta H_c \quad (3.41)$$

and

$$\Delta H_2 = \frac{-\sigma_1^2(\Delta w_d C_{d2} + \Delta w_\ell C_{\ell 2}) + C_{1,2}(\Delta w_d C_{d1} + \Delta w_\ell C_{\ell 2})}{\sigma_1^2 \sigma_2^2 - C_{1,2}^2}. \quad (3.42)$$

Now, if the currencies are uncorrelated with the assets, the incremental allocation to the first currency becomes $-\Delta H_c$ and the incremental allocation to the second currency will be zero. The minimum-tracking-error basket will allocate a fully offsetting hedge corresponding to the incremental currency position associated with the underlying asset. No allocation is made to the other currency in the basket.

The array of possible assumptions that can be made in structuring the optimal currency positions can sometimes be difficult to keep in perspective. Figure 3.4 shows a simple framework to keep track of various assumptions used in constructing minimum-risk currency positions. The most general case allows for a full set of currencies to be used in constructing the hedge while accounting for the full correlations between assets and currencies. If only a subset of currencies is used to create a proxy for the fully matched hedge, the minimum-risk hedge is usually referred to as a basket hedge. If the correlations between assets and currencies are assumed to be zero, the minimum-risk positions result in either no

---

Currency Basket Hedge with Minimum Tracking Error

Suppose, as in the previous basket hedge, the core currency position is French francs and a basket hedge is desired using British pounds and German marks to track the position in the franc. The benchmark currency positions are equal to zero for each currency, and the actual currency position for the French franc represents full exposure at 1.0. Using Equations 3.31 and 3.32 to calculate the optimal basket allocations gives the weights for the pound and the mark in the following table, which illustrates the trade-off between the incremental cost of the hedge and the tracking error for various values of γ:

γ	$\Delta H_\pounds$	ΔH_{DM}	ΔH_{FF}	Hedge Impact on Return	$\sigma_{\Delta R}$
1	0.87	−0.31	1.0	6.1%	16.0%
2	0.37	−0.52	1.0	3.7	8.9
5	0.07	−0.64	1.0	2.3	5.4
10	−0.02	−0.69	1.0	1.9	4.7
100	−0.11	−0.72	1.0	1.4	4.5
Basket with minimum tracking error	−0.12	−0.73	1.0	1.4	4.5
Matched hedge	0.00	0.00	0.0	0.0	0.0

Varying γ allows the investor to choose the most appealing trade-off between incremental cost and risk. Notice that all of the basket-hedge configurations increase the portfolio return at the expense of increasing the tracking error.

Figure 3.4. Minimum-Risk Hedging

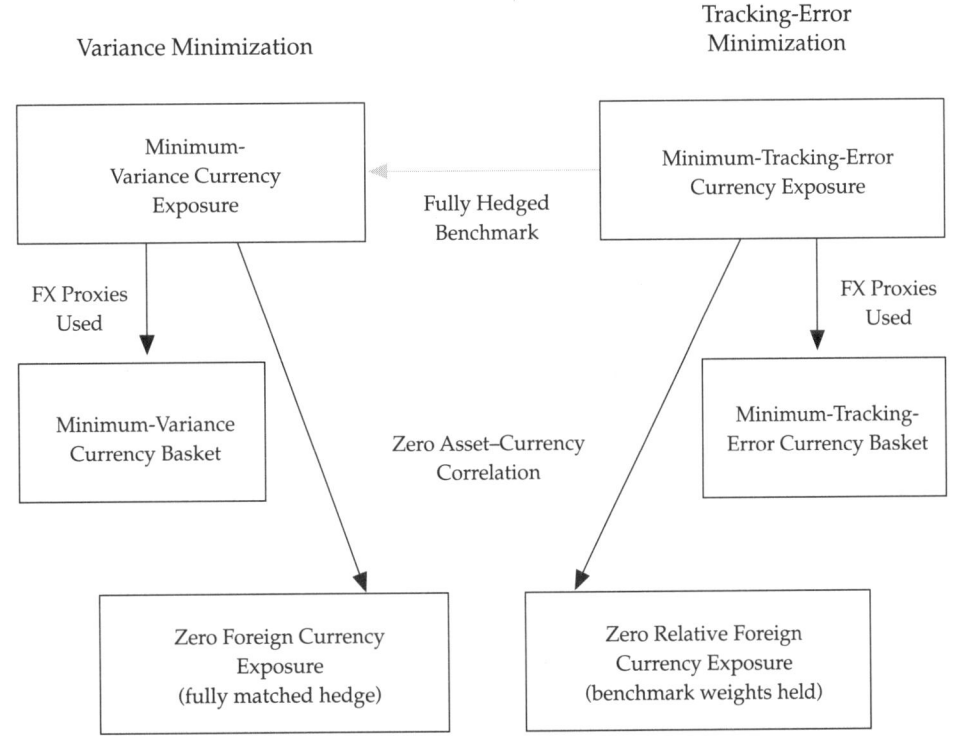

Variance Minimization

Minimum-Variance Currency Exposure
— Fully Hedged Benchmark →
Minimum-Tracking-Error Currency Exposure

Tracking-Error Minimization

FX Proxies Used ↓ → Minimum-Variance Currency Basket

FX Proxies Used ↓ → Minimum-Tracking-Error Currency Basket

Zero Asset–Currency Correlation

↓ Zero Foreign Currency Exposure (fully matched hedge)

↓ Zero Relative Foreign Currency Exposure (benchmark weights held)

currency exposure (a fully matched hedge) or no incremental exposure relative to the currency benchmark position. Note that if the currency benchmark is fully hedged ($H^B = 0$), the solution for minimizing tracking error is the same as for minimizing variance.

Note also that the previous examples were somewhat simplified in order to illustrate basic principles. Actual portfolios may involve many different asset and currency positions. The algebra becomes increasingly complex, but the optimization approach can continue to be applied to construct minimum-variance hedging positions. For applications involving many assets and currencies, in practice, the optimization is typically carried out on a computer. Always keep in mind that the effectiveness of the hedge will depend to a great extent on the accuracy of the investor's estimates of the cross-correlations between currencies and assets.

Minimum-Variance Basket Hedge for the Italian Lira

As a final example of the issues involved in constructing a basket of currencies to hedge an underlying currency position, consider the case of a U.S. investor using the German mark, the Swiss franc, and the British pound to create a minimum-variance basket hedge for the Italian lira in 1992. The minimum-variance hedge proportions based on the previous 36 months of returns are given by the coefficients in the regression equation:

$$r_{IL} = 0.0082 + 0.77 r_{DM} + 0.02 r_{SF} + 0.12 r_{£},$$
$$\quad\quad (6.97) \quad\quad (8.91) \quad\quad (0.23) \quad\quad (1.73)$$

with an adjusted R^2 of 0.96 (numbers in parenthesis represent the t-statistics for each coefficient). Table 3.1 compares the hedging returns from using the Italian lira with the hedging returns from using the basket of currencies, with the proportions determined by these regression coefficients. Figure 3.5 shows the monthly and cumulative differential returns. Notice that the basket actually outperformed the full Italian lira hedge until the correlations collapsed during the September 1992 Exchange Rate Mechanism crisis. The basket hedge then performed poorly for a few months.

Currency Management: Concepts and Practices

Table 3.1. Differential Return between the Italian Lira and the Currency Basket, January 1992–January 1993

Month	Lira Hedge Return	Basket Return	Differential Return	Cumulative Differential Return
1992				
January	−3.38%	−4.01%	0.62%	0.62%
February	−1.46	−1.75	0.29	0.92
March	−0.07	−0.47	0.40	1.32
April	2.16	1.33	0.83	2.17
May	2.61	2.34	0.27	2.44
June	6.87	5.81	1.06	3.52
July	3.83	2.54	1.29	4.85
August	6.24	5.74	0.50	5.37
September	−12.74	−2.63	−10.11	−5.28
October	−6.60	−8.19	1.59	−3.77
November	−3.02	−0.24	−2.78	−6.45
December	−3.65	−1.39	−2.26	−8.57
1993				
January	−1.63	−1.21	−0.41	−8.94

Note: Returns are calculated from the perspective of a U.S. investor.

Figure 3.5. Results of a Basket-Hedged Italian Lira Investment: German Mark, Swiss Franc, and British Pound Proxy

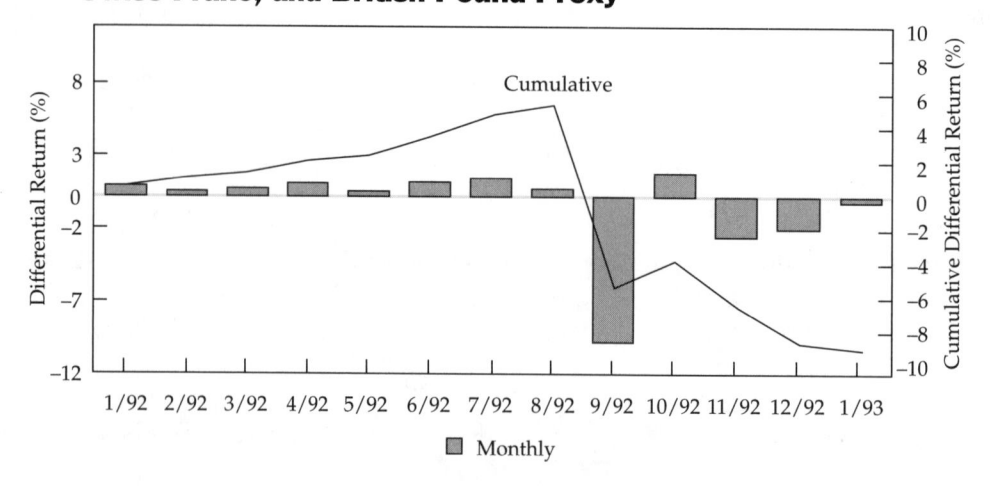

Constructing Asymmetrical Hedges

The construction of an asymmetrical hedge that responds to positive currency returns differently from the way it responds to negative currency returns usually requires the use of foreign exchange options or strategies that replicate options. The two most common strategies to hedge currency exposure are the protective put and the range forward (collar).

Protective Put. The protective put is constructed by purchasing foreign exchange put options with a strike price set at the desired level of protection for the hedge horizon. Like futures and forward contracts, simple put options have a defined maturity date and a specified exercise price. If the foreign exchange rate falls below the strike price at maturity, the put option pays the difference between the spot foreign exchange rate and the strike price. If the foreign exchange rate stays above the strike price, the put option expires worthless. Purchasing the put option allows the investor to hedge against negative currency returns but leaves the investor with the benefits if returns are positive.

Figure 3.6. Currency Hedge Using a Protective Put

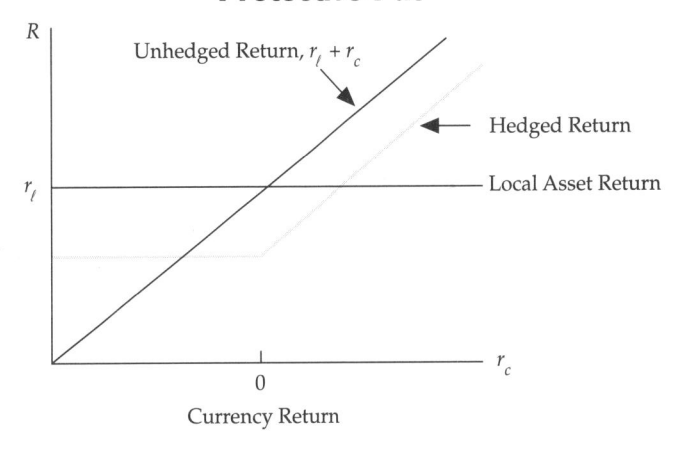

Figure 3.6 illustrates the asymmetrical impact of a protective put on returns.

Note that the put preserves much of the currency return if returns are positive but protects the asset from negative currency returns. The cost of the option itself reduces the full return somewhat and keeps the asset from participating fully in positive currency returns. A short discussion of the pricing of currency options is found in the section of this chapter on implementation vehicles.

Protective Put Currency Hedge

For an illustration of the impact of currency options to hedge currency exposure, consider an extension of the previous matched hedge example. The situation has the following characteristics:

	USD/DM Exchange Rate	Portfolio Value (DM thousands)	Percent Change in DM	Unhedged Portfolio Value (US$ thousands)	Percent Change in USD
Current	0.60	10,000	na	6,000	na
After six months	0.63	11,000	10.0%	6,930	15.5%
After six months	0.57	11,000	10.0	6,270	4.5

na = not applicable.

Suppose now that the investor hedges the currency risk by purchasing a six-month put option with a strike price of 0.60 USD/DM at a cost of US$207,000. If the exchange rate declines, the value of the put option at expiration will be

$$10,000,000(0.60 - 0.57) = US\$300,000.$$

The net value of the portfolio in U.S. dollar terms will be

$$6,270,000 + 300,000 - 207,000 = US\$6,363,000,$$

which represents an increase of 6.1 percent. The option will finish in the money and contributes value to the portfolio. Without the option position, the unhedged value of the portfolio would have increased by only 4.5 percent. The value of the portfolio in U.S. dollar terms has increased by less than the 10 percent increase in local currency terms because of the initial cost of the option and because only the DM10,000,000 principal amount was hedged.

If the exchange rate increases, the value of the option at expiration will be zero, resulting in a net value of the portfolio in U.S. dollar terms of

$$6,930,000 - 207,000 = US\$6,723,000.$$

This figure represents an increase of 12.1 percent. Because of the cost of the option, the hedged portfolio underperforms the unhedged portfolio, which returns 15.5 percent.

Range Forward. The range forward (collar) is constructed by selling a call option in addition to buying a put option. The maturity of the call option is typically the same as that of the put, but the call has a higher strike price. Figure 3.7 illustrates the return impact of a range forward.

The sale of the call option eliminates the benefit of positive currency returns above the level of the call's strike price. In exchange, the sale of the call brings in cash, which offsets some of the cost of purchasing the put option. Selling a call option with the same strike price as the put option would protect against downside losses but would also eliminate any upside participation. This approach would make the hedge symmetrical and similar to selling a futures or forward contract. Indeed, the short-call and long-put position with the same strike price creates a synthetic futures or forward contract that produces a symmetrical hedge.

Figure 3.7. Currency Hedge Using a Range Forward

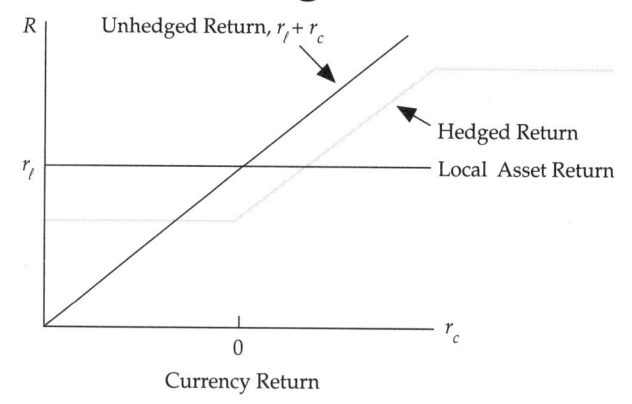

Range Forward Currency Hedge

For an illustration of how the range forward works, suppose that in the previous example, the investor sold a call option at a strike price of 0.62 USD/DM for US$135,000 in addition to purchasing the put option at a strike price of 0.60 USD/DM. If the exchange rate were to decline to 0.57 USD/DM, the put option would have value but the call option would expire worthless. The net value of the portfolio would be

$$6,270,000 + 300,000 - 207,000 + 135,000 = US\$6,498,000,$$

which represents an increase of 8.3 percent (compared with the local portfolio return of 10.0 percent and a return of 6.1 percent with the put option alone). The sale of the call option has helped offset the cost of the put option hedge.

On the other hand, if the exchange rate were to increase, the put option would expire worthless and the loss from the value of the call option at expiration would be

$$10,000,000 \times (0.62 - 0.63) = -US\$100,000.$$

> The net value of the portfolio would be
>
> 6,930,000 − 207,000 + 135,000 − 100,000 = US$6,758,000,
>
> which represents a net increase of 12.6 percent.
>
> Comparing the protective put strategy with the collar shows that with the collar, the investor is better off if the exchange rate declines, but if the exchange rate increases much beyond the strike price of the call option, the investor may be worse off. If the exchange rate increases beyond 0.6335, the loss on the call option will be greater than its cost, causing the collar to perform worse than the protective put strategy. In this USD/DM example, the loss on the intrinsic value of the call option is not quite as great, however, as the premium received when the option was sold; so, even though the exchange rate increased, the investor did slightly better than with the straight protective put.

Implementation Vehicles

A full discussion of the theoretical pricing of options and forward contracts is beyond the scope of this presentation, but a short summary will help explain the return implications of the hedging strategies. Both forward and options contracts derive their value from the level of the underlying exchange rate, the relative interest rates between the two countries, and the time to maturity of the contracts. The price of an option also depends on the strike price of the option and the estimated volatility of currency returns.

Forward and Futures Contracts. The pricing of foreign exchange forward and futures contracts is driven by the covered interest arbitrage relationship, which was discussed in Chapter 1. Although the two types of contracts contain important differences, they can be treated as equivalent for purposes of pricing. The fair forward or futures price is

$$F = \frac{S_o(1 + i_d t)}{1 + i_\ell t}, \quad (3.43)$$

where

F = the current forward foreign exchange rate
S_o = the current spot foreign exchange rate
i_d = the annualized domestic interest rate
i_ℓ = the annualized foreign interest rate
t = the time to expiration of the forward contract (fraction of a year).

The equivalent expression for the pricing of a forward contract using continuous compounding instead of discrete compounding is

$$F = S_o e^{(i_d^* - i_\ell^*)t}. \quad (3.44)$$

> ### Pricing a Forward or Futures Contract
>
> Suppose the current exchange rate between the U.S. dollar and the Japanese yen is 105.00 yen/USD or 0.009524 USD/yen. If annualized U.S. interest rates are 6 percent and Japanese interest rates are 4 percent, the forward rate for a contract with six months to expiration will be
>
> $$F = \frac{S_o(1 + i_{US}t)}{1 + i_{JP}t}$$
>
> $$= \frac{0.009524[1 + (0.06/2)]}{1 + (0.04/2)}$$
>
> $$= 0.009617 \text{ USD/yen}.$$
>
> Because the U.S. interest rate is higher than the Japanese rate, if the American quotation convention is used, the forward exchange rate will be higher than the current spot rate. The reciprocal will give the forward rate quotation in terms of yen/USD (European quotation) as
>
> $$\frac{1}{0.009617} = 103.98 \text{ yen/USD}.$$

A foreign currency futures or forward contract calls for future delivery of a specified amount of foreign exchange at a fixed time and price. The buyer of the contract has the obligation to receive the foreign exchange amount; the seller has the obligation to deliver the specified amount.

In the United States, the majority of foreign currency futures contracts are traded in Chicago on the International Monetary Market (IMM), which was organized in 1972 as a division of the Chicago Mercantile Exchange. Since 1985, contracts traded on the IMM have been interchangeable on the Singapore International Monetary Exchange.

Currency futures contracts have standardized features in order to concentrate trading liquidity into common size and maturity specifications. Table 3.2 shows the most common contracts traded on the IMM, their contract sizes, and minimum price fluctuation per contract. IMM currency futures contracts follow a quarterly expiration cycle, with expirations on the third Wednesday in March, June, September, and December.

Futures contract prices are quoted American style (USD/FX), and the purchase or sale of one contract on a particular currency corresponds to the associated contract size. Gains and losses caused by changes in the futures prices are settled on a daily basis between individual investors and the exchanges through the brokers.

For example, suppose an investor purchases 100 futures contracts on the Japanese yen at a price of 0.0100 USD/yen (100.0 yen/USD). If the yen appreciates from 0.0100 to 0.0101 USD/yen (99.0 yen/USD), the investor will gain US$125,000 (that is, 100 contracts × (0.0101 − 0.0100) × ¥12,500,000 per contract).

Table 3.3 provides a brief summary of the major differences between futures and forward contracts. Whereas currency futures contracts are traded on an organized exchange, currency forward contracts are negotiated in the interbank market. Both are used for investment and hedging purposes, although the volume of trading in forward contracts greatly exceeds that of futures contracts. Forward contracts provide more flexibility in their size and maturity specifications than futures contracts because forward contracts need not be standardized. Gains and losses are usually not marked to market on a daily basis but are settled at the expiration of each contract or when terminated with the original counterparty.

Another important difference between the two is the investor's credit risk. In the case of futures contracts, the exchange bears the obligation of making good on the daily mark to market. In the case of forward contracts, the counterparty bank bears the risk of settling gains and losses at maturity.

Option Contracts. Standard foreign currency option contracts have the following features:

- The option contract gives the option purchaser the right (but not the obligation) to buy or sell a given amount of foreign exchange in the underlying currency at a fixed price per unit (strike or exercise price) within a specified period of time (set by the maturity or expiration date).
- A call option gives the investor the right to buy the foreign currency; a put option gives the investor the right to sell the foreign currency.
- An American option gives the buyer the right to exercise at any time up to the exercise date; a European option can be exercised only on the expiration date.
- The cost of the option is usually referred to as the option premium.
- Options on futures contracts give the

Table 3.2. Currency Futures Contract Specifications at the IMM

Currency	Contract Size (home-country currency)	Minimum US$ Price Fluctuation per Contract
Australian dollar	100,000	$10.00
British pound	62,500	31.25
Canadian dollar	100,000	10.00
French franc	250,000	12.50
Japanese yen	12,500,000	12.50
Dutch guilder	125,000	12.50
Swiss franc	125,000	12.50
German mark	125,000	12.50

Table 3.3. Comparison of Foreign Currency Futures and Forward Contracts

	Futures Contract	Forward Contract
Contract size	Standardized per currency	Flexible
Maturity	Fixed maturities, usually in three-month increments	Flexible
Pricing	Open outcry at the futures exchange	Bid and offer quotes by each bank
Collateral	Initial margin and daily mark to market	Standing bank lines of credit
Counterparty	Exchange serves as guarantor of the trade	Individual bank with whom contract negotiated makes settlement
Liquidity	Liquid for relatively small transactions	Liquid for much larger transactions
Commissions	Fixed rate per contract paid to broker	Embedded in bid/offer quotation
Settlement	Position usually reversed by offsetting transaction in futures market	Foreign currency usually delivered at expiration of contract through spot market or offset with the original counterparty

buyer the option to purchase currency futures contracts instead of the underlying currency itself.

- The intrinsic value of an option depends on the relationship between the strike price and the exchange rate of the underlying currency. A call option has an intrinsic value equal to the maximum of zero or the difference between the underlying exchange rate and the exercise price. A put option has an intrinsic value equal to the maximum of zero or the difference between the strike price and the underlying exchange rate.

- An option with a positive intrinsic value is said to be in the money. Options with no intrinsic value are said to be out of the money. An at-the-money option is one whose strike price is equal to the underlying exchange rate.

Option Intrinsic Values

As an illustration of option values, suppose the current exchange rate between the U.S. dollar and the German mark, S, is 0.62 USD/DM. A put option with a strike price, K, of 0.64 would have an intrinsic value of

$$\text{Put option value} = \max[0, (K - S)]$$

$$= \max[0, (0.64 - 0.62)]$$

$$= 0.02 \text{ USD/DM}.$$

If the option contract covers DM62,500, the dollar amount of the intrinsic value is

$$0.02 \text{ USD/DM} \times \text{DM62,500} = \text{US\$1,250}.$$

On the other hand, the intrinsic value of a call option with the same strike price would be zero:

> Call option value = max[0, (S − K)]
> $$= \max[0, (0.62 - 0.64)]$$
> $$= 0.$$
>
> In this instance, the put option would be in the money whereas the call option would be out of the money.

■ *Currency option markets.* Foreign currency options are available in three markets in the United States:

- options on the physical currency in the over-the-counter (interbank) market;
- options on the physical currency on organized exchanges;
- options on futures contracts at the IMM in Chicago.

The most common *over-the-counter* (*OTC*) options written by banks are for U.S. dollars against the British pound, the German mark, the Swiss franc, the Japanese yen, and the Canadian dollar. The size, maturity, and strike price of the options can be tailored to meet the specific needs of the investor, and the market is quite liquid for transactions in multiples of US$5–US$10 million. OTC options do expose the investor, however, to counterparty risk—the risk of the bank not being able to fulfill its obligation in the option contract.

In the OTC market, option prices are typically quoted as a percentage of the home currency amount of the transaction evaluated at the strike price of the option in home currency units. For example, a put option to exchange US$41,875,000 for DM62,500,000 at an exchange rate of 0.67 USD/DM quoted at 1.76 percent would cost $737,000 (that is, 0.0176 [US$41,875,000]), which is equivalent to quoting the option as a percentage of the exercise price of the option in home currency units. When considered in this way, the cost of the option would also be US$737,000 (that is, 0.0176[0.67 × DM62,500,000], where 0.67 × DM62,500,000, or US$41,875,000, represents the home currency value of the strike price).

Options on the underlying physical currency are *traded on several exchanges* around the world. In the United States, the greatest volume is traded on the Philadelphia Stock Exchange. The exchange clearing house serves as the guarantor behind the options contracts, and members of the clearing house bear the financial responsibility. Table 3.4 shows the major individual currency options that are traded on the exchange and their contract sizes. Options are typically quoted in U.S. cents per foreign currency unit (except for the French franc and the Japanese yen, which for convenience, are quoted in tenths of a cent per franc and hundredths of a cent per yen). Expiration months are March, June, September, and December plus the two nearest additional months to the contract date. Each option expires on the Saturday preceding the third Wednesday of the expiration month.

The number of exchange-traded options needed to cover a particular amount of foreign exchange is calculated by dividing the amount of foreign exchange by the amount covered by each option.

Table 3.4. Currency Option Contract Specifications on the Philadelphia Stock Exchange

Currency	Contract Size (home-country currency)
Australian dollar	50,000
British pound	31,250
Canadian dollar	50,000
German mark	62,500
French franc	250,000
Japanese yen	6,250,000
Swiss franc	62,500

> **Calculating the Number of Exchange-Traded Options Needed**
>
> If an investor wants to purchase exchange-traded put options on DM1,000,000, with each option covering DM62,500, 16 options would be needed. If each option is quoted at 1.18 U.S. cents to the mark (1.18¢/DM), the cost of the 16 options would be $11,800 (that is, 16 × 1.18¢/DM × DM62,500).

Options on futures contracts are traded on the IMM. Options are available on the futures contracts that expire according to the quarterly expiration cycle (March, June, September, and December), but the futures options carry monthly expiration dates. As a result, an investor can purchase option contracts on the March futures contract, for example, that will expire in January, February, and March. Options expire two Fridays before the third Wednesday of the expiration month. As with exchange-traded options on the physical currency, prices for futures options are quoted in cents per unit of the foreign currency.

■ *Pricing put and call currency options.* The pricing of currency options is somewhat more complex than the pricing of futures and forward contracts, and it involves a few more parameters. Garman and Kohlhagen (1983) showed that, under certain assumptions, the price of a European call option on spot foreign exchange rates is given by

$$C = S_o e^{-i_\ell^* t} N(d) - K e^{-i_d^* t} N(d - \sigma_c \sqrt{t}), \quad (3.45)$$

where

$$d = \frac{\ln(S_o/K) + (i_d^* - i_\ell^* + \sigma_c^2/2)t}{\sigma_c \sqrt{t}}$$

- $N(\bullet)$ = the cumulative normal distribution function
- C = the price of the European call option
- S_o = the current spot exchange rate
- K = the strike price
- t = the time remaining to expiration (fraction of a year)
- i_ℓ^* = the annualized foreign interest rate (continuous compounding)
- i_d^* = the annualized domestic interest rate (continuous compounding)
- σ_c = the annualized standard deviation of the percentage change in the spot exchange rate.

The arbitrage relationship between a put and call option, *put–call parity*, allows the price of a put option to be written as

$$\begin{aligned} P &= C + K e^{-i_d^* t} - S_o e^{-i_\ell^* t} \\ &= S_o e^{-i_\ell^* t}[N(d) - 1] \\ &\quad - K e^{-i_d^* t}[N(d - \sigma_c \sqrt{t}) - 1]. \end{aligned} \quad (3.46)$$

Of particular interest is the sensitivity of the option price to a change in the underlying exchange rate. This sensitivity is referred to as the option's *delta*. Delta measures the change in the option price for a one-unit change in the underlying exchange rate. The delta of the European call option of Equation 3.45 is

$$\Delta_{call} = e^{-i_\ell^* t} N(d). \quad (3.47)$$

The put–call parity relationship in Equation 3.46 also shows that the delta of a European put option will be given as

$$\begin{aligned} \Delta_{put} &= \Delta_{call} - e^{-i_\ell^* t} \\ &= e^{-i_\ell^* t}[N(d) - 1]. \end{aligned} \quad (3.48)$$

Notice that the theoretical values of the options in Equations 3.45 and 3.46 require the use of annualized, continuously compounded interest rates. Option traders typically use LIBOR (the London Interbank Offered Rate) to value currency options. Because these rates are quoted using a 360-day convention with no compounding, the rate must be converted to a continuously compounded, 365-day rate by using

$$i^* = \left(\frac{365}{360\tau}\right) \ln[1 + r_{LIBOR}(\tau)] \quad (3.49)$$

where τ is the maturity of the LIBOR rate selected to value the option (fraction of a year

Currency Management: Concepts and Practices

based on a 360-day year). For example, for a 30-day LIBOR rate quoted at 5.74 percent, the corresponding annualized, continuously compounded rate would be

$$i^* = \frac{365}{360(30/360)} \ln[1 + 0.0574(30/360)]$$
$$= 5.81\%.$$

Pricing Put and Call Currency Options

Suppose an investor wants to price put and call options on the German mark with the following parameters:

$t = 36/365$
$K = 58.00¢/DM$
$S_o = 58.93¢/DM$
$i_d^* = 5.81\%$
$i_\ell^* = 8.81\%$
$\sigma_c = 13.00\%.$

The theoretical price of the put and call options requires the calculation of the cumulative normal distribution function. The inputs give

$$d = \frac{\ln(S_o/K) + (i_d^* - i_\ell^* + \sigma_c^2/2)t}{\sigma_c\sqrt{t}}$$

$$= \frac{\ln(58.93/58.00) + [0.0581 - 0.0881 + (0.13)^2/2](36/365)}{0.13\sqrt{36/365}}$$

$$= 0.3376$$

and

$$d - \sigma_c\sqrt{t} = 0.3376 - 0.13\sqrt{36/365} = 0.2967.$$

With the use of the interpolated values from Table 3.5, the cumulative normal distribution functions are found to be

$N(d) = 0.6321$

and

$N(d - \sigma_c\sqrt{t}) = 0.6167.$

Using these values in Equations 3.45 and 3.46 gives

$$C = S_o e^{-i_\ell^* t} N(d) - K e^{-i_d^* t} N(d - \sigma_c\sqrt{t})$$
$$= 1.37¢/DM$$

and

$$P = S_o e^{-i_\ell^* t}[N(d) - 1] - K e^{-i_d^* t}[N(d - \sigma_c\sqrt{t}) - 1]$$
$$= 0.62¢/DM.$$

The delta of the put and call options would be

$$\Delta_{call} = e^{-i_\ell^* t} N(d)$$
$$= 0.63$$

and

$$\Delta_{put} = \Delta_{call} - e^{-i_\ell^* t}$$
$$= -0.37.$$

Table 3.5. Standard Normal Distribution: Prob($r \le d$) = $N(d)$

d	0.00	0.01	0.02	0.03	0.04	0.05	0.06	0.07	0.08	0.09
0.0	0.5000	0.5040	0.5080	0.5120	0.5160	0.5199	0.5239	0.5279	0.5319	0.5359
0.1	0.5398	0.5438	0.5478	0.5517	0.5557	0.5596	0.5636	0.5675	0.5714	0.5753
0.2	0.5793	0.5832	0.5871	0.5910	0.5948	0.5987	0.6026	0.6064	0.6103	0.6141
0.3	0.6179	0.6217	0.6255	0.6293	0.6331	0.6368	0.6406	0.6443	0.6480	0.6517
0.4	0.6554	0.6591	0.6628	0.6664	0.6700	0.6736	0.6772	0.6808	0.6844	0.6879
0.5	0.6915	0.6950	0.6985	0.7019	0.7054	0.7088	0.7123	0.7157	0.7190	0.7224
0.6	0.7257	0.7291	0.7324	0.7357	0.7389	0.7422	0.7454	0.7486	0.7517	0.7549
0.7	0.7580	0.7611	0.7642	0.7673	0.7704	0.7734	0.7764	0.7794	0.7823	0.7852
0.8	0.7881	0.7910	0.7939	0.7967	0.7995	0.8023	0.8051	0.8078	0.8106	0.8133
0.9	0.8159	0.8186	0.8212	0.8238	0.8264	0.8289	0.8315	0.8340	0.8365	0.8389
1.0	0.8413	0.8438	0.8461	0.8485	0.8508	0.8531	0.8554	0.8577	0.8599	0.8621
1.1	0.8643	0.8665	0.8686	0.8708	0.8729	0.8749	0.8770	0.8790	0.8810	0.8830
1.2	0.8849	0.8860	0.8888	0.8907	0.8925	0.8943	0.8962	0.8980	0.8997	0.9015
1.3	0.9032	0.9049	0.9066	0.9082	0.9099	0.9115	0.9131	0.9147	0.9162	0.9177
1.4	0.9192	0.9207	0.9222	0.9236	0.9251	0.9265	0.9279	0.9292	0.9306	0.9319
1.5	0.9332	0.9345	0.9357	0.9370	0.9382	0.9394	0.9406	0.9418	0.9429	0.9441
1.6	0.9452	0.9463	0.9474	0.9484	0.9495	0.9505	0.9515	0.9525	0.9535	0.9545
1.7	0.9554	0.9564	0.9573	0.9582	0.9591	0.9599	0.9688	0.9616	0.9625	0.9633
1.8	0.9641	0.9649	0.9656	0.9664	0.9671	0.9678	0.9686	0.9693	0.9699	0.9706
1.9	0.9713	0.9719	0.9726	0.9732	0.9738	0.9744	0.9750	0.9756	0.9761	0.9767
2.0	0.9772	0.9778	0.9783	0.9788	0.9793	0.9798	0.9803	0.9808	0.9812	0.9817
2.1	0.9821	0.9826	0.9830	0.9834	0.9838	0.9842	0.9846	0.9850	0.9854	0.9857
2.2	0.9861	0.9864	0.9868	0.9871	0.9875	0.9878	0.9881	0.9884	0.9887	0.9890
2.3	0.9893	0.9896	0.9898	0.9901	0.9904	0.9906	0.9909	0.9911	0.9913	0.9916
2.4	0.9918	0.9920	0.9922	0.9925	0.9927	0.9929	0.9931	0.9932	0.9934	0.9936
2.5	0.9938	0.9940	0.9941	0.9943	0.9945	0.9946	0.9948	0.9949	0.9951	0.9952
2.6	0.9953	0.9955	0.9956	0.9957	0.9959	0.9960	0.9961	0.9962	0.9963	0.9964
2.7	0.9965	0.9966	0.9967	0.9968	0.9969	0.9970	0.9971	0.9972	0.9973	0.9974
2.8	0.9974	0.9975	0.9976	0.9977	0.9977	0.9978	0.9979	0.9979	0.9980	0.9981
2.9	0.9981	0.9982	0.9982	0.9983	0.9984	0.9984	0.9985	0.9985	0.9986	0.9986
3.0	0.9987	0.9987	0.9987	0.9988	0.9988	0.9989	0.9989	0.9989	0.9990	0.9990

Because of covered interest arbitrage between the forward rate and the spot rate, the pricing of options can also be expressed in terms of the forward rate. Equations 3.50 and 3.51 give the prices of European options on futures contracts instead of on the underlying exchange rate:

$$C = e^{-i_d^* t}[FN(y) - KN(y - \sigma_c\sqrt{t})] \quad (3.50)$$

and

$$P = e^{-i_d^*t}\{F[N(y) - 1] - K[N(y - \sigma_c\sqrt{t}) - 1]\}, \quad (3.51)$$

where

$$y = \frac{\ln(F/K) + \sigma_c^2 t/2}{\sigma_c\sqrt{t}}.$$

Synthetic Option Positions. The return effects of an option can be mimicked by using futures or forward contracts to adjust the hedge ratio in a systematic way as exchange rates move. Selling more futures contracts as the exchange rate falls creates the protection a put option provides. Buying futures as the exchange rate rises reduces the impact of the hedge and allows some upside participation in currency returns. On the other hand, selling futures contracts as the exchange rate rises will create the effect of having sold a call option to truncate upside returns.

The effectiveness of these *dynamic hedges* in mimicking the price movement of an option depends on knowing how the price of the option will respond to a change in exchange rates and on being able to change the hedge effectively and smoothly. Although both the actual option position and the synthetic option position protect the portfolio against adverse currency returns and capture some favorable currency returns, the effectiveness of the synthetic option is uncertain because it is only an approximation. Sharp market moves or gaps do not allow the investor to change the hedge ratio smoothly, and in such a circumstance, the tracking error of the synthetic option will increase relative to the actual option, which will increase the cost of the dynamic replication. If the *ex post* volatility of exchange rates is less than the volatility implied in pricing the actual option, the cost of the synthetic option will generally be less than the cost of the actual option. Actual volatility greater than the implied volatility will increase the cost of the synthetic option.

For example, suppose a U.S. investor has a portfolio currently valued at US$100,000,000 exposed to the German mark and wishes to ensure that the portfolio will not decline more than 5 percent one year from now in the event of depreciation of the mark. Germany's one-year riskless rate is 5 percent, and the one-year riskless rate in the United States is 6 percent. The mark's annualized standard deviation equals 10 percent.

The investor wishes to replicate a protective put option on the mark. Hence, the investor must determine this option's value and its delta.

The value of a one-year put option on the US$100,000,000 with a strike price equal to US$95,000,000 is given by Equation 3.46 and equals US$1,521,916. Now, the investor has a problem. The investor seeks protection from a loss in excess of 5 percent, but the cost of the put option, together with a US$95,000,000 strike price, implies a potential maximum loss of 6.5 percent; therefore, the amount of the portfolio that can be protected needs to be decreased so that the combination of its cushion and the cost of the option is no greater than US$5,000,000. Combined, the amount required to purchase the option and the amount of the portfolio that is protected should be equal to the total portfolio value, US$100,000,000.

The investor carries out an iterative procedure to determine the right mix between the portfolio amount that can be protected and the option cost. This procedure reveals that the investor can purchase a put option to prevent US$97,896,730 of the portfolio from declining below US$95,000,000 for US$2,103,270. The US$2,896,730 cushion between the floor of US$95,000,000 and the initial value of the portfolio and the US$2,103,270 cost of the option ensure a total maximum loss of US$5,000,000.

Instead of purchasing this option, however, the investor can replicate it by dynamically changing the hedge ratio. The next step, therefore, is to invest an amount equal to 1 plus the put's delta times the exposure in the mark and invest the balance in a U.S.-denominated riskless asset.

The delta of the put option in this example is equal to -0.3476; therefore, the investor's exposure to the mark should equal US$63,867,827. Because the portfolio already has a US$97,896,730 exposure to the mark, the investor achieves the required exposure by selling the mark short in an amount equal to US$34,028,903. As the value of the underlying portfolio and the mark change over time, the new hedge ratio must be reestimated from the currency option formula and the portfolio must be rebalanced to accord with the new hedge ratio.

In theory, investors following a dynamic hedge strategy carry out trading continuously as time passes and the value of the portfolio and the foreign exchange rate change. In practice, continuous trading is impossible, so investors impose transaction filters to balance the cost of frequent trading against the imprecision that can result from infrequent trading.

For example, suppose that after one year, the mark depreciates 10 percent. The resulting depreciation in the example portfolio's value will be partially offset by the short position in the mark forward contract, so the net depreciation in the portfolio's value because of the change in the mark will not exceed 5 percent. If, in contrast, the mark appreciates 10 percent, the portfolio's mark exposure and the short forward position should capture 97.9 percent of the terminal value of the portfolio attributable to the rise in the mark. In other words, if the local value of the portfolio remains unchanged but the mark declines 10 percent, the ending dollar value of the hedged portfolio should equal US$95,000,000. If the mark rises 10 percent and the local value of the portfolio remains unchanged, the ending dollar value of the hedged portfolio should equal US$107,686,403.

A Portfolio of Options versus an Option on a Portfolio. When a portfolio contains exposure to multiple currencies, the investor may be able to use an option on the portfolio of currencies instead of using options on each individual currency to create a hedge. Such a possibility has an important benefit, namely, an option on a portfolio is theoretically less expensive than options on the individual pieces. The reason is that the option on the portfolio will deliver the same protection as the portfolio of options when each currency falls below its floor but the option on the portfolio will not perform as well as the portfolio of options when some currencies are above and some are below their strike prices. As a result, the portfolio of options should, in theory, cost more than the option on the portfolio.

Consider the following simple case of a two-currency portfolio with spot exchange rates S_1 and S_2. The total value of the currency exposure with individual exposures w_1 and w_2 is

$$S = w_1 S_1 + w_2 S_2 \qquad (3.52)$$

Each currency has a put option with a strike price K_i; the portfolio has a corresponding put option with a strike price of

$$K = w_1 K_1 + w_2 K_2. \qquad (3.53)$$

Now, consider the three possible cases: at expiration, both put options are in the money, both options are out of the money, or only one of the options is in the money.

■ *Case 1: Both options expire in the money.* If both options expire in the money, the payoff from the portfolio of options at time t will be

$$w_1(K_1 - S_1^t) + w_2(K_2 - S_2^t) = (w_1 K_1 + w_2 K_2)$$
$$- (w_1 S_1^t + w_2 S_2^t) = K - S^t,$$
$$(3.54)$$

where

$$S^t = w_1 S_1^t + w_2 S_2^t.$$

This formula provides the same payoff an option on the portfolio would give, so the structures result in equivalent payoffs.

■ *Case 2: Both options expire out of the money.* If both options expire out of the money, the payoff will be zero for the portfolio of options. This result will also be true for the option on the portfolio because, for each currency, S_i^t is equal to or greater than K_i. These conditions imply that in using an option on the portfolio, the portfolio value will be greater than or equal to the portfolio strike price, so the put option will expire out of the money. That is,

$$S = w_1 S_1^t + w_2 S_2^t \geq w_1 K_1 + w_2 K_2 = K. \qquad (3.55)$$

■ *Case 3: One option expires in the money.* If only one option expires in the money (say, Option 1), the payoff from the portfolio of options will be $w_1(K_1 - S_1^t)$ because S_1^t is less than K_1 and S_2^t is greater than K_2. In this case, the payoff from the option on the portfolio will depend on whether the portfolio is above its strike price or not:

$$S^t = w_1 S_1^t + w_2 S_2^t \leq K. \qquad (3.56)$$

If the in-the-money currency falls proportionally less in the weighted portfolio than the out-of-the-money currency rises, the portfolio at expiration of the option will be greater than the option's strike price. Consequently, the option on the portfolio will expire worthless and the portfolio of options will have a greater payoff than the option on the portfolio.

If the in-the-money currency falls proportionally more in the weighted portfolio than the out-of-the-money currency rises, the portfolio option will expire in the money and the payoff will be $K - S^t$. This payoff will be less than that on the portfolio of options, however, as can be seen in the equation

$$K - S^t = w_1(K_1 - S_1^t) + w_2(K_2 - S_2^t)$$
$$< w_1(K_1 - S_1^t) \quad (3.57)$$

because the out-of-the-money option implies that $K_2 - S_2^t$ is less than zero.

The probability of the portfolio falling into each of these cases is related to the correlation between the two currencies. Less-than-perfect positive correlation allows the diversification to create a portfolio with a smaller variance than the average variance of the individual components. This reduction in the variance of the portfolio helps reduce the cost of the option on the portfolio relative to the sum of the individual options.

For an illustration of this phenomenon, consider a portfolio containing equal proportions of two securities, each of which has a volatility of 20 percent. Table 3.6 shows the volatility of the portfolio for various values of the correlation between the two securities. Note that the volatility of the portfolio is always smaller than the volatility of the individual securities as long as the securities are not perfectly positively correlated.

Table 3.6 also shows the value of an at-the-money put option on the portfolio compared with a portfolio of two individual at-the-money put options. Except for the case of perfect positive correlation, the portfolio of put options is always worth more than the put option on the portfolio.

Nevertheless, hedging with a portfolio of options may be an acceptable choice. First, an option on a portfolio of currencies may not always be easily available, so the investor is forced to purchase the more expensive individual options to create the hedge. Second, the

Table 3.6. Option Prices as a Percentage of Portfolio Value

Correlation	Portfolio Volatility	Put Option on the Portfolio	Portfolio of Individual Put Options
1.0	20.0%	3.37%	3.37%
0.8	19.0	3.17	3.37
0.6	17.9	2.96	3.37
0.4	16.7	2.72	3.37
0.2	15.5	2.49	3.37
0.0	14.1	2.22	3.37
−0.2	12.6	1.93	3.37
−0.4	11.0	1.62	3.37
−0.6	8.9	1.22	3.37
−0.8	6.3	0.71	3.37
−1.0	0.0	na	3.37

Note: At-the-money three-month European put options are priced using the Black–Scholes model. Individual options are priced assuming a volatility of 20 percent and an annualized, continuously compounded riskless rate of 5 percent. The portfolio is equally weighted between the two securities.

na = not applicable.

dispersion of individual currency returns may present opportunities to restructure the positions periodically during the course of the hedge to lower the overall cost. These opportunities exist if the dispersion between currency returns embodied in cross-rate movements is large enough that the gains from one option position more than offset the losses from another option position. This situation can occur because the price changes in an option for up and down moves of equal percentage in the underlying currency are not symmetrical. Gains in a put option from an equal percentage move down will be larger than the losses from the same percentage move up. This difference often allows the investor to restructure the portfolio of options to provide the same floor but at a lower cost, even after taking into account transaction costs.

Hedging with a Portfolio of Options

For an example of this technique, consider a simple two-currency portfolio composed of half German mark exposure and half Japanese yen exposure. Suppose individual put options are initially purchased to protect the portfolio for a six-month time horizon. The annualized interest rates for that horizon are assumed to be 4 percent in the United States, 8 percent in Germany, and 3 percent in Japan. Suppose also that after one month, the mark has depreciated by 2 percent while the yen has appreciated by 2 percent, leaving the total portfolio value the same:

	Initial Value			Value One Month Later		
	Exchange Rate	FX	USD	Exchange Rate	FX	USD
DM exposure	0.6000 USD/DM	8,333,333	5,000,000	0.588 USD/DM	8,333,333	4,900,000
Yen exposure	0.0100 USD/yen	500,000,000	5,000,000	0.0102 USD/yen	500,000,000	5,100,000
Total			10,000,000			10,000,000

Furthermore, assume that an at-the-money put option on DM8,333,333 with 180 days to expiration costs US$240,000 and an at-the-money put option on ¥500,000,000 costs US$190,000. After 30 days, when the mark has depreciated by 2 percent and the yen has appreciated by 2 percent, the respective options will be worth US$280,833 and US$101,000.

These options could be sold and replaced by new at-the-money options with 150 days to expiration for a reduced cost, as shown in the following table (option prices estimated using Equation 3.46 and assuming a 12 percent volatility):

	Initial At-the-Money Options with 180 Days to Expiration	Initial Options with 150 Days to Expiration	New At-the-Money Options with 150 Days to Expiration
DM option	US$240,000	US$280,833	US$190,000
Yen option	190,000	101,000	145,000
Total	US$430,000	US$381,833	US$335,000

Because the total portfolio value of the currency positions has not changed, replacing the initial put options with new at-the-money options maintains the portfolio protection, but at a cost savings of US$46,833 (that is, US$381,833 − US$335,000). The cash generated by replacing the original options thus reduces the initial outlay of US$430,000. If the currency returns diverge again, the process can be repeated to generate additional cost savings.

Experience shows that this technique can be used effectively to create portfolio protection without using an option on the portfolio as a whole. The greatest cost savings are achieved as the component currencies diverge in their returns around each initial exchange rate level.

Summary

- If currency hedging is desired, either active or passive hedging strategies can be designed. Passive strategies can be characterized as either symmetrical or asymmetrical hedges. An asymmetrical hedge leaves some upside potential as the currency appreciates, whereas a symmetrical hedge eliminates this upside while protecting the downside.
- Futures or forward contracts are typically used to create symmetrical hedges. Direct options or dynamic option replication are needed for an asymmetrical hedge.
- A basket hedge uses a collection of currencies as a proxy for individual hedges. The diversified basket may lower hedging costs

but at the risk of some tracking error.
- Minimum-variance hedge ratios depend on the size of the foreign asset positions, the correlations between local asset returns, and the volatility of currency returns.
- If correlations between local asset returns and currency returns are zero, a fully matched hedge gives the minimum-variance currency position for the portfolio.
- Because of the natural diversification within a portfolio, which reduces the portfolio volatility, a put option on a portfolio of currencies is less expensive than a portfolio of put options with similar parameters on each individual currency.
- A portfolio of options on individual currencies may allow some restructuring over time so as to reduce the total cost of the individual hedges to be closer to the cost of an option on the entire portfolio.

4. Actively Managing Currencies to Enhance Return

Managing currency exposure is an unavoidable issue for investors who allocate a fraction of their portfolios to foreign assets. Even if these investors have no views about the returns of currencies, they are still faced with a decision about how to control the risk that comes from currency exposure.

In contrast to those investors with no views about currencies, many investors approach currencies, whether or not their portfolios have embedded currency exposure, as an opportunity to generate profits. In this chapter, we describe a general model for exploiting a view that currencies have nonzero returns, and we show how to exploit some of the empirical tendencies of currencies discussed in Chapter 2.

A General Model for Exploiting Views about Currency Returns

Simple optimization can be used to implement any currency-hedging strategy based on the assumption that forward contracts have nonzero expected returns and that the investor does not wish to change the composition of the underlying asset portfolio. The general procedure allows one to balance a hedging strategy's effects on a portfolio's expected return and risk. Equation 4.1 shows how this balance is achieved for a simple foreign asset portfolio:

$$E(U) = E(R_H) + H[E(r_c) - f] \\ - \lambda(\sigma_\ell^2 + H^2\sigma_c^2 + 2HC_{\ell c}), \quad (4.1)$$

where

$E(U)$ = expected utility or risk-adjusted return
$E(R_H)$ = expected return on the currency-hedged asset portfolio = $E(r_\ell) + f$
$E(r_\ell)$ = expected foreign local asset return
f = the currency forward premium or discount
$E(r_c) - f$ = expected return of the currency forward contract
$E(r_c)$ = expected currency return
H = currency exposure ratio
λ = investor's risk-aversion penalty
σ_ℓ^2 = variance of the foreign local asset portfolio
σ_c^2 = variance of the currency return
$C_{\ell c}$ = covariance between the foreign local asset return and the currency return.

Equation 4.1 defines the expected risk-adjusted return (expected utility) as a function of a portfolio's expected return, risk, and the investor's risk aversion using the simple optimization structure presented in Chapter 3. We will explore this approach more fully in Chapter 5 using multiple assets and currencies and also allowing the composition of the asset portfolio to change.

By taking the partial derivative of Equation 4.1 with respect to the weighting of the currency forward contract, setting it equal to zero, and rearranging terms, we define the exposure to a currency forward contract that achieves the optimal balance between a currency forward contract's contribution to the portfolio's expected return and its contribution to the portfolio's risk. The result is

$$H = \frac{E(r_c) - f - 2\lambda C_{\ell c}}{2\lambda \sigma_c^2}$$
$$= \frac{E(r_c) - f}{2\lambda \sigma_c^2} - \frac{\rho_{\ell c}\sigma_\ell}{\sigma_c}, \quad (4.2)$$

where $\rho_{\ell c}$ is the correlation between the foreign local asset return and the currency return.

Equation 4.2, which can easily be expanded to accommodate multiple currencies, specifies precisely how much an investor should allocate to a currency forward contract in light of the investor's particular view about that contract's expected return. The investor's risk aversion can often be inferred from the composition of the underlying portfolio in conjunction with the investor's assumptions about the component assets' expected returns, standard deviations, and correlations.

How to Exploit the Forward Rate Bias

As documented in Chapter 2, the historical record shows that the forward exchange rate, on average, has overpredicted the subsequent changes in the spot rate for the major currencies. Thus, an investor could have profited historically by selling forward contracts that were priced at a premium (low-interest-rate currency) and purchasing forward contracts that were priced at a discount (high-interest-rate currency). Equivalently, investors could have hedged more of a premium currency and less of a discount currency.

Table 4.1 shows the performance of a strategy that bought or sold five separate forward contracts each month. The strategy bought the

Table 4.1. Strategy Exploiting the Forward Rate Bias

Five Years Ended	Annualized Return	Standard Deviation
1978	−0.14%	5.71%
1979	0.62	5.39
1980	1.67	6.68
1981	6.26	7.70
1982	8.53	7.65
1983	9.96	6.54
1984	10.50	6.81
1985	8.23	5.90
1986	2.75	5.04
1987	0.59	4.84
1988	1.85	5.81
1989	0.69	5.68
1990	4.42	5.81
1991	6.75	7.65
1992	7.06	9.29
1993	6.13	9.30
1974–93	4.38	7.08

Note: The strategy calls for purchasing discount contracts and selling premium contracts using the British pound, the German mark, the French franc, the Swiss franc, and the Japanese yen.

forward contracts when they were priced at a discount and sold them when they were priced at a premium. The exposures were equally weighted. As shown, this strategy added value in all but 1 five-year period out of 16 overlapping five-year periods. The average annualized value added during the entire 20-year period was 4.4 percent, with a standard deviation of 7.1 percent. If this strategy had been overlaid on a Treasury bill portfolio, it would have produced a total annualized return of 11.9 percent. Clearly, such a strategy would have made an attractive addition to the typical institutional portfolio, especially considering that its implementation would have required little capital.

The forward rate bias can also be exploited by selectively hedging a portfolio's embedded currency exposure. Suppose an investor wishes to hedge the currency exposure of a Morgan Stanley Capital International EAFE (Europe/Australia/Far East) Index fund. The investor could optimize the exposure to forward contracts conditioned on the forward contracts' discounts or premiums. For example, if a currency forward contract is selling at a 1 percent discount, the investor would assume that its expected return is 1 percent. If it is selling at a 1 percent premium, the investor would assume that its expected return equals −1 percent (that is, that $E[r_c^j] - f_j = -f_j$). The optimizer hedges less, on balance, when the forward contract has a positive expected return than when it has a negative expected return.

Table 4.2 compares the results of two optimization strategies (and a dynamic strategy to be discussed later) as applied to the EAFE Index. The naive optimization strategy assumes that the forward contracts' expected returns are always equal to zero, and the "conditional" optimization strategy assumes that the forward contracts' expected returns are equal to their discounts or premiums. The naive optimization assumes that uncovered interest arbitrage holds, whereas the conditional optimization assumes that currency returns are a random walk with a zero mean.

The naive optimization uses five forward currency contracts to hedge the portfolio—the British pound, German mark, French franc, Swiss franc, and Japanese yen. (These five countries account for about 77 percent of the total EAFE Index weight, on average.) It constrains the exposure to each forward contract to range from minus the weighting of the country allocation (full hedging) to zero (no hedging), and it does not allow cross-hedging. The naive optimization also assumes that annualized implementation costs equal 50 basis points and that the investor's marginal risk aversion equals 1; that is, the investor is willing to incur one unit of *incremental trading cost* in order to lower the portfolio's variance by one unit. The expected returns of the forward contracts are set equal to zero (that is, $E[r_c^j] - f_j = 0$), and their variances and covariances are based on the entire history of prior monthly returns up to the time of the optimization. The portfolio is reoptimized monthly, and the first optimization occurs in July 1974; hence, the covariance matrix is based on the 12 monthly observations following July 1973. The next monthly optimization is based on the prior 13 monthly observations.

The conditional optimization is almost identical to the naive optimization; it differs only in that the expected returns of the forward contracts are conditioned on the discounts or premiums. A forward contract that sells at a discount is assumed to have a positive expected return equal to the annualized discount; a forward contract that sells at a premium is assumed to have a negative expected return equal to the annualized premium (that is, $E[r_c^j] - f_j = -f_j$). These assumptions are tantamount to the view that the current spot rate is the unbiased estimate of the future spot rate or, equivalently, that the expected change in the spot rate is zero.

Notice that the conditional optimization under the assumption that expected currency returns are zero performs better than the naive optimization with less risk. The result is consistent with the tendency for currencies to exhibit a forward rate bias and consistent with the fact that uncovered interest arbitrage has not held during the floating-rate period since 1974. Investors would have been better off to hedge premium currencies and leave discount currencies unhedged at the margin.

How to Exploit Nonrandomness in Currency Returns

Chapter 2 contained evidence that currency returns are positively serially correlated; that is, they trend. Here, we describe a trading rule to exploit the nonrandomness of currency returns.

For the approach to be useful, the historical presence of trends must, of course, be more than a period-specific phenomenon. One reason to believe that currencies will in fact continue to trend is the conclusion that the trending arises from central bank interventions. The reasoning for such a conclusion is as follows. Central banks prefer stable exchange rates. Thus, whenever an economic or political shock occurs, they intervene to prevent exchange rates from moving abruptly. Generally, they do not prevent the

Table 4.2. Returns from Three Hedge Strategies Applied to the EAFE Index, July 1974–December 1993

	Annualized Return	Standard Deviation
Naive optimization	13.8%	16.2%
Conditional optimization	14.8	15.7
Dynamic strategy	14.5	16.1

Figure 4.1. Payoff Diagram for Dynamic Strategy versus Buy-and-Hold Strategy

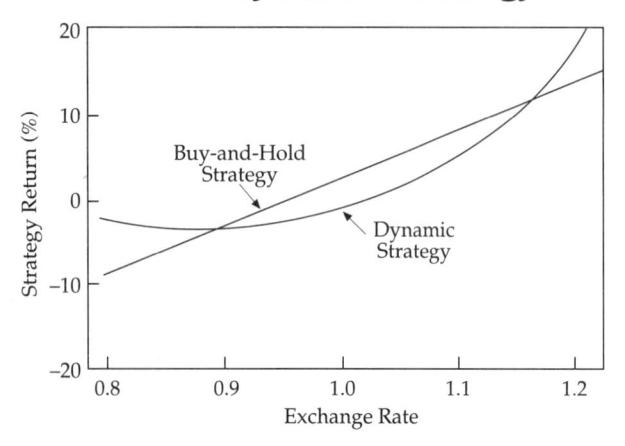

currency from eventually reaching its market-determined price, but by "leaning against the wind," they stretch out the change in a currency's value over time. They cushion its movement to the new price.

If an investor believes that central banks will continue to promote stable exchange rates and accepts the argument that central bank interventions promote currency trending, then that investor will believe a profit can be made by purchasing a currency after it rises and selling it after it falls. The rationale is that, because of the central bank's intervention, the currency's value will continue to move in the direction it has been going until underlying market forces gradually overcome the central bank's dampening efforts.

If currency returns trend, adding value to a buy-and-hold exposure may be possible by following a dynamic strategy that generates a convex payoff function. This notion is illustrated in Figure 4.1. The horizontal axis is the exchange rate of a hypothetical currency, and the vertical axis represents the returns—the conditional return of a buy-and-hold exposure to the currency and the return of a dynamic strategy that produces a convex payoff function.

The buy-and-hold strategy produces a straight-line payoff function with a slope of 0.5 (because it is assumed to begin with a 50 percent exposure to the currency); thus, if the currency were to move from a value of 1.0 to 1.2, the buy-and-hold strategy would generate a return of 10 percent.

As can be seen, the convex strategy outperforms the buy-and-hold strategy when the exchange rate moves significantly away from its value at inception (1.0), and the direction of that move does not matter. Thus, the dynamic strategy is appealing in an environment in which currencies trend, because trending increases the likelihood that the currency's exchange rate will move to one extreme or the other rather than fluctuate within a narrow interval.

An investor can generate a convex payoff function by following a linear investment rule that increases exposure to a currency as it appreciates and decreases exposure to a currency as it depreciates. For example, suppose an investor starts out with a 50.0 percent exposure to a currency and the currency appreciates 1.2 percent. The change in the value of the currency by itself increases the buy-and-hold exposure to 50.6 percent. The investor can increase this exposure by multiplying the currency's return by a multiple greater than 1 and then adding this value to the initial exposure. If the multiple equals 5, the new exposure to the currency would equal 56.0 percent; that is, 50.0 percent + (1.2 percent × 5). If the currency declines by 1.2 percent, the new exposure under this rule would equal 43.0 percent. As long as the currency trends, the rule produces a convex payoff function and adds value to a buy-and-hold strategy.

The value added as the currency trends in one direction is lost, however, during turning points when the trend changes direction unless the investor imposes a ceiling and a floor to constrain the exposure to the currency. Suppose, for example, that the investor's neutral exposure is 50 percent. The investor might impose a 75 percent ceiling and a 25 percent floor. As the currency appreciates, the investor increases exposure to the currency until the ceiling is reached. As the currency continues to trend up, the exposure remains at 75 percent, thus adding value relative to the buy-and-hold exposure. At some point, the currency changes direction, however, so with this rule, the investor begins to reduce exposure to the currency. During this transition, some of the profits that accrued to the strategy as the currency appreciated are lost, but because the maximum exposure was constrained to 75 percent, the strategy returns to a neutral exposure relatively quickly, before all of the profits are lost. It then begins to add additional value as the exposure is reduced

Figure 4.2. Risk and Return for Alternative Hedging Strategies Using the EAFE Index

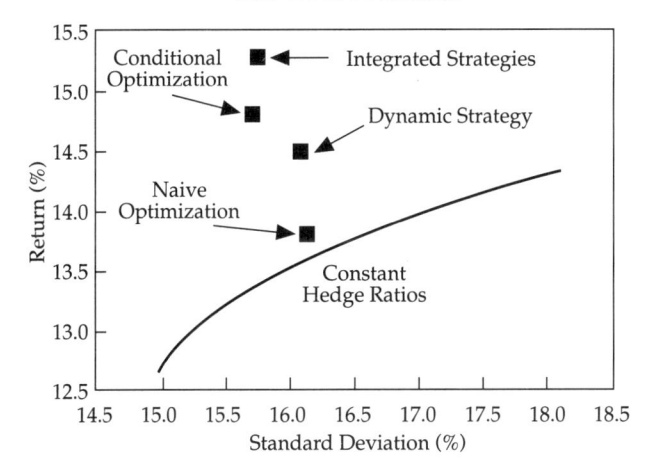

[Chart showing Return (%) vs Standard Deviation (%) with points labeled: Conditional Optimization, Integrated Strategies, Dynamic Strategy, Naive Optimization, and a curve labeled Constant Hedge Ratios]

below the neutral exposure. In the same fashion, as the currency's move once again changes direction, the 25 percent floor serves to protect some of the added value. In general, if the ceiling or floor is reached before the trend changes direction, this strategy will add value beyond a buy-and-hold strategy.

Table 4.2 compares the results of the dynamic strategy with the naive and conditional optimizations described earlier. The same assumptions about transaction costs apply. The dynamic strategy changes the hedge ratio each month by an amount equal to 10 times the preceding month's return up to constraints 25 percent greater than or less than the neutral exposure determined by the optimizer.

Figure 4.2 illustrates the relative performance of alternative hedging strategies for controlling the risk and enhancing the return of the EAFE Index. The constant hedge ratios assume that a constant percentage ranging from 100 percent to 0 percent of the five major currencies (the pound, the mark, the French franc, the Swiss franc, and the yen) is hedged each month. The other currency exposures in the index are left unhedged. The naive optimization, conditional optimization, and dynamic strategy are as described previously. The "integrated strategies" alternative combines the conditional optimization with the dynamic strategy.

Although the value obtained by combining the conditional and dynamic strategies is not perfectly additive, the strategies are sufficiently independent to generate a higher combined return for the integrated strategies than either of them generates individually. Moreover, the combined risk of the integrated strategies is only marginally higher than the risk of the conditional optimization. Remember, however, that the future success of these active strategies depends on the persistence of the empirical tendencies described in Chapter 2.

Technical Analysis

One of the most popular approaches to managing currencies is technical analysis. In general, in the securities markets, technical analysts attempt to forecast the direction of a security's price by examining the security's past price behavior and its trading volume. The rationale for technical analysis is that price patterns combined with volume offer clues about the supply and demand for a security and the market's sentiment regarding that security. Many also argue that certain price patterns are a product of investors' psychological tendencies that repeat over time. Once they detect the start of a pattern, traders take action on the assumption that the market will complete that pattern as it typically has in the past.

For many types of assets, there is little evidence that technical analysis adds value with any significant degree of consistency. (Of course, a particular analyst may have a unique approach for interpreting technical signals that researchers are unable to simulate in their tests of the efficacy of technical analysis.) In currency management, however, the application of technical analysis does appear to generate successful results, even without the aid of superior interpretive skills.[1]

The most popular techniques for applying technical analysis to currency management rely on moving averages, filters, or momentum indicators. The objective is to detect when a sustainable trend has begun or to detect critical turning points in the market.[2]

---

[1] See Levich and Thomas (1993) and Silber (1994) for examples of technical trading strategies.

[2] A more complete discussion than is possible here of various technical indicators can be found in Pring (1985).

Figure 4.3. Buy and Sell Signals from Moving Averages

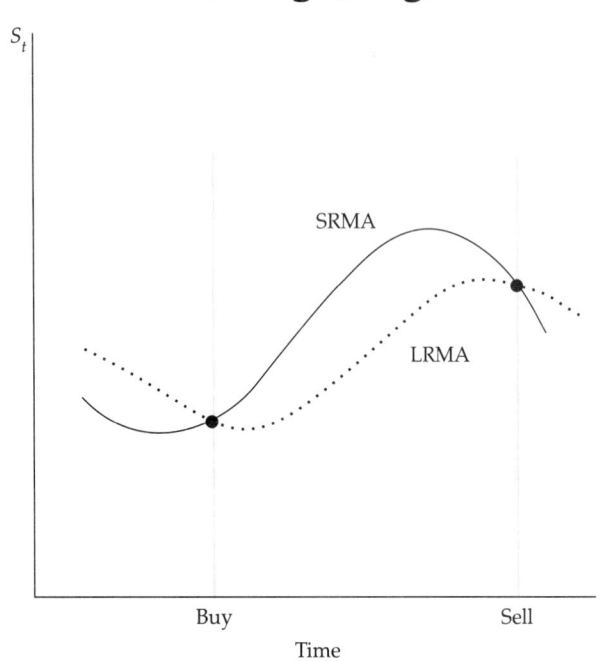

Figure 4.4. Buy and Sell Signals from an X Percent Filter Rule

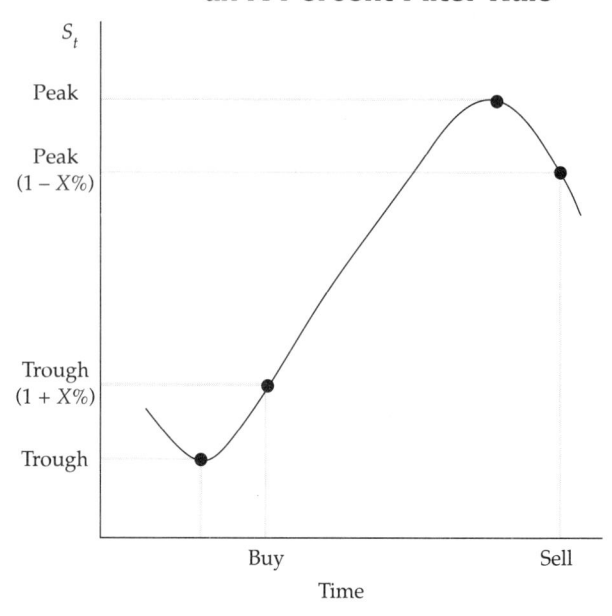

■ *Moving averages.* The aim of using moving averages is to smooth out some of the erratic daily swings of market prices (in this case, currency market spot prices) in order to spot the signals of major trends. The moving average approach is often implemented by computing a long-run moving average (LRMA) and a short-run moving average (SRMA). The assumption implied by the moving average approach is that prices will continue their trends in the prevailing direction of the SRMA. A long-run moving average will always lag a short-run moving average because it gives a smaller weight to recent movements than does the short-run moving average. As Figure 4.3 shows, a buy signal occurs when the SRMA price (or spot price at time t, S_t) moves above the LRMA and a sell signal occurs when the SRMA moves below LRMA.

■ *Filters.* Filter methods generate buy signals when a market price rises a set percentage (the filter) above its most recent low, and they generate sell signals when the price falls a set percentage below the previous high. The idea is to smooth out, or filter, daily fluctuations in order to detect lasting trends. Figure 4.4 illustrates how filter rules will put an investor into a market position once a trend has begun and will reverse positions after a trend has changed.

Filter rules can generate many false signals, however, causing losses if market movements do not continue in one direction long enough after the position is initiated for gains to outweigh losses once the market changes direction.

■ *Momentum models.* The purpose of momentum models is to determine the strength of a market by examining the change in velocity of exchange rate movements. A buy signal is generated by market prices climbing at an increasing rate. When the market loses its momentum, the position can be eliminated or reversed. Figure 4.5 shows one type of momentum indicator; it is calculated by taking the ratio of two market prices n days apart. If the market has been rising for the past n days, the ratio will be increasing above 1. If the market has been decreasing, the ratio will fall below 1. A change in market momentum will be indicated by the peak or trough in the relative exchange rates. A market that accelerates to a higher level and stays there will first show positive momentum; momentum will reach a peak; then, with the passage of time, it will fall back toward the zero point. The investor may decide to liquidate a long position when the market momentum peaks or to hold on until the momentum accelerates downward.

Figure 4.5. Buy and Sell Signals from Relative Momentum

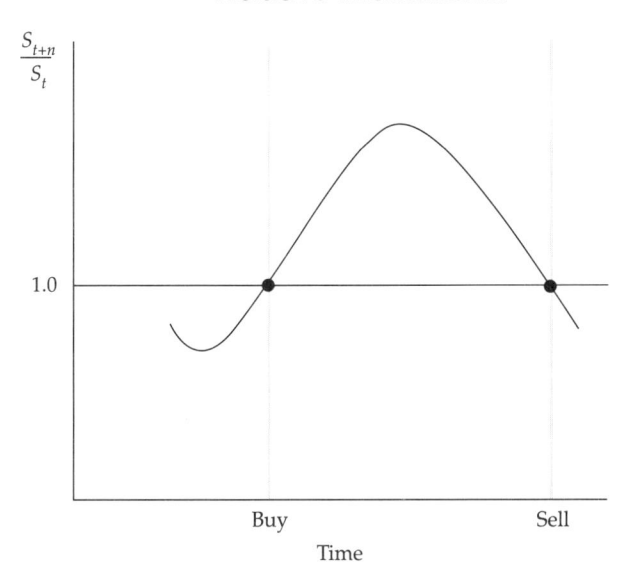

Note that a good deal of discretionary judgment is inherent in designing and using these technical indicators. Trading signals are sensitive to the time intervals used to construct the indicators. Also, certain indicators may perform well in some market environments but poorly in others. For example, trend-following signals work well when trends are well defined and persist for some period of time. They generally do not perform well when markets are in a choppy, transition period with no clear direction. If the market begins a price pattern but maintains it only long enough to generate a trading signal and then reverses itself, the technical investor will lose money on the signaled trade.

Technical analysis has succeeded in currency management probably for the same reason that dynamic strategies have successfully added value—central bank actions. Central bank interventions in the currency markets cause prices to adjust to new information relatively slowly, which affords traders the opportunity to transact in advance of full price responses. Technical traders who rely on trend-following approaches increase exposure to currencies as they appreciate and reduce exposure as the currencies fall in value. They trade in the same direction as investors who follow a dynamic strategy to generate a convex payoff function.

Summary

- Exploiting empirical tendencies often involves a trade-off between risk and return in the portfolio. The exploitation can be structured in terms of an investment decision to add incremental return or a hedging decision to reduce risk.
- The forward rate bias can be exploited by allowing the discount or premium in the forward rate to influence the expected return on a currency position. Investors will tend to be more positive about incurring currency exposure (or hedging less) for high-interest-rate currencies than for low-interest-rate currencies.
- Nonrandomness in currency returns can be exploited by testing for the presence of trends in the exchange rate over time. Currency moves have tended to persist from one month to the next but are prone to have some day-to-day reversals.
- Periods of serial correlation in currency returns lend themselves to the use of trend-following strategies common to many forms of technical analysis.

This chapter focused on active management to exploit the empirical tendencies of currencies. Note, however, that the framework for balancing the expected return of currencies with their contribution to a portfolio's risk need not be restricted to expected returns that arise from empirical tendencies. Chapter 7 will review the fundamental factors that might lead to various convictions about the direction of exchange rates.

5. Combining Return-Enhancement and Hedging Strategies

The focus in Chapter 3 was primarily on reducing the risk of currency exposure in a portfolio. Risk can be altered by constructing either symmetrical or asymmetrical hedges. Symmetrical hedges can be formed by choosing currency exposures that either minimize the portfolio variance or minimize tracking error relative to a benchmark.

Risk minimization may not be the desired goal for some investors. Indeed, in a fashion similar to the return-enhancement strategies discussed in Chapter 4, an investor may have developed particular forecasts of currency returns that may be helpful in structuring the optimal currency position. To use these forecasts, the investor requires a procedure for making trade-offs between risk and expected return.

We noted in Chapter 3 some of the different assumptions that can be made in structuring a minimum-variance currency position. In that chapter, as well as in Chapter 4, the asset positions were taken as fixed while the investor was free to structure the currency exposures given those asset positions. This chapter develops a framework for the more general case in which the investor is free to choose both the assets and the currency exposures.

The broad array of assumptions that can be made in structuring the optimal asset and currency decisions can sometimes be difficult to keep track of. In solutions to currency-hedging questions, however, it is important to recognize what assumptions have been made in structuring the problem and what constraints have been imposed. Figure 5.1 outlines the array of potential assumptions.

Depending on where one is working along the assumption tree, different solutions can emerge. The most general case occurs at the top, where the investor is free to choose both asset and currency positions and choose them simultaneously. As one works along the branches, the optimization is subject to more and more restrictions. Along one path, when only currency exposure can be altered and the portfolio benchmark is fully hedged, the benchmark-relative solution converges to the mean–variance solution. Along another path, the benchmark-relative optimization produces the optimal currency exposures for a basket hedge to minimize the tracking error against a benchmark currency portfolio. If the investor has very high aversion to tracking error, if currencies are uncorrelated with assets, and if all currencies are allowed to be part of the solution, the minimum-variance currency positions will result in a fully matched hedge. Allowing only a subset

Currency Management: Concepts and Practices

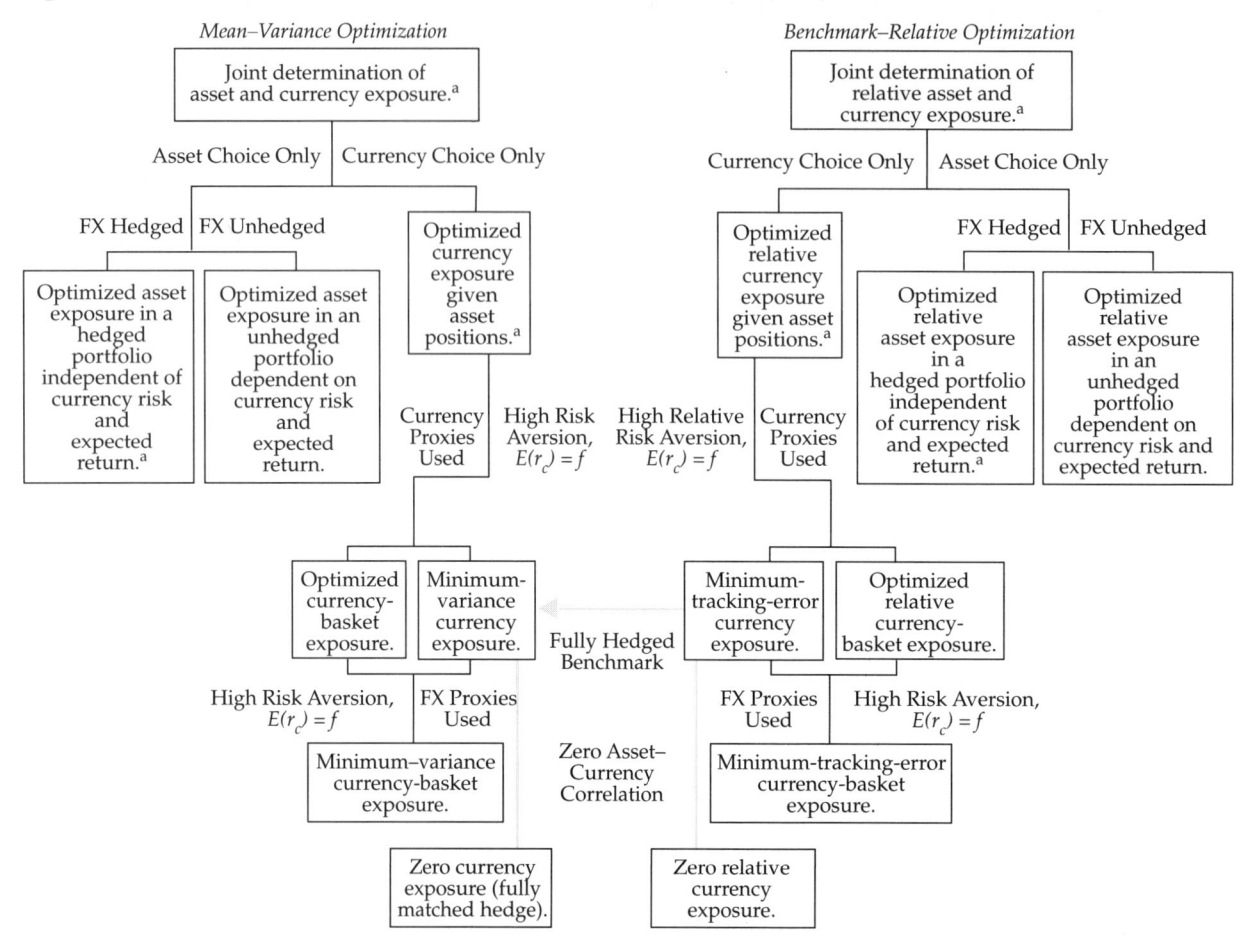

Figure 5.1. Mean–Variance and Benchmark-Relative Optimization

Mean–Variance Optimization

- Joint determination of asset and currency exposure.[a]
  - Asset Choice Only
    - FX Hedged: Optimized asset exposure in a hedged portfolio independent of currency risk and expected return.[a]
    - FX Unhedged: Optimized asset exposure in an unhedged portfolio dependent on currency risk and expected return.
  - Currency Choice Only
    - Optimized currency exposure given asset positions.[a]
      - Currency Proxies Used
        - Optimized currency-basket exposure.
        - High Risk Aversion, $E(r_c) = f$
          - Minimum–variance currency-basket exposure.
      - High Risk Aversion, $E(r_c) = f$
        - Minimum-variance currency exposure.
        - FX Proxies Used
        - Zero currency exposure (fully matched hedge).

Benchmark–Relative Optimization

- Joint determination of relative asset and currency exposure.[a]
  - Currency Choice Only
    - Optimized relative currency exposure given asset positions.[a]
      - High Relative Risk Aversion, $E(r_c) = f$
        - Minimum-tracking-error currency exposure.
        - FX Proxies Used
          - Minimum-tracking-error currency-basket exposure.
      - Currency Proxies Used
        - Optimized relative currency-basket exposure.
        - High Risk Aversion, $E(r_c) = f$
          - Zero relative currency exposure.
  - Asset Choice Only
    - FX Hedged: Optimized relative asset exposure in a hedged portfolio independent of currency risk and expected return.[a]
    - FX Unhedged: Optimized relative asset exposure in an unhedged portfolio dependent on currency risk and expected return.

Fully Hedged Benchmark ← Zero Asset–Currency Correlation

---

[a]Currency and asset decisions will be independent if currency and asset returns are uncorrelated.

FX = foreign currency.

of currency positions to be part of the solution results in a basket of currencies that tracks the benchmark with minimum tracking error. The sections that follow illustrate each of the branches.

Optimal Allocation of Asset and Currency Exposure

The optimal combination of asset and currency exposures in a portfolio composed of domestic and foreign assets depends on three categories of parameters:

- the expected returns to both assets and foreign currencies,
- the variances and covariances of the assets and currencies, and
- the investor's risk-aversion penalty.

In the traditional mean–variance framework, the investor chooses the asset weights and currency exposures to maximize the expected return of the portfolio minus a penalty for the risk. The investor solves the following problem:

$$\text{Maximize } E(R) - \lambda \sigma_R^2 \quad (5.1)$$

subject to

$$\sum_i w_i = 1.0$$

and

$$\sum_j H_j = 1.0,$$

where

$$E(R) = \sum_i w_i[E(r_\ell^i) + f_i] + \sum_j H_j[E(r_c^j) - f_j] \quad (5.2)$$

w_i = the portfolio weight held in asset i
$E(r_\ell^i)$ = the expected local asset return of asset i
f_i = the forward premium or discount for currency i
H_j = the portfolio currency exposure for currency j
$E(r_c^j)$ = the expected currency return for currency j
λ = the investor's risk-aversion penalty
σ_R^2 = the variance of the portfolio return.

The sum of all asset weights is typically constrained to be equal to 1.0; total currency exposure is also set equal to 1.0.[1]

A variety of other constraints related to maximum and minimum exposures for individual assets, individual currencies, or combinations of them can also be incorporated into a general optimization framework. To illustrate some of the basic principles and to keep the algebraic complexity to a minimum, we will use just two assets, however—one domestic asset and one foreign asset, with its associated currency—and impose only the budget constraint that the portfolio remain fully invested. Additional constraints are often needed in practical applications, but the general principles will remain the same.

Joint Optimization of the Asset and Currency Decisions. The joint optimization of asset and currency exposure can be illustrated by solving for the optimal asset and currency weights in the simple two-asset portfolio. The weights for the domestic asset, the foreign asset, and currency exposure from the unconstrained optimization conditions are

$w_d =$
$$\frac{E(r_d) - [E(r_\ell) + f] - [E(r_c) - f](C_{dc} - C_{\ell c})/\sigma_c^2 - 2\lambda[C_{d\ell} - \sigma_\ell^2 - (C_{dc} - C_{\ell c})C_{\ell c}/\sigma_c^2]}{2\lambda[\sigma_d^2 + \sigma_\ell^2 - 2C_{d\ell} - (C_{dc} - C_{\ell c})^2/\sigma_c^2]},$$
(5.3)

$$w_\ell = 1 - w_d, \quad (5.4)$$

and

$$H = \frac{E(r_c) - f - 2\lambda[w_d C_{dc} + w_\ell C_{\ell c}]}{2\lambda\sigma_c^2}. \quad (5.5)$$

Notice that in the joint optimization problem, the optimal asset and currency weights depend on all three factors referred to previously. The optimal weights depend on the expected asset and currency returns, asset and currency variances and covariances, and finally, the investor's risk-aversion parameter, λ.

Joint optimization of the asset and currency decisions allows the correlations between asset and currency returns to drive the final solution. This approach provides the most flexibility in forming positions and the best risk–return trade-offs.

Investment policies, however, often subordinate the currency decision to the asset decisions, and the usual result is a suboptimal solution. In some cases, investment policy dictates that currency exposure be always either hedged or unhedged, in which case, currency allocations are dictated by the asset allocation decisions. In other cases, instead of being predetermined, the currency-hedging decisions are addressed after the assets are in place, and correlations between assets and currencies may or may not be taken into account when decisions are made about how much currency exposure to have in the portfolio.

Only if currencies are uncorrelated with asset returns can asset and currency decisions be made independently and still lead to the same optimal results as joint decisions. Jorion (1994), in an interesting discussion of these issues, provides some estimates of the extent of inefficiency caused when decisions are not made jointly.

---

[1] The structure is flexible enough to allow currency exposure to be different from the asset exposure corresponding to that currency. The sum of the currency exposures can be constrained to be equal to 1.0 if the investor's base currency absorbs the residual between the aggregate foreign currency exposure and 1.0. The expected currency return and the forward premium for the base currency are identically zero in this framework.

Asset and Currency Exposure Determined Jointly

Suppose a U.S. investor decides to allocate a portfolio between U.S. and Japanese (JP) stocks using the following assumptions (percents):

$$E(r_{US}) = 14.3 \quad \sigma_{US} = 14.0$$
$$\text{Japanese stocks} \quad E(r_{JP}) = 15.6 \quad \sigma_{JP} = 18.0$$
$$\text{Currency} \quad E(r_\text{¥}) = 2.4 \quad \sigma_\text{¥} = 10.0$$
$$f = 1.2$$

	Correlation Matrix		
	U.S. Stocks	Japanese Stocks	Yen
U.S. stocks	1.0	0.3	−0.1
Japanese stocks		1.0	0.2
Yen			1.0

	Covariance Matrix		
U.S. stocks	0.0196	0.0076	−0.0014
Japanese stocks		0.0324	0.0036
Yen			0.0100

Using Equations 5.3, 5.4, and 5.5 to solve for the optimal asset weights and currency exposure gives the values in the following table for the various risk-aversion parameters:

λ	w_d	w_ℓ	H	E(R)	σ_R
1	39.4	60.6	43.7	16.3	14.8
2	53.2	46.8	20.6	15.7	13.1
5	61.5	38.5	6.8	15.3	12.6
10	64.3	35.7	2.1	15.2	12.6
100	66.8	33.2	−2.0	15.1	12.5
Minimum variance	67.1	32.9	−2.5	15.1	12.5

In this case, in which the asset and currency positions are determined jointly, note that as the investor's risk aversion increases, the allocation to the higher-risk Japanese stock, together with exposure to the yen, decreases. The minimum-variance allocation suggests that about two-thirds of the portfolio should be allocated to U.S. stocks, with about one-third allocated to Japanese stocks. Yen exposure in the minimum-variance allocation is slightly negative because of the yen's positive correlation with Japanese stocks and low expected return.

The trade-off between risk and expected return in the portfolio can be plotted as shown in Figure 5.2. The trade-off forms the efficient frontier that represents the best return for any given level of risk. The upward slope indicates that more risk is taken on to achieve additional return. Figure 5.2 also shows the fully hedged efficient frontier, which does not allow for any foreign currency exposure. This case is discussed later.

Asset Selection with Predetermined Currency Policy. Suppose the investor has chosen a currency policy that keeps currency exposure proportional to foreign asset exposure in the portfolio. Under this assumption, the minimum-variance allocation to domestic and foreign assets is

$$w_d = \frac{\begin{array}{c}E(r_d) - \{E(r_\ell) + f + p[E(r_c) - f]\} \\ - 2\lambda[C_{d\ell} + p(C_{dc} - C_{\ell c}) \\ - pC_{\ell c} - p^2\sigma_c^2 - \sigma_\ell^2]\end{array}}{\begin{array}{c}2\lambda\{\sigma_d^2 + \sigma_\ell^2 + p^2\sigma_c^2 \\ - 2[C_{d\ell} - p(C_{dc} - C_{\ell c})]\}\end{array}} \quad (5.6)$$

and

$$w_\ell = 1 - w_d, \quad (5.7)$$

where p is the currency proportionality constant. Equation 5.6 differs from Equation 5.3 because Equation 5.6 takes into account the constraint that the currency exposure be maintained proportional to the foreign asset exposure. With this constraint, two special cases are of particular interest: A fully hedged policy sets p equal to zero, and a fully unhedged policy sets p equal to 1.0.

■ *Fully hedged currency exposure ($p = H = 0$).* *If the currency exposure of the foreign asset position is assumed to be fully hedged as a matter of policy, the optimal allocation to domestic and foreign assets is*

$$w_d = \frac{E(r_d) - [E(r_\ell) + f] - 2\lambda(C_{d\ell} - \sigma_\ell^2)}{2\lambda(\sigma_d^2 + \sigma_\ell^2 - 2C_{d\ell})} \quad (5.8)$$

and

$$w_\ell = 1 - w_d. \quad (5.9)$$

The optimal asset allocation does not depend on the currency risk or cross-correlations with domestic or foreign assets. The forward premium is a factor, however, because of the cost to hedge the foreign asset.

It is interesting to note the conditions under which the asset weights in a jointly optimized portfolio are the same as those when currency policy is to fully hedge the currency exposure. A

Figure 5.2. Portfolio Efficient Frontier

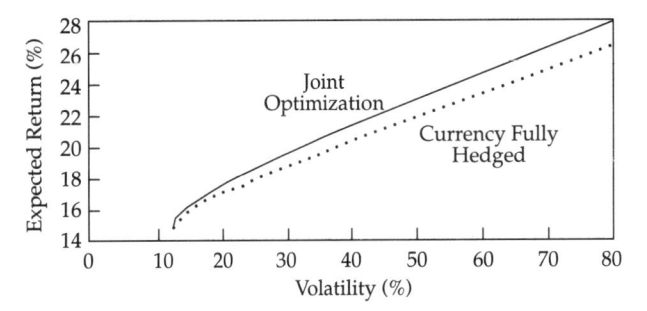

comparison of Equation 5.8 with Equation 5.3 shows that the two will be the same if the covariances of asset returns with currency returns are all zero. In this circumstance, the asset and currency decisions could be made independently and would give the same solution as if made jointly.

■ *Unhedged currency exposure ($p = 1$ and $H = w_\ell$).* If the currency exposure of any foreign asset position is always left unhedged as a matter of policy, the allocation to domestic assets depends on the currency risk and expected return as given in Equation 5.10:

$$w_d = \frac{\begin{array}{c}E(r_d) - [E(r_\ell) + E(r_c)] \\ - 2\lambda[C_{d\ell} + C_{dc} - 2C_{\ell c} \\ - \sigma_\ell^2 - \sigma_c^2]\end{array}}{\begin{array}{c}2\lambda[\sigma_d^2 + \sigma_\ell^2 + \sigma_c^2 \\ - 2(C_{d\ell} + C_{dc} - C_{\ell c})]\end{array}}. \quad (5.10)$$

The forward premium does not enter into the solution because no hedging is contemplated. Currency risk enters into the decision, even though asset returns are uncorrelated with currency returns, because incremental foreign asset exposure also adds incremental currency exposure. These allocations will generally not be the same as those that result from joint optimization of assets and currencies.

Asset Decision with Predetermined Currency Policy

Suppose the investor uses the same basic portfolio data as in the previous example except that the currency decision is tied to the underlying asset decision. The following table gives the optimal asset weights for the portfolio for various risk-aversion parameters based on using Equations 5.8 through 5.10. In one case, the currency policy is to be fully hedged; in the other case, the currency is unhedged.

| | Fully Hedged ||||| Unhedged |||||
λ	w_d	w_ℓ	H	$E(R)$	σ_R	w_d	w_ℓ	H	$E(R)$	σ_R
1	33.4	66.6	0.0	16.0	14.1	43.8	56.2	56.2	16.4	15.0
2	53.2	46.8	0.0	15.5	12.8	60.1	39.9	39.9	15.8	13.4
5	61.5	38.5	0.0	15.3	12.6	69.9	30.1	30.1	15.4	12.9
10	64.3	35.7	0.0	15.2	12.5	73.2	26.8	26.8	15.3	12.8
100	66.8	33.2	0.0	15.1	12.5	76.1	23.9	23.9	15.2	12.8
Minimum variance	67.1	32.9	0.0	15.1	12.5	76.4	23.6	23.6	15.2	12.8

Note that the fully hedged and unhedged asset allocations are different for the same risk-aversion parameter, but because the asset return correlations relative to currency returns are assumed to be small, the jointly determined allocations are reasonably close to those assigned using a fully hedged currency policy.

The fully hedged efficient frontier is plotted in Figure 5.2 relative to the frontier when assets and currencies are jointly determined. Any constraints placed on the portfolio positions typically result in a less desirable frontier relative to an unconstrained allocation.

Optimal Currency Selection with Predetermined Asset Exposure. If the currency exposure decision is made after the asset positions are already decided, the optimal currency exposure is not a function of the expected asset returns directly but is influenced through the previously decided asset allocations w_d and w_ℓ. This type of approach is used by many currency overlay managers because they cannot alter the asset mix in the portfolio. In this sequential case, the optimal currency exposure is a function of the asset correlations with currency returns and is given by

$$H = \frac{E(r_c) - f - 2\lambda[w_d C_{dc} + w_\ell C_{\ell c}]}{2\lambda \sigma_c^2}. \quad (5.11)$$

The effects of two additional assumptions are interesting to note. First, in the event that correlations between asset and currency returns are assumed to be zero, the optimal currency exposure is independent of the underlying asset positions and is equal to

$$H = \frac{E(r_c) - f}{2\lambda \sigma_c^2}. \quad (5.12)$$

This assumption of independence allows currency overlay programs to be structured without regard to the underlying asset portfolio. If correlations are truly nonzero, however, currency overlay programs structured without regard to the underlying assets in the portfolio will sacrifice some effectiveness. The assumption of uncorrelated asset and currency returns is unlikely to be accurate—especially if the underlying portfolio contains foreign bonds, because bond and currency correlations have tended to be high. The choice of how much currency exposure to hedge when asset and currency decisions are made sequentially will be suboptimal when the currency returns are not independent of the asset returns (see Jorion 1994).

The second assumption with interesting effects concerns risk aversion. If the investor has a high aversion to risk (chooses risk minimization without regard to expected return or cost), the optimal currency exposure will be

$$H = -\left[\frac{w_d C_{dc} + w_\ell C_{\ell c}}{\sigma_c^2}\right], \quad (5.13)$$

which is the same result as for the minimum-variance hedge noted in Chapter 3. Now, if asset returns are uncorrelated with currency returns, the optimal currency exposure is zero (implying fully hedged exposure).

Currency Decision with Predetermined Asset Exposure

Suppose the investor uses the same basic portfolio data as in the example in "Joint Optimization of the Asset and Currency Decisions" except that the assets are held fixed at 70 percent U.S. stocks and 30 percent Japanese stocks. Using Equation 5.11 produces the following optimal currency exposure for the portfolio for various risk-aversion parameters:

λ	w_d	w_ℓ	H	E(R)	σ_R
1	70.0	30.0	59.0	15.8	13.9
2	70.0	30.0	29.0	15.4	12.9
5	70.0	30.0	11.0	15.2	12.6
10	70.0	30.0	5.0	15.1	12.5
100	70.0	30.0	−0.4	15.0	12.5
Minimum variance	70.0	30.0	−1.0	15.0	12.5

Notice that the more risk averse the investor is, the less currency exposure is desired. Notice also that with the asset positions already determined, the expected returns are slightly less for the same amount of risk than when allocations are jointly determined as in the previous example.

Optimization Relative to a Benchmark

Optimization relative to a benchmark can be done using a framework similar to the traditional mean–variance optimization. In this framework, the investor chooses the optimal deviation from a benchmark position in order to maximize the expected incremental return minus a penalty for the tracking error of the portfolio. The investor solves the following problem:

$$\text{Maximize } E(\Delta R) - \gamma \sigma^2_{\Delta R} \quad (5.14)$$

subject to

$$\sum_i \Delta w_i = 0$$

and

$$\sum_j \Delta H_j = 0,$$

where

$$E(\Delta R) = \sum_i \Delta w_i[E(r^i_\ell) + f_i]$$
$$+ \sum_j \Delta H_j[E(r^j_c) - f_j] \quad (5.15)$$

Δw_i = the difference between the portfolio and the benchmark asset exposure for asset i

ΔH_j = the difference between the portfolio and the benchmark currency exposure for currency j

γ = the investor's tracking-error penalty

$\sigma_{\Delta R}$ = the tracking error of the portfolio.

As before, we illustrate the basic principles through the use of only two assets in order to avoid extensive algebraic complexity, but keep in mind that similar flexibility in structuring constraints on asset and currency weights is possible in the benchmark-relative optimization as is available in the mean–variance optimization.

Joint Optimization of the Asset and Currency Decisions. This section, as in previous sections, uses a simple two-asset portfolio to illustrate the joint optimization of asset and currency decisions relative to a benchmark. Solving for the optimal incremental exposures for the domestic asset and currency from the maximization conditions produces

$$\Delta H = \frac{E(r_c) - f - 2\gamma[\Delta w_d C_{dc} + \Delta w_\ell C_{\ell c}]}{2\gamma \sigma^2_c} \quad (5.16)$$

and

$$\Delta w_d = \frac{E(r_d) - [E(r_\ell) + f] - [E(r_c) - f](C_{dc} - C_{\ell c})/\sigma^2_c}{2\gamma[\sigma^2_d + \sigma^2_\ell - 2C_{d\ell} - (C_{dc} - C_{\ell c})^2/\sigma^2_c]}, \quad (5.17)$$

Currency Management: Concepts and Practices

with the deviation from the foreign asset benchmark equal to

$$\Delta w_\ell = -\Delta w_d. \qquad (5.18)$$

The last condition follows from the fact that any deviation from the benchmark by the domestic asset position would have to be absorbed by the foreign asset in order to keep the portfolio fully invested.

Figure 5.3. Relative Efficient Frontier

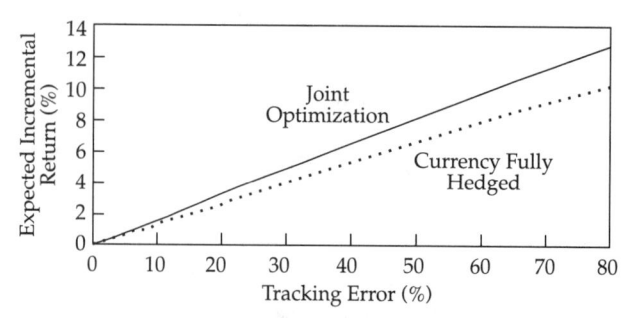

Relative Asset and Currency Exposure Determined Jointly

Optimization relative to a benchmark can be illustrated using the same basic portfolio data as in the previous examples. For instance, suppose the investor's benchmark portfolio is 70 percent in U.S. stocks and 30 percent in Japanese stocks with the benchmark currency exposure unhedged. Using Equations 5.16, 5.17, and 5.18, the following table gives the optimal relative asset and currency allocations for various tracking-error parameters:

γ	Δw_d	Δw_ℓ	ΔH	$E(\Delta R)$	$\sigma_{\Delta R}$
1	−27.7	27.7	46.2	1.3	7.9
2	−13.9	13.9	23.1	0.6	4.0
5	−5.5	5.5	9.2	0.3	1.6
10	−2.8	2.8	4.6	0.1	0.8
100	−0.3	0.3	0.5	0.0	0.1
Minimum tracking error	0.0	0.0	0.0	0.0	0.0

Notice that as the investor's aversion to tracking error increases, the recommended deviations from the benchmark become smaller and smaller. The trade-off between incremental return and tracking error when assets and currencies are treated jointly is plotted in Figure 5.3 (which also contains the data for the fully hedged currency decision, to be discussed later). This trade-off forms the efficient benchmark-relative frontier. The frontier passes through the intercept, indicating that if the portfolio is held in benchmark proportions, there is no tracking error and no incremental return can be expected.

Joint optimization of the asset and currency decisions relative to the benchmark allows the correlations between assets and currencies to influence the marginal allocations in a way similar to the full mean–variance procedure. Joint optimization provides the most flexibility in structuring positions and the best trade-off between incremental return and tracking error.

As we show in the next sections, making the currency decision after the asset decisions are already made does not produce the same allocation produced by joint decision making unless asset returns are uncorrelated with currency returns. If returns are uncorrelated, then asset and currency decisions can be made independently without loss of efficiency.

Optimal Relative Asset Selection with Predetermined Currency Policy. Suppose that in the relative optimization framework, the investor has decided upon a currency policy that keeps relative currency exposure proportional to relative foreign asset exposure. Under this assumption, the optimal relative asset allocation would be

$$\Delta w_d = \frac{E(r_d) - \{E(r_\ell) + f + p[E(r_c) - f]\}}{2\gamma\{\sigma_d^2 + \sigma_\ell^2 + p^2\sigma_c^2 - 2[C_{d\ell} - p(C_{dc} - C_{\ell c})]\}} \quad (5.19)$$

and

$$\Delta w_\ell = -\Delta w_d,$$

where p again represents the proportionality constant between incremental currency exposure and foreign asset exposure. Two special policies of interest are the fully hedged on an incremental basis and the fully unhedged on an incremental basis.

■ *Fully hedged incremental asset exposure* $(p = \Delta H = 0)$. If the currency policy is to hedge incremental foreign asset exposure fully, the optimal deviation from the domestic asset benchmark is

$$\Delta w_d = \frac{E(r_d) - [E(r_\ell) + f]}{2\gamma(\sigma_d^2 + \sigma_\ell^2 - 2C_{d\ell})}. \quad (5.20)$$

Note that the optimal incremental domestic asset exposure is a function of the relative expected asset returns and the forward premium or discount, but no expected currency return enters into the decision because all incremental currency risk is hedged.

In the event that the covariances between asset returns and currency returns are zero, a comparison of Equations 5.17 and 5.20 shows that the relative asset weights when they are determined jointly with currency exposure will be equal to those determined when incremental currency exposure is assumed to be fully hedged. As a result, deviations from asset benchmark positions in a joint optimization process will be as if incremental asset positions were always fully hedged.

■ *Unhedged incremental asset exposure* $(p = 1 \text{ and } \Delta H = \Delta w_\ell)$. If the incremental currency exposure is always maintained at the same level as the incremental foreign asset exposure, the optimal deviation from the domestic asset benchmark is

$$\Delta w_d = \frac{E(r_d) - [E(r_\ell) + E(r_c)]}{2\gamma[\sigma_d^2 + \sigma_\ell^2 + \sigma_c^2 - 2(C_{d\ell} - C_{dc} + C_{\ell c})]}. \quad (5.21)$$

In this case, the optimal asset decision is affected by the expected currency return in addition to the currency variance and correlation with foreign and domestic assets. Currency risk again enters into the asset decision because incremental foreign asset exposure also adds incremental currency exposure. These allocations will not be the same as those resulting from a joint optimization even if asset returns are assumed to be uncorrelated with currency returns.

Relative Asset Decision with Predetermined Currency Policy

If the investor's benchmark portfolio is composed of the same 70/30 percentages of U.S. stocks and Japanese stocks as in the previous example, Equations 5.20 and 5.21 will give the optimal marginal allocation to U.S. stocks when the currency policy is to be fully hedged or unhedged:

	Fully Hedged Incremental Asset Exposure				
γ	Δw_d	Δw_ℓ	ΔH	$E(\Delta R)$	$\sigma_{\Delta R}$
1	−34.0	34.0	0.0	0.9	6.5
2	−17.0	17.0	0.0	0.4	3.3
5	−6.8	6.8	0.0	0.2	1.3
10	−3.4	3.4	0.0	0.1	0.7
100	−0.3	0.3	0.0	0.0	0.1
Minimum tracking error	0.0	0.0	0.0	0.0	0.0

Currency Management: Concepts and Practices

	Unhedged Incremental Asset Exposure				
γ	Δw_d	Δw_ℓ	ΔH	$E(\Delta R)$	$\sigma_{\Delta R}$
1	−32.6	32.6	32.6	1.2	7.8
2	−16.3	16.3	16.3	0.6	3.9
5	−6.5	6.5	6.5	0.2	1.6
10	−3.7	3.7	3.7	0.1	0.8
100	−0.3	0.3	0.3	0.0	0.1
Minimum tracking error	0.0	0.0	0.0	0.0	0.0

Notice that the two allocations for assets are not very different. Unhedged asset exposure adds some additional risk but does not affect the solution much because the correlations between assets and the currency are small and the expected currency return is small.

The relative efficient frontier for the fully hedged benchmark is plotted in Figure 5.3. The constraint imposed by forcing currency exposure to be fully hedged results in a less desirable relative efficient frontier than in the case of joint optimization of the relative asset and currency allocations.

Optimal Relative Currency Selection with Predetermined Asset Exposure.

The choice of the currency exposure that will generate the minimum tracking error when asset positions are held fixed is found by solving

$$\Delta H = \frac{E(r_c) - f - 2\gamma[\Delta w_d C_{dc} + \Delta w_\ell C_{\ell c}]}{2\gamma \sigma_c^2}. \quad (5.22)$$

The optimal currency positions are a function of the expected currency return, the forward premium or discount, and the volatility and correlation of currency returns. As noted previously, this allocation will not necessarily be the same as the allocation when the asset and currency decisions are made jointly. Sequential decisions result in some loss of efficiency.

Two special cases here are of interest. First, if correlations between asset and currency returns are assumed to be zero, or asset positions are held at benchmark exposures, the optimal incremental currency exposure is independent of the underlying asset positions and is given by

$$\Delta H = \frac{E(r_c) - f}{2\gamma \sigma_c^2}. \quad (5.23)$$

In this special case, the relative currency allocation will be the same as when the currency decision is made jointly with the relative asset allocation decisions.

Second, if the investor has a high aversion to tracking error, the optimal relative currency exposure will be

$$\Delta H = -\frac{[\Delta w_d C_{dc} + \Delta w_\ell C_{\ell c}]}{\sigma_c^2}. \quad (5.24)$$

This result is the same as the result noted in Chapter 3 that minimizes the tracking error. Now, if asset returns are uncorrelated with currency returns, the optimal position is to take on no incremental currency exposure.

Combining the Mean–Variance and Benchmark-Relative Approaches

The mean–variance approach can be combined with the benchmark-relative optimization in one process. In this case, the investor solves

$$\text{Maximize } E(\Delta R) - \lambda \sigma_R^2 - \gamma \sigma_{\Delta R}^2$$

subject to

$$\sum_i w_i = 1.0$$

and

$$\sum_j H_j = 1.0.$$

In the simple two-asset case with asset positions already predetermined, the optimal incremental currency exposure is

Relative Currency Decision with Predetermined Asset Exposure

For the final example in this series, suppose the investor's portfolio holds 70 percent in U.S. stocks and 30 percent in Japanese stocks against a benchmark of 70/30 with the benchmark currency exposure unhedged. Using Equation 5.22 provides the optimal incremental currency exposures for various risk–return trade-offs in the relative optimization framework:

γ	Δw_d	Δw_ℓ	ΔH	H	$E(\Delta R)$	$\sigma_{\Delta R}$	$E(R)$	σ_R
1	0.0	0.0	60.0	90.0	0.7	6.0	16.1	15.5
2	0.0	0.0	30.0	60.0	0.4	3.0	15.8	13.9
5	0.0	0.0	12.0	42.0	0.1	1.2	15.6	13.2
10	0.0	0.0	6.0	36.0	0.1	0.6	15.5	13.1
100	0.0	0.0	0.6	30.6	0.0	0.1	15.4	12.9
Minimum tracking error	0.0	0.0	0.0	30.0	0.0	0.0	15.4	12.9

Notice that even though asset positions are held at benchmark weights, some trade-off between risk and return is possible by taking on incremental currency exposure. At the extreme, no incremental exposure reduces the tracking error to zero.

If both total variance and tracking error are important to the investor, Equation 5.25 shows the optimal incremental currency exposure for various risk–return trade-offs against an unhedged currency benchmark to be

γ and λ	Δw_d	Δw_ℓ	ΔH	H	$E(\Delta R)$	$\sigma_{\Delta R}$	$E(R)$	σ_R
1	0.0	0.0	14.5	44.5	0.2	1.4	15.6	13.3
2	0.0	0.0	−0.5	29.5	0.0	0.1	15.4	12.9
5	0.0	0.0	−9.5	20.5	−0.1	1.0	15.3	12.7
10	0.0	0.0	−12.5	17.5	−0.2	1.3	15.3	12.7
100	0.0	0.0	−15.2	14.8	−0.2	1.5	15.2	12.6

The interplay between tracking error and total risk can be seen in this case; the reduction in variance is achieved by taking on additional tracking error.

$$\Delta H = \frac{E(r_c) - f - 2\lambda(w_d C_{dc} + w_\ell C_{\ell c}) - 2\gamma(\Delta w_d C_{dc} + \Delta w_\ell C_{\ell c})}{2\sigma_c^2(\lambda + \gamma)} - \frac{\lambda H^B}{\lambda + \gamma}, \quad (5.25)$$

where H^B represents the benchmark currency exposure. Now, the optimal relative currency exposure is a function of both the absolute asset exposures and the asset exposures relative to their respective benchmark positions. One can easily see that Equation 5.25 collapses to either Equation 5.11 or Equation 5.22, depending on whether total variance or tracking error is most important.[2]

---

[2] This type of approach, in which both risks are important to the investor, is discussed by Chow (1995). Whether expected total return or expected incremental return is used in the objective function makes no difference to the solution because the portfolio benchmark return in the relative optimization is a constant and drops out in the optimization procedure.

Extensions beyond Simple Portfolios

The simple examples so far in this chapter are structured so that the allocations can be derived using the algebraic solutions. Few portfolios, however, are so simple. When portfolios contain many asset and currency positions, the simplest approach is to use the computer to find an optimal solution, which was done for the optimization in this section. Computer solutions require the use of a nonlinear optimizer to find the efficient frontier using a procedure similar to the traditional Markowitz portfolio analysis.

Figure 5.1 demonstrated that, no matter how complex the portfolio, the objective function to be optimized can be defined in at least two ways. Optimal portfolio positions can be constructed either by maximizing the total portfolio return subject to a penalty for portfolio variance or by maximizing total return (or incremental return) subject to a penalty for tracking error relative to a benchmark allocation. A variety of different constraints and assumptions can be made in setting up the problem. For a few examples of the many possibilities, consider that assets can be held in fixed proportions while currency exposure is allowed to vary; assets can be assumed to be uncorrelated with currency returns; currency exposure can be limited by asset exposure; or baskets of currencies can be used to proxy for another currency. The solutions that result depend on the assumptions made and the constraints imposed by the investor in structuring the problem. The optimization process is flexible enough to be tailored to individual objectives and preferences. (A general portfolio allocation that meets the needs of all investors is not likely to exist, even when the same assumptions are made about risk and return.)

Figure 5.4 illustrates the relative efficient frontier for a more complex portfolio than has been addressed up to this point in the chapter. This portfolio includes multiple assets and currencies from seven countries. Table 5.1 contains the expected local one-month returns for each asset and currency from a U.S. perspective. The covariance matrix used in the optimization was developed using historical monthly returns.

The optimization is structured relative to the investor's benchmark portfolio so that the port-

Figure 5.4. Portfolio Efficient Frontier Relative to a Benchmark

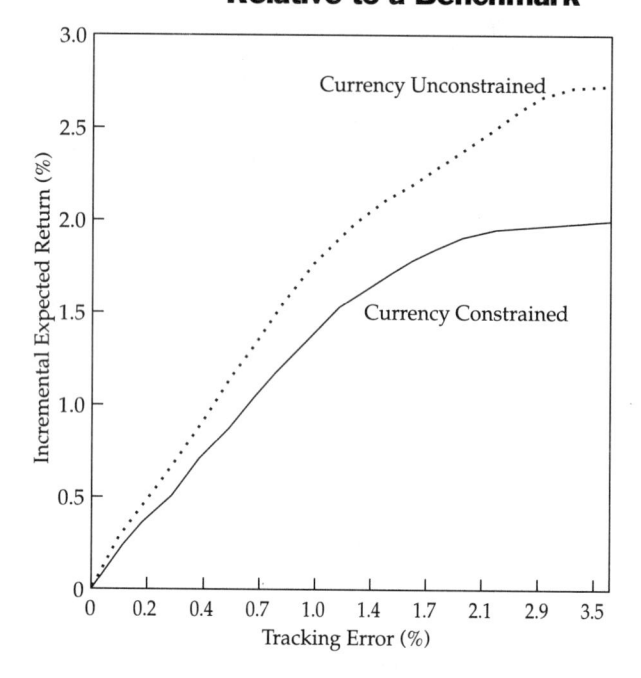

folio allocation maximizes the expected portfolio return less a penalty for tracking error relative to the benchmark. Table 5.1 shows both the benchmark allocation and the recommended portfolio allocation using a specific penalty for tracking error ($\gamma = 20$). Notice that the unconstrained portfolio is underweighted in assets and currencies with low expected returns and overweighted in assets and currencies with high expected returns.

Notice also that some currency allocations in the unconstrained portfolio are greater than the assets allocated from their corresponding countries while others are less. In this unconstrained case, currency positions are not constrained by the size of the asset positions. More currency exposure can be held than the allocation to assets in the corresponding country.

Table 5.1 also shows the recommended allocations if currency exposure is constrained by the corresponding asset exposure. When this type of constraint is imposed, the optimizer may choose to increase exposure to an unattractive asset in order to gain exposure to an attractive currency. Such is the case in Table 5.1 for German bonds in the constrained portfolio. Asset exposure is increased in order not to lose the attractive German mark exposure. Notice that, as a result of the constraints, the expected

5. Combining Return-Enhancement and Hedging Strategies

Table 5.1. Optimal Portfolio Allocation Relative to a Benchmark

Country (and Currency)	Asset Class	Expected One-Month Hedged Return	Benchmark	Currency Unconstrained Portfolio	Currency Unconstrained Difference	Currency Constrained Portfolio	Currency Constrained Difference
United States (US$)	Stocks	0.57%	25.5%	0.0%	−25.5%	0.0%	−25.5%
	Bonds	−0.31	25.5	0.0	−25.5	0.0	−25.5
	Cash	0.42	0.0	0.0	0.0	0.0	0.0
Germany (DM)	Stocks	1.01	11.0	4.7	−6.3	2.0	−9.0
	Bonds	1.46	11.0	0.0	−11.0	0.0	−11.0
United Kingdom (£)	Stocks	1.46	1.8	17.7	15.9	7.2	5.4
	Bonds	0.35	1.7	0.0	−1.7	0.0	−1.7
Japan (¥)	Stocks	1.87	7.5	14.2	6.7	13.3	5.8
	Bonds	1.54	7.5	0.0	−7.5	0.0	−7.5
Australia (AU$)	Stocks	−1.68	0.7	0.0	−0.7	0.0	−0.7
	Bonds	2.41	0.8	15.6	14.8	8.9	8.1
Canada (CA$)	Stocks	1.06	0.5	0.0	−0.5	0.0	−0.5
	Bonds	2.31	0.5	47.8	47.3	39.9	39.4
France (FF)	Stocks	−5.62	3.0	0.0	−3.0	0.0	−3.0
	Bonds	1.15	3.0	0.0	−3.0	28.7	25.7
Total assets			100.0%	100.0%	0.0%	100.0%	0.0%

Currency Exposure	Expected One-Month Forward Contract Return					
US$	0.00	51.0	41.6	−9.4	69.3	18.3
DM	−0.26	22.0	0.0	−22.0	2.0	−20.0
£	−0.63	3.5	0.0	−3.5	0.0	−3.5
¥	−0.54	15.0	0.0	−15.0	0.0	−15.0
AU$	−0.19	1.5	0.0	−1.5	0.0	−1.5
CA$	−0.69	1.0	0.0	−1.0	0.0	−1.0
FF	0.77	6.0	58.4	52.4	28.7	22.7
Total currencies		100.0%	100.0%	0.0%	100.0%	0.0%

Monthly portfolio statistics						
Expected return		0.39	2.50	2.11	2.06	1.66
Total volatility		3.03	3.07	4.04	2.28	−0.75
Tracking error			1.46		1.46	

return on the constrained portfolio is slightly lower than the return on the unconstrained portfolio. Constraints on asset or currency positions typically reduce the effective risk–return trade-off a portfolio can achieve.

One of the easiest ways to structure the joint optimization problem is to follow the formulations in Equation 5.2 or Equation 5.15 to separate the asset weights from the currency weights. Using these formulations, the asset returns are treated as fully hedged while the currencies are treated as if futures or forward contracts are purchased to gain currency exposure. In the mean–variance formulation of Equation 5.2, the sum of the asset weights is typically constrained to equal 100 percent, as is the sum of the currency exposures, to keep the portfolio fully invested and avoid leveraging. The home currency of the investor effectively serves as a residual currency allocation; once the foreign currency allocations are calculated, the home currency makes up the difference so that the currency allocations sum to 100 percent.

In the mean–tracking error formulation of Equation 5.15, the decision variables are the deviations from benchmark allocations. The sum of the deviations from benchmark asset positions and the sum of the deviations from benchmark currency positions are each typically constrained to equal zero to avoid leveraging the portfolio and keep it fully invested.

Whether mean–variance or benchmark-relative optimization is used, the expected local asset returns are adjusted to a fully hedged basis by adding back the forward premium or discount and expected forward contract returns are calculated by subtracting the forward premium or discount from the expected currency return. The interaction between local asset and currency returns comes through the covariance matrix. This separation of asset and currency positions makes the structure of the optimization somewhat easier and reinforces the concept that currency positions can be implemented independently of asset decisions. As Equation 1.20a demonstrated, some of this intuition is lost if the returns in the objective function are structured so that the currency position is coupled with the asset position.

Summary

- A fully integrated solution to the currency-hedging problem involves a joint decision process in which asset positions and currency exposures are determined at the same time.
- Currency decisions are often made after the assets are already in place. This sequential approach gives a less efficient trade-off between risk and return than the joint decision because it does not recognize that the choice of currency exposure may influence the choice of asset exposure, especially if currency exposure is constrained by the size of the asset positions.
- The choice of currency exposure will be independent of asset positions only if currency positions are unconstrained by asset positions and currency returns are uncorrelated with domestic and foreign local asset returns. Under these conditions, sequential decisions for asset and currency allocations will give the same results as if they were made jointly.
- Optimal currency positions can be structured with risk defined as total portfolio variance or as tracking error relative to a benchmark. The solutions to the asset and currency allocation decisions will generally not be the same unless the benchmark is fully hedged. In that case, tracking error and total variance are the same, so the allocations that minimize total variance will also minimize tracking error.
- When asset positions are fixed, the optimal currency positions collapse to the risk-minimizing solutions if the investor has very high risk aversion. Otherwise, some trade-off will exist between expected return and risk.

6. Performance Attribution for Actively Managed Portfolios

Investors and investment managers naturally want to know how an active investment strategy has performed and which active decisions have contributed the most value to performance. Measuring total value added is relatively simple: The total value added from active management can be calculated by comparing the portfolio's total return with the portfolio's benchmark return. Decomposition of the total added value into its component parts is sometimes more complex.

In this chapter, we demonstrate alternative performance attribution methodologies. The first section describes two techniques that can be used when the portfolio allocations have not changed during the measurement period and the portfolio is invested in physical assets. If portfolio positions have changed during the measurement period, using beginning-of-period allocations to evaluate each individual contribution will produce only an approximation of the performance attribution. The greater the interim changes in allocations, the less precise the estimated attribution will be.

The second section describes a technique for measuring performance when derivatives have been used in the portfolio to implement changes in portfolio exposure while holding the underlying asset positions constant. This technique can be used whether derivatives alter the net market exposures during the performance period or not.

Each of the three performance attribution techniques gives the same total added value, but they partition it in slightly different ways. No way is necessarily "right," because in a portfolio in which the allocations sum to 100 percent, the decisions are interdependent. An overweight position in one market means another position must be underweighted. Performance attribution can identify the contribution to performance from each market segment, but additional information is needed to elucidate the underlying rationale for the decisions.

Performance Attribution When Underlying Asset Composition Is Constant

As long as the composition of a physical-asset portfolio is held constant during the measurement period, two methods are available to measure value added to that portfolio's returns, relative to the returns of a benchmark, by active management. Although both formulations give the same total added value, they partition that value among markets in different ways.

The first technique describes the value added for each asset as the absolute contribution to incremental return from an over- or underweight position. An overweight position will have a positive contribution when market returns are above zero and a negative contribution when market returns are below zero. The second technique describes the added value as the contribution relative to the benchmark return. In this technique, an overweight position will have a positive contribution when market returns are above the benchmark return and a negative contribution when market returns are below the benchmark return.

The development of these two techniques begins with calculating the total portfolio return, which weights the fully hedged return from each asset and each individual currency exposure in the portfolio. The total portfolio return found by using the return formulation in Equation 1.20b, which separates the currency returns from the underlying hedged local asset returns, is

$$R \approx \sum_i w_i(r_\ell^i + f_i) + \sum_j H_j(r_c^j - f_j) \qquad (6.1)$$

where

w_i = the portfolio weight held in asset i
r_ℓ^i = the local asset return of asset i
f_i = the forward premium for currency i[1]
r_c^j = the currency return for currency j
H_j = the currency exposure of the portfolio to currency j.

Similarly, the return on the benchmark portfolio can be represented as

$$R_B \approx \sum_i w_i^B(r_B^i + f_i) + \sum_j H_j^B(r_c^j - f_j)$$
$$= R_A^B + R_c^B, \qquad (6.2)$$

where

w_i^B = the benchmark portfolio weight in asset i
r_B^i = the local asset return in the benchmark for asset i
H_j^B = the currency exposure of the benchmark portfolio to currency j.

The hedged asset and currency benchmark returns are represented as

$$R_A^B = \sum_i w_i^B(r_B^i + f_i) \qquad (6.3)$$

and

$$R_c^B = \sum_j H_j^B(r_c^j - f_j). \qquad (6.4)$$

The difference between the local asset return in each market attributed to active management and the corresponding local asset benchmark return is captured by α_i:

$$\alpha_i = r_\ell^i - r_B^i. \qquad (6.5)$$

Absolute Contribution Analysis. The value added is found by subtracting the benchmark return from the total portfolio return. Using Equations 6.1, 6.2, and 6.5 and separating the total added value into parts gives the following:

$$\begin{aligned}\text{Value added} &= R - R_B \\ &= \sum_i w_i \alpha_i + \sum_i \Delta w_i(r_B^i + f_i) \\ &\quad + \sum_j \Delta H_j(r_c^j - f_j) + e \end{aligned} \qquad (6.6)$$

where

$$\Delta w_i = w_i - w_i^B \qquad (6.7)$$

and

$$\Delta H_j = H_j - H_j^B. \qquad (6.8)$$

The first term in Equation 6.6 represents the value added by active asset management within each market segment. Passive, indexed asset management will generate no incremental asset returns, producing no value added from this source.

The second term represents the absolute value added by active asset allocation within the asset portfolio, market by market, using hedged asset returns. The value added by active asset allocation is equal to the sum of the active asset allocation weights relative to the benchmark times the hedged asset return. Hedged asset returns are used in order to separate the asset allocation contribution from the currency contribution. This second term will be zero if the assets are held at benchmark weights.

The third term represents the absolute value added from active currency allocation within the portfolio, market by market. It is equal to the sum of the active currency allocation weights

---

[1] In this notation, the forward premium and currency return for the investor's home currency are identically zero.

relative to the benchmark times the respective forward currency surprise in each market. This term will also be zero if each currency exposure is held at its benchmark weight.

A final error term is usually added to capture the cross-products caused by the interaction between asset returns and currency returns, which have been ignored in Equations 6.1 and 6.2. This error term is typically small relative to the other terms because it involves the products of returns; it is usually either disregarded or used as a plug figure to make everything balance.

Absolute Contribution Analysis

Consider the performance of a simple portfolio composed of U.S. and Japanese stocks with the following results for the measurement period from the perspective of a U.S. investor (percents):

$$r_{US} = 5.0 \qquad \alpha_{JP} = [-2.0 - (-3.0)] = 1.0$$
$$r_{JP} = -2.0 \qquad w_{US} = 60.0$$
$$r_¥ = 3.0 \qquad w_{JP} = 40.0$$
$$f_¥ = 0.3 \qquad H_¥ = 30.0$$
$$r^B_{US} = 4.0 \qquad w^B_{US} = 50.0$$
$$r^B_{JP} = -3.0 \qquad w^B_{JP} = 50.0$$
$$\alpha_{US} = (5.0 - 4.0) = 1.0 \qquad H^B_¥ = 50.0.$$

In the aggregate, Equation 6.1 gives the following total return of the portfolio:

		Weighted Contribution
U.S. stocks	$w_{US}r_{US} = 0.6(5.0)$	3.0%
Japanese stocks	$w_{JP}(r_{JP} + f_¥) = 0.4(-2.0 + 0.3)$	−0.7
Yen	$H_¥(r_¥ - f_¥) = 0.3(3.0 - 0.3)$	0.8
Portfolio return		3.1%

The total return to the benchmark, from Equation 6.2, is

		Weighted Contribution
U.S. stocks	$w^B_{US}r^B_{US} = 0.5(4.0)$	2.0%
Japanese stocks	$w^B_{JP}(r^B_{JP} + f_¥) = 0.5(-3.0 + 0.3)$	−1.4
Yen	$H^B_¥(r_¥ - f_¥) = 0.5(3.0 - 0.3)$	1.3
Benchmark return		1.9%

Therefore, the absolute value added by active management is

$3.1 - 1.9 = 1.2\%$.

The absolute contribution of each segment of added value can be broken out as follows:

			Weighted Contribution
Active asset management:			
U.S. stocks	$w_{US}\alpha_{US}$	$= (0.6)(1.0)$	0.6%
Japanese stocks	$w_{JP}\alpha_{JP}$	$= (0.4)(1.0)$	0.4
Subtotal			1.0%
Asset allocation:			
U.S. stocks	$\Delta w_{US} r^B_{US}$	$= (0.6 - 0.5)(4.0)$	0.4
Japanese stocks	$\Delta w_{JP}(r^B_{JP} + f_¥)$	$= (0.4 - 0.5)(-3.0 + 0.3)$	0.3
Subtotal			0.7%
Currency allocation: yen	$\Delta H_¥(r_¥ - f_¥)$	$= (0.3 - 0.5)(3.0 - 0.3)$	−0.5
Cross-product error term			0.0
Total added value			1.2%

The underlying assets contributed 1.0 percent to portfolio value because the active management of both U.S. and Japanese stocks added value. The total value added from asset allocation was 0.7 percent, with a portion coming from U.S. equities and a portion from Japanese equities. The currency decision reduced value, however, because the yen was underweighted, relative to the benchmark, when the yen was contributing a positive return. The cross-product term contributed 0.0 percent. Summing all the components gives a total added value of 1.2 percent.

Relative Contribution Analysis. An alternative way of measuring the value added by each component is to begin with Equation 6.6 and rearrange the algebra to show market returns relative to benchmark returns:

$$R - R_B = \sum_i w_i \alpha_i + \sum_i \Delta w_i (r^i_B + f_i - R^B_A)$$
$$+ \sum_j \Delta H_j (r^j_c - f_j - R^B_c) + e, \quad (6.9)$$

where

$$R^B_A = \sum_i w^B_i (r^i_B + f_i) \quad (6.10)$$

and

$$R^B_c = \sum_j H^B_j (r^j_c - f_j). \quad (6.11)$$

Equations 6.10 and 6.11 represent the aggregate benchmark returns to hedged asset positions and benchmark currency exposures.

This form of contribution analysis changes the way the individual value added by asset allocation and currency is calculated. These values are based not only on the portfolio's incremental exposure but also on whether the particular market had returns higher or lower than the aggregate benchmark return for assets and currencies, respectively. The contribution of each market is now represented relative to whether the market outperformed the benchmark rather than whether the market had a positive or negative return in an absolute sense. In this approach, a positive contribution will be generated when a market is overweighted at a time when it outperforms the benchmark return or is underweighted when it underperforms the benchmark return.

Relative Contribution Analysis

From the previous data, the benchmark return for the assets is

		Weighted Contribution
U.S. stocks	$w_{US} r_{US}^B = 0.5(4.0)$	2.0%
Japanese stocks	$w_{JP}(r_{JP}^B + f_¥) = 0.5(-3.0 + 0.3)$	-1.4
Benchmark asset return		0.6%

and the benchmark return for the currency exposure is

Yen $\quad H_¥(r_¥ - f_¥) = 0.5(3.0 - 0.3) \quad\quad 1.4\%$

Therefore, in the relative performance attribution approach, the contribution to added value by the asset allocation and currency decisions would be as follows

		Weighted Contribution
Asset allocation:		
U.S. stocks	$\Delta w_{US}(r_{US}^B - R_A^B) = (0.6 - 0.5)(4.0 - 0.6)$	0.3%
Japanese stocks	$\Delta w_{JP}(r_{JP}^B + f_¥ - R_A^B) = (0.4 - 0.5)(-3.0 + 0.3 - 0.6)$	0.3
Subtotal		0.6%
Currency allocation:		
U.S. dollar	$\Delta H_{US}(-R_C^B) = (0.7 - 0.5)(-1.4)$	-0.3
Yen	$\Delta H_¥(r_¥ - f_¥ - R_C^B) = (0.3 - 0.5)(3.0 - 0.3 - 1.4)$	-0.3
Subtotal		-0.6%

Note that the total contribution to the value added (within rounding error) by asset allocation and currency is the same whether one is using the absolute contribution approach or the relative contribution approach. The individual contributions, however, are slightly different. In the relative contribution analysis, U.S. stocks added 0.3 percent, whereas they added 0.4 percent in the absolute contribution analysis. Japanese stocks added the same 0.3 percent when performance was measured by the relative approach as they did when performance was measured by the absolute approach.

The relative contribution for the currency allocation decision will also generally result in a somewhat different partitioning of the value added when the different measurement techniques are used, even though the total will be the same. In this particular example, however, with only one currency pair, the U.S. dollar decision and the yen decision are really the same decision. A portfolio with more currency pairs would generally manifest differences in attributions for each nonbase currency.

Performance Attribution When Derivatives Are Used

The use of derivative contracts (options, futures, forwards, and swaps) allows an investor to change the asset and currency exposures without altering the physical-asset mix in the underlying portfolio. Because the use of derivatives changes the effective asset mix without changing the mix of the underlying assets, performance attribution when derivatives are used is difficult to carry out with either the relative or absolute techniques illustrated in the previous section. The technique described in this section facilitates performance evaluation when derivatives are included.

To capture the effect on performance of the use of derivative instruments, the total return to the portfolio can be written as

$$R = (1 - m)(R_B + \alpha_u) + mR_c + \sum_i D_i^A$$
$$+ \sum_j D_j^c, \qquad (6.12)$$

where

- m = proportion of the total fund segregated in a cash reserve at the beginning of the period to service derivatives transactions, margin requirements, and mark-to-market flows
- R_B = benchmark return for the portfolio
- α_u = value added through management of the underlying assets[2]
- R_c = average interest rate earned on the cash reserve
- D_i^A = net gains or losses on derivative contracts, including any mark-to-market flows, during the period (converted to the base currency) for asset market i, as a percentage of the initial portfolio value
- D_j^c = net gains or losses on derivative contracts, including any mark-to-market flows, during the period (converted to the base currency) for currency market j, as a percentage of the initial portfolio value.

The value added of the portfolio relative to the benchmark can be written as

$$R - R_B = (1 - m)\alpha_u - m(R_B - R_c) + \sum_i D_i^A$$
$$+ \sum_j D_j^c + e \qquad (6.13a)$$
$$= (1 - m)\alpha_u + \sum_i [D_i^A - mw_i^B(r_B^i + f_i$$
$$- R_c)] + \sum_j [D_j^c - mH_j^B(r_c^j - f_j)] + e, \qquad (6.13b)$$

where e is a residual error term reflecting tracking error on derivative contracts relative to benchmark returns, the interest earned on realized gains or losses during the measurement period, and any currency translation gains or losses from daily margin flows.

The transformation of Equation 6.13a to Equation 6.13b results from decomposing the benchmark returns into their component parts and regrouping terms. The value added for the total portfolio in Equation 6.13b is composed of several parts. The first term represents the fact that m proportion of the portfolio set aside in the cash reserve does not participate in any incremental return generated by the management of the underlying asset portfolio. The cash reserve is assumed to be overlaid with derivative exposure invested at benchmark weights in the respective asset and currency markets, which earn the benchmark return before any active positions are taken.

The second term in Equation 6.13b represents the contribution to total value added from an incremental allocation to each asset market. This contribution is captured by the total net gain or loss in the respective derivative positions for the period. A slight adjustment is needed to account for the fact that some of the total gains or losses are generated by the appropriate number of derivative contracts used to keep the cash reserve fully invested at benchmark weights before any active allocations are made.

The third term in Equation 6.13b represents a contribution from active currency management similar to the return to each asset market. The total net gains or losses in derivative positions for each currency are, again, adjusted for the fact that part of the daily variation margin may represent flows from currency contracts used to keep the cash reserve fully invested at benchmark weights before any active allocation.

The last term in Equation 13b captures any residual error in the performance calculation. This error, in addition to accounting for the interest earned on any realized gains or losses during the measurement period and currency translation gains or losses on daily margin flows, can result from tracking error in the pricing of the derivative contracts relative to the benchmark returns.

---

[2]The α_u term may be decomposed by using either the relative or absolute performance attribution techniques discussed in the previous section if the physical-asset positions have been kept constant during the measurement period. The value added for the underlying portfolio can then be examined using either Equation 6.6 or 6.9.

Performance Analysis with the Use of Derivatives

To illustrate this technique, we use the basic data for the portfolio of U.S. and Japanese stocks from the previous examples and add the use of derivatives. The underlying asset portfolio is assumed to have outperformed the benchmark by 1.0 percent through management of the underlying assets. Thus, the performance data are as follows (percents):

$$
\begin{array}{llll}
r_¥ = & 3.0 & D^A_{JP} = & -0.2 \\
f_¥ = & 0.3 & D^c_¥ = & -0.3 \\
r^B_{US} = & 4.0 & R_B = & 1.9 \\
r^B_{JP} = & -3.0 & m = & 15.0 \\
R_c = & 3.2 & w^B_{US} = & 50.0 \\
\alpha_u = & 1.0 & w^B_{JP} = & 50.0 \\
D^A_{US} = & 1.2 & H^B_¥ = & 50.0
\end{array}
$$

where α_u is the value added on the underlying portfolio.

The return on the total portfolio including the derivative positions is

$$R = (1 - m)(R_B + \alpha_u) + mR_c + D^A_{US} + D^A_{JP} + D^c_¥$$
$$= (1 - 0.15)(1.9 + 1.0) + 0.15(3.2) + 1.2 - 0.2 - 0.3$$
$$= 3.6\%,$$

giving a total added value relative to the benchmark of

$$3.6 - 1.9 = 1.7\%.$$

The components of this added value are as follows:

		Weighted Contribution
Underlying assets	$(1 - m)\alpha_u = (1.0 - 0.15)(1.0)$	0.9%
Asset allocation:		
U.S. stocks	$D^A_{US} - mw^B_{US}(r^B_{US} - R_c) = 1.2 - (0.15)(0.5)(4.0 - 3.2)$	1.1
Japanese stocks	$D^A_{JP} - mw^B_{JP}(r^B_{JP} + f_¥ - R_c) = -0.2 - [(0.15)(0.5) \times (-3.0 + 0.3 - 3.2)]$	0.2
Subtotal		1.3%
Currency management:		
yen	$D^c_¥ - mH^B_¥(r_¥ - f_¥) = -0.3 - (0.15)(0.5)(3.0 - 0.3)$	−0.5
Error term		0.0
Total added value		1.7%

Note that the underlying assets contributed 0.9 percent to the added value of the portfolio even though the management of the underlying assets resulted in outperformance of 1.0 percent. The difference lies in the fact that a portion of the total assets did not participate in earning the extra return because that portion was set aside in a cash reserve to service any margin requirements for the derivative positions. Asset allocation decisions involving U.S. and Japanese stocks added 1.3 percent, and currency decisions subtracted 0.5 percent, resulting in a net value for the portfolio of 1.7 percent above the benchmark return.

Summary

- The evaluation of performance and the contribution of returns by active management are usually carried out relative to a benchmark portfolio. The benchmark portfolio defines the standard of performance in the absence of any active decisions.
- Performance attribution is easiest to do when portfolio allocations are held constant during the measurement period relative to the benchmark. If the portfolio positions are restructured during the measurement period, the evaluation of each individual contribution using beginning-of-period allocations will be only an approximation.
- When portfolio allocations are held constant for the period, *absolute contribution analysis* will report positive value added for each market allocation when the respective market return is positive and the portfolio is overweighted in that market relative to the benchmark. *Relative contribution analysis* will report positive value added for each market allocation when the respective market return is greater than the benchmark return and the portfolio is overweighted in that market. Both techniques result in the same total value added, but they apportion it differently depending on whether each market return is greater than zero or greater than the benchmark return.
- Assessing performance contributions when derivatives are used to allocate market exposure requires adding the net gains and losses and/or mark-to-market flows from each market segment to the analysis.
- The absolute, relative, and derivatives-included performance attribution techniques all give the same total added value, but each partitions it in a slightly different way.

7. Structural Models of Exchange Rate Determination

In this chapter, we discuss five structural models that are commonly used to explain the behavior of exchange rates. Although all of these models might seem reasonable, the factors on which they rely often act on exchange rates simultaneously but with offsetting influences, different lead times, and confusing feedback responses. Disentangling the influences of the various factors, therefore, and determining which model will best explain exchange rate behavior over any particular horizon are sometimes difficult.

Model Descriptions

The five models are the purchasing power parity, the international Fisher effect, the balance-of-payments, the monetary, and the portfolio balance models. Each model suggests a conceptual relationship between exchange rates and underlying economic variables. Table 7.1 summarizes the key relationships.

Purchasing Power Parity. The concept of *absolute* purchasing power parity (PPP) states that if the exchange rates are allowed to adjust freely, then after allowing for the exchange rate conversion, the price of a commodity in one country should be equal to the price of that same commodity in another country. That is,

$$P_d = P_f S_o, \tag{7.1}$$

where

- P_d = the current price of a commodity in home currency units
- P_f = the current price of a commodity in foreign currency units
- S_o = the current spot exchange rate (home currency/foreign currency).

If this relationship holds over time, then in order to restore the balance between prices, expected changes in the relative prices of the commodities will be reflected in the expected change in the exchange rate. This incremental relationship is often referred to as *relative* purchasing power parity and can be written as

$$E(S) = S_o \frac{(1 + \pi_d t)}{(1 + \pi_f t)}, \tag{7.2}$$

where π_d is the expected annualized percentage change in the price of the commodity in the home country during time period t and π_f is the expected annualized percentage change in the price of the commodity in the foreign country during time period t. In this relationship, the expected future spot exchange rate will be equal to the current exchange rate times the ratio of expected relative gross price changes between the two countries.

Experience has shown that the PPP relationship, unlike the covered interest arbitrage rela-

Table 7.1. Key Model Relationships

Model	Sensitivity of Exchange Rate to Economic Variables	Change in the Value of Foreign Currency (holding constant other factors)
Purchasing power parity	Domestic prices rise	Increase
International Fisher effect	Nominal domestic interest rates rise	Decrease
Balance of payments	Domestic current account deficit	Increase
Monetary	Domestic money supply rises (flexible prices)	Increase (consistent with PPP)
	Domestic money supply rises (sticky prices)	Increase (overshoots PPP)
Portfolio balance	Investor wealth rises because of expansive monetary policy	Increase
	Investor wealth rises because of expansive fiscal policy • Wealth effect • Interest rate effect	Could increase or decrease

tionship, has not held well in the past.[1] The financial arbitrage required by the covered interest arbitrage relationship is relatively easy to create; marshaling economic forces to drive commodity prices between countries into a proper balance is much more difficult. In a perfectly frictionless world, if prices did not conform to the PPP relationship, people would purchase the commodity that was undervalued and sell it in the country where it was overvalued. This process would continue until the relative prices of the two commodities came into balance with the expected exchange rate between the two currencies, thus restoring the PPP relationship. In a realistic world, where the costs of transportation between countries may be substantial and barriers to trade and other regulatory restrictions may exist, market forces may not keep the PPP relationship in line. Prices and exchange rates can deviate from their theoretical relationship for extended periods of time.

An additional complication results from trying to define the index of price changes for entire baskets of commodities, some of which may be more desirable in one country than in another. In practice, therefore, most analyses of purchasing power parity have used relative inflation rates to represent aggregate price changes between countries; that is, the analyses have concerned relative PPP.

During the floating-rate period as a whole, rising *ex post* inflation has been associated with increased currency depreciation. The average relationship predicted by relative PPP has not held for most countries, as illustrated in Figure 7.1. With the exception of Japan, the relationship between *ex post* inflation and the depreciation of the currency during the same period has been less pronounced than one might have expected. The depreciation in the foreign currency has been less than the difference in inflation from a U.S. investor's perspective. As a result, many foreign goods have become relatively less expensive for U.S.-dollar-based consumers during this period.

Because of the difficulties in measuring PPP and in implementing effective arbitrage strategies, purchasing power parity has had little empirical relevance for exchange rate movements, except perhaps over very long time horizons. Other forces seem to dominate the relationship between exchange rates in the short run.

---

[1] See Frankel (1989) for a review of recent experience versus theory.

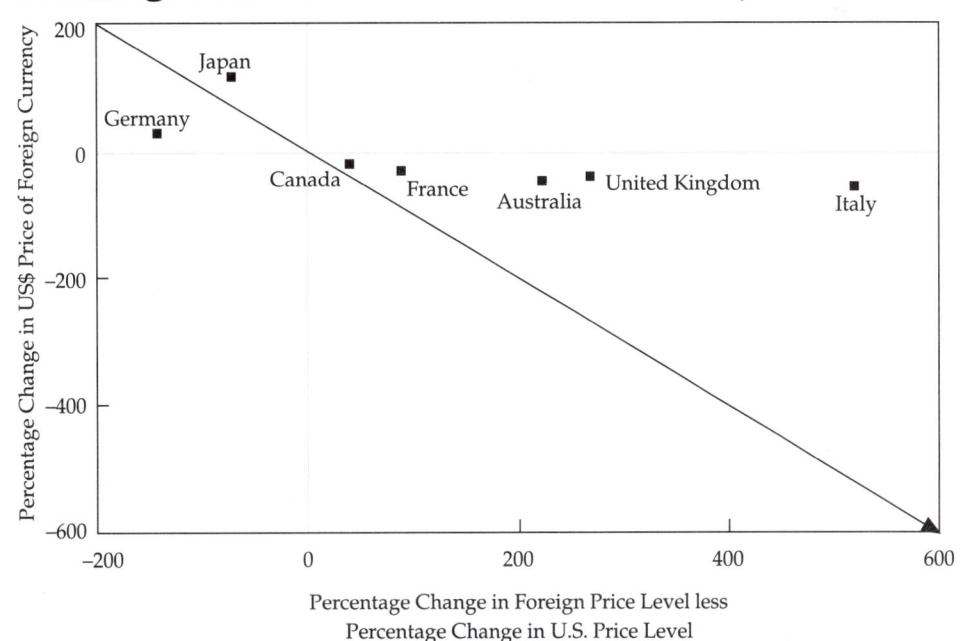

7. Structural Models of Exchange Rate Determination

Figure 7.1. Exchange Rate Trends and Inflation Differentials, 1973–93

International Fisher Effect. Irving Fisher postulated that nominal interest rates in a country are related to real interest rates and the expected level of inflation. The Fisher effect within a country can be written as

$$(1 + it) = (1 + i_r t)(1 + \pi t), \quad (7.3)$$

where

- i = the annualized nominal interest rate
- i_r = the annualized real interest rate
- π = the expected annualized inflation rate over time period t.

If real interest rates are the same between countries, the ratio of gross nominal interest rates will be equal to the ratio of gross expected inflation rates:

$$\frac{(1 + i_d t)}{(1 + i_f t)} = \frac{(1 + \pi_d t)}{(1 + \pi_f t)}, \quad (7.4)$$

where the subscript d means domestic and the subscript f means foreign.

The addition of the relative PPP relationship in Equation 7.2 to Equation 7.4 ties the expected future spot exchange rate to the ratio of nominal interest rates. That is,

$$E(S) = S_o \frac{(1 + i_d t)}{(1 + i_f t)}. \quad (7.5)$$

This relationship is referred to as the international Fisher effect.

Because it depends on the strength of the PPP relationship in addition to the Fisher effect assumptions, not surprisingly, the relationship between changes in exchange rates and relative interest rates has not been a completely dependable empirical relationship. Large interest rate differentials have sometimes led to large currency returns, but this relationship has often been dominated by other, more powerful forces for extended time periods.

Note that the international Fisher effect has the same form as the covered interest arbitrage relationship, which relates the current spot exchange rate to the forward exchange rate. As a result, if the international Fisher effect were to hold exactly, the forward rate would be an unbiased predictor of the expected future spot rate, which is sometimes referred to as *uncovered interest arbitrage*. As noted in Chapter 2, historical evidence suggests that uncovered interest arbitrage has generally not held, which implies that either the international Fisher effect or PPP or both are not accurate descriptors of changes in foreign exchange rates.

Currency Management: Concepts and Practices

Figure 7.2. Foreign Exchange Relationships

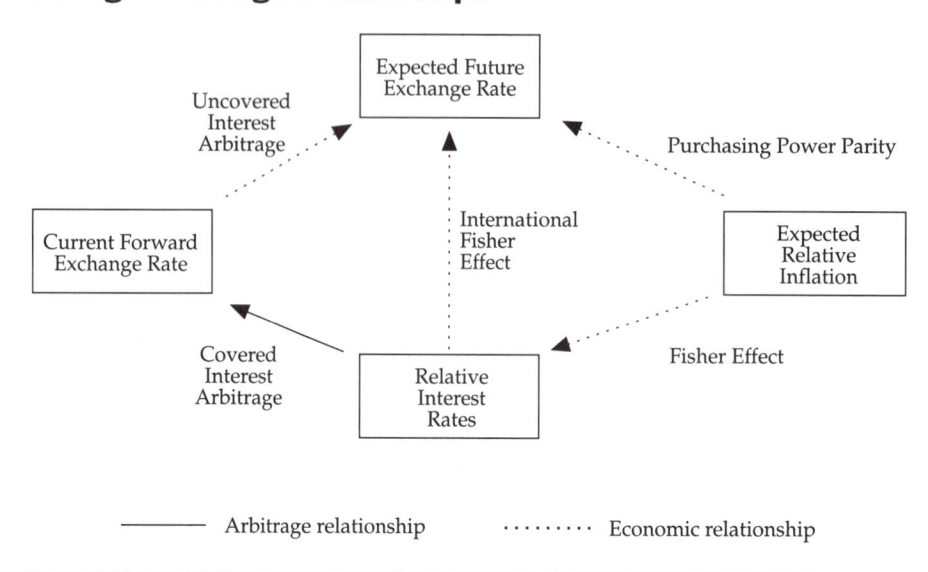

```
                    Expected Future
                    Exchange Rate
    Uncovered       ▲    ▲    ▲
    Interest       ·     |     ·
    Arbitrage     ·      |      ·     Purchasing Power Parity
                 ·       |       ·
                ·   International  ·
 Current Forward·      Fisher       ·    Expected
 Exchange Rate         Effect            Relative
                ▲        |               Inflation
                 \       |              ·
     Covered      \      |             ·  Fisher Effect
     Interest      \     |            ·
     Arbitrage    Relative
                  Interest
                   Rates
```

────── Arbitrage relationship   ·········· Economic relationship

PPP, Fisher Effects, and Covered and Uncovered Interest Arbitrage

The equations and relationships for these theories are summarize as follows:

Covered interest arbitrage (CIA)	$F = S_o \dfrac{(1 + i_d t)}{(1 + i_f t)}$
Purchasing power parity (PPP)	$E(S) = S_o \dfrac{(1 + \pi_d t)}{(1 + \pi_f t)}$
Fisher effect (FE)	$\dfrac{(1 + i_d t)}{(1 + i_f t)} = \dfrac{(1 + \pi_d t)}{(1 + \pi_f t)}$
International Fisher effect (IFE = PPP + FE)	$E(S) = S_o \dfrac{(1 + i_d t)}{(1 + i_f t)}$
Uncovered interest arbitrage (CIA + IFE)	$E(S) = F$

Figure 7.2 summarizes the theoretical relationships between relative expected inflation, relative nominal interest rates, the current forward exchange rate, and the expected future exchange rate. Empirical evidence confirms the effectiveness of the covered interest arbitrage relationship but does not support the strong link among the factors that would validate the PPP, the international Fisher effect, or uncovered interest arbitrage relationships.

Balance of Payments. The balance of payments measures all financial flows across a country's borders. It is partitioned into a current account, which consists mainly of a country's trade balance, and a capital account, which accounts for a country's borrowing and lending.

If a country experiences a trade deficit (it imports more goods and services than it exports), it must balance this deficit with a surplus in its capital account by borrowing more foreign currency than it lends. When other factors are controlled for, a current account deficit would be expected to lead to a decrease in the value of the home currency. The excess demand for foreign goods and services would lead to an excess demand for the foreign currency. The excess demand for the foreign currency would, in turn, cause the foreign currency to appreciate relative to the domestic currency.

Monetary. The monetary model of exchange rate determination is simply an extension of the quantity theory of money to an open economy. The monetary approach has two variations. One is called the *flexible price monetary model* and is attributed to Frenkel (1976), Kouri (1976), and Mussa (1979). This model assumes that PPP holds continuously and that the demand for money in both countries is a stable function of income and interest rates. This variation posits that a change in the money supply will lead to a proportionate change in the price level. If PPP holds continuously, the change in the domestic country's price level relative to the change in the foreign country's price level will automatically translate into a change in the exchange rate. Therefore, the monetary authorities can support a currency's value by restraining growth in the domestic money supply relative to growth in the money supply of the foreign country.

The second variation of the monetary approach is called the *sticky price monetary model* and is attributed to Dornbusch (1976). Dornbusch argued that prices are sticky in the short run because goods markets respond more slowly than asset markets to monetary shocks. Because prices in the goods markets do not adjust in the short run, a change in the nominal money supply causes a change in the real money supply. This change in the real money supply causes interest rates to change, which in turn, leads to capital flows. These capital flows amplify the change in the exchange rate that would have occurred had prices adjusted instantaneously; thus, changes in the exchange rate overshoot the changes that would be consistent with long-run purchasing power parity.

Suppose, for example, that the monetary authorities decrease the money supply. This action leads, given sticky prices, to a decrease in the real money supply, which causes interest rates to rise. The increase in interest rates attracts foreign capital, and the domestic currency appreciates. Foreign investors continue to buy the domestic bonds until these investors anticipate a depreciation in the domestic currency sufficient to offset the interest rate differential. The mere fact that they expect the exchange rate to depreciate implies that it overshot its long-run PPP value. Eventually, goods prices fall in response to the decrease in the money supply, and the exchange rate slowly converges to its PPP value.

Portfolio Balance. The portfolio balance model posits that the exchange rate is determined by the supply and demand for financial assets. If the change in demand for financial assets arises from a change in the money supply, the effect on the exchange rate is relatively straightforward. If the money supply falls, for example, investors will demand fewer foreign assets. As they sell foreign assets, the domestic currency appreciates.

If the change in investor wealth arises from a shift in fiscal policy, the effect on the exchange rate is ambiguous. Suppose the government pursues an expansionary fiscal policy by increasing the supply of bonds. This policy induces both a wealth effect and an interest rate effect. The increase in wealth increases the demand for foreign assets and, therefore, exerts upward pressure on the value of the foreign currency. The increase in government borrowing, however, raises domestic interest rates, which might induce investors to switch from foreign assets to domestic assets. This shift would tend, of course, to increase the value of the domestic currency. The net impact on the exchange rate would depend on the relative elasticities in the demand functions for domestic and foreign assets.

Empirical Tests of Structural Models

To validate structural models with empirical tests is difficult, at least if one is using exchange rate data covering the modern floating-rate era.[2] The following results underscore this point.

Purchasing Power Parity. PPP implies that a domestic country's exchange rate should decline if its rate of inflation increases at a faster rate than the rate of inflation in the foreign country or if its rate of inflation decreases at a slower rate. Table 7.2 shows that a simple test of this argument using the British pound, the German mark, and the Japanese yen fails to offer support.

---

[2] One of the most important studies on this topic was performed in the 1980s by Meese and Rogoff (1983a).

Table 7.2. Test of Purchasing Power Parity

Dependent variable: monthly return of forward contract
Independent variable: monthly percentage change in ratio of 1 plus foreign inflation rate to 1 plus U.S. inflation rate

Currency	Alpha	Beta	t-Statistic	R^2	Period
Coincident regression					
Pound	0.0004	0.0016	0.0623	0.0000	7/73–12/93
Mark	−0.0004	−0.0074	−0.9936	0.0040	7/73–12/93
Yen	0.0018	−0.0104	−0.8922	0.0033	7/73–12/93
One-month-lagged regression					
Pound	0.0005	−0.0103	−0.3987	0.0007	7/73–12/93
Mark	−0.0004	−0.0025	−0.3436	0.0005	7/73–12/93
Yen	0.0017	0.0009	0.0740	0.0000	7/73–12/93

The results in Table 7.2 reveal essentially no relationship between the change in a country's relative inflation rate and the return on the forward contract of a currency. (We use the forward contract return in order to control for interest rate differentials.) The adjusted-R^2 statistics are very low, and the slope coefficient statistics do not indicate that the relationship between the forward contract returns and inflation differentials are different from zero with any reasonable degree of confidence. This result seems to hold for both contemporaneous and one-month-lagged relationships.

International Fisher Effect. The international Fisher effect posits that the forward discount or premium is an unbiased predictor of the future return on the spot rate. One can easily test this theory by regressing monthly spot returns on the forward discount or premium as of the beginning of the month. If the forward discount or premium is unbiased, its coefficient will equal 1 and the intercept term will equal 0. Table 7.3 shows these results using the pound, the mark, and the yen.

Not only are the coefficients less than 1 in Table 7.3, but in the case of the pound and the mark, they are negative. This result implies that the spot rate increased, on balance, when the forward contract sold at a discount and that it decreased when the forward contract sold at a premium.

The evidence from these regressions is consistent with the evidence shown in Tables 2.9 and 2.10, which revealed that an investor could have profited by selling forward contracts when they were at a premium and purchasing them when they were at a discount.

Monetary. The monetary model holds that an increase in the money supply of the domestic country relative to the foreign country will result in the depreciation of the domestic country's currency. Table 7.4 shows that, again, the evidence is not particularly compelling; relative changes in money supply apparently do not explain returns on forward contracts. Although the pound has a significant t-statistic, the coefficient is positive, which implies that an increase in the U.K. money supply relative to the change

Table 7.3. Test of the International Fisher Effect: Coincident Regression

Dependent variable: monthly return of spot rate
Independent variable: forward discount or premium as of prior month end

Currency	Alpha	Beta	t-Statistic	R^2	Period
Pound	−0.0072	−1.8299	−2.3949	0.0230	7/73–12/93
Mark	0.0025	−0.6748	−0.9791	0.0039	7/73–12/93
Yen	0.0031	0.1943	0.4362	0.0008	7/73–12/93

Table 7.4. Test of the Monetary Model

Dependent variable: monthly return of forward contract
Independent variable: percentage change in foreign country's money supply less percentage change in U.S. money supply

Currency	Alpha	Beta	t-Statistic	R^2	Period
Coincident regression					
Pound	0.0003	0.5800	2.1201	0.0353	7/82–11/92
Mark	0.0034	0.1367	0.4909	0.0026	1/86–12/93
Yen	0.0059	−0.5911	−2.1311	0.0183	7/73–12/93
One-month-lagged regression					
Pound	0.0002	0.6265	2.2858	0.0411	7/82–11/92
Mark	0.0047	−0.3158	−1.1854	0.0149	1/86–12/93
Yen	−0.0008	0.3410	1.2224	0.0061	7/73–12/93

in the U.S. money supply is positively correlated with the return on the pound. This relationship contradicts the thesis of the monetary model, of course, which holds that a relative increase in the money supply will lead to a depreciation of the currency.

Portfolio Balance. The final test concerns the portfolio balance model, which holds that rising asset values in the domestic country relative to the foreign country will contribute to a rise in the value of the domestic currency. Little evidence supports this model of exchange rate determination. In Table 7.5, only the yen has a significant t-statistic with the appropriate sign. Unfortunately, it pertains to a coincident relationship, which implies that an investor would have to forecast successfully the relative performance of the U.S. and Japanese stock markets in order to gain insight into the direction of the yen. The one-month-lagged relationship, however, does seem to have a significant negative coefficient for the pound.

Summary

Over the years, researchers have put forth a number of theories about what factors should influence exchange rates. The primary theories are

- purchasing power parity,
- the international Fisher effect,
- the balance-of-payments model,
- the monetary model, and
- the portfolio balance model.

None of the model results offers much encouragement to use structural models to antici-

Table 7.5. Test of the Portfolio Balance Model

Dependent variable: monthly return of forward contract
Independent variable: percentage change in foreign country's stock market index less percentage change in U.S. stock index

Currency	Alpha	Beta	t-Statistic	R^2	Period
Coincident regression					
Pound	0.0010	0.0885	1.3661	0.0098	2/78–12/93
Mark	−0.0003	−0.0742	−1.8271	0.0315	7/73–12/93
Yen	0.0017	0.0877	2.3391	0.0219	7/73–12/93
One-month-lagged regression					
Pound	0.0011	−0.1316	−2.0223	0.0213	2/78–12/93
Mark	−0.0005	0.0246	0.6005	0.0015	7/73–12/93
Yen	0.0017	−0.0106	−0.2778	0.0003	7/73–12/93

pate exchange rate movements. The empirical evidence indicates that exchange rate movements are not well anchored to the postulated fundamental economic variables. In many periods, in fact, the relationships often seem to have been the opposite of what would be expected.

One should not conclude from these results, however, that these structural models are invalid. The regression analyses shown here are based on relatively short time periods and are simple specifications of the structural models. Moreover, the independent variables are not adjusted to disentangle the anticipated component of their change from the unanticipated component. More complex models applied to a larger data set could quite conceivably show stronger relationships between macroeconomic activity and currency returns.

Nevertheless, the prudent investor should proceed with caution when confronted with currency forecasts based on simple economic relationships. The lack of consistent fundamental relationships leaves currency markets particularly vulnerable to emotional forces and speculative behavior.

8. Commonly Asked Questions about Currency Hedging

In this chapter, we respond to 17 commonly asked questions about currency management.

1. *Should one have separate currency-hedging policies for stocks and bonds?*

In an unconstrained environment, when asset positions are fixed, it makes no difference whether currency-hedging policy is set separately for each asset class or set for the portfolio exposure as a whole. The investor will end up hedging some fraction of each currency exposure even though the proportions for stocks and bonds may be different. This result assumes that both domestic and foreign assets are included in the portfolio so that the hedge ratios will also take into account the correlations with domestic assets. The explanation for this invariance principle is that the optimal hedge ratio for each currency is a function of the relationship of each asset class with respect to each currency, each currency's return and risk, and the investor's risk aversion. Because currency risk and return, and the investor's risk aversion, are the same for each asset class and because covariances are additive, the weighted average of the optimal currency hedge ratios for each asset class will sum to the optimal currency hedge ratio for the combined exposure of stocks and bonds in each currency.

A frequent assertion is that one should hedge the currency exposure of a foreign bond portfolio but not the currency exposure of a foreign stock portfolio because the currency component of return and risk is greater for foreign bonds than it is for foreign stocks. However, although the currency contribution to total risk does seem to be greater for bonds than for stocks, the impact of currency exposure on total portfolio risk is the same whether it arises from the bond component's currency exposure or from the stock component's currency exposure.

2. *Should the hedging policy be developed within the context of the total portfolio, including domestic assets, or only with respect to the foreign assets?*

Unless the domestic asset returns are independent of all currency returns, the currency-hedging policy should be developed within the context of the total portfolio—foreign and domestic assets. Mathematically, such a total approach will produce a more efficient hedging policy than considering foreign assets alone; that is, if the currency risk is managed from the perspective of the total portfolio, lower total portfolio risk will result.

A nonzero correlation between domestic asset returns and currency returns implies that the domestic assets are sensitive to currency returns. If the domestic asset returns are positively correlated with currency returns, more of the portfolio's total currency exposure should be hedged than if only the currency exposure of the foreign assets is considered. If the domestic asset returns are negatively correlated with currency returns, then to take advantage of the natural diversification, less of the total portfolio's currency exposure should be hedged. Note the impact of these effects on the optimal currency exposure in Equations 5.5 and 5.11.

3. *Should the currency-hedging policy be developed simultaneously with the choice of the portfolio assets or as a separate process after the portfolio has already been selected?*

Ideally, the currency-hedging policy should be developed simultaneously with the choice of the portfolio assets. The determination of the optimal currency-hedging policy can be thought of as an optimization process in which the currency exposures are selected with the portfolio assets. If the portfolio assets are preselected and thus fixed in the optimization process, the optimizer's choices for diversification are reduced and the optimizer will be forced to select a less efficient portfolio than had it not been constrained. Constraints almost always reduce portfolio efficiency. Note the examples in Chapter 5 that showed the impact of holding the asset weights constant versus the impact of joint optimization.

Valid reasons do exist, however, for optimizing the currency exposures while holding the weights of the portfolio assets constant. The empirical evidence about the forward rate bias suggests that changes in the expected returns of currency forward contracts may be more predictable than changes in the expected returns of portfolio assets. Thus, the investor might wish to rebalance the currency exposures more frequently than the portfolio assets. Also, the investor might rebalance currency exposures more frequently because trading currency forward contracts is less expensive than trading assets or is less disruptive to the fund managers. Differences in trading costs can be incorporated in the optimization algorithm, however; so, this reason is not as compelling as the predictability of forward contract returns as justification for a constrained optimization.

4. *Should each currency exposure have a specific hedge ratio?*

Yes. The optimal amount to hedge for each currency is specific to the currency forward contract's expected return, standard deviation, and correlations with the portfolio assets and other currencies. These values differ from currency to currency and are likely to result in a different hedge ratio for each currency. The integrated example at the end of Chapter 5 showed the divergence between individual currency allocations in a portfolio. Therefore, each currency exposure should have a separate hedge ratio, and it is dependent on which other assets and currencies are included in the portfolio.

5. *If currency exposure introduces diversification to a portfolio, why should it be hedged away?*

The relevant issue is the trade-off between diversification from currency exposure and the volatility it introduces in the portfolio. This point is especially confusing because some analysts consider the correlation between currency returns and the foreign assets' local returns whereas other analysts consider the correlation between currency returns and the foreign assets' dollar-denominated returns. Because part of the dollar-denominated return is the currency return, currencies hardly ever introduce enough diversification to overcome the volatility they bring to a portfolio of foreign assets. Thus, in almost all cases, to minimize portfolio risk, at least some of a foreign portfolio's currency exposure should be hedged.

If a portfolio is composed of mostly domestic assets, with only a small allocation to foreign assets, and if the domestic asset returns are negatively correlated with the currency returns, then the diversification that currency exposure introduces might not overcome the additional volatility that it introduces, which would render hedging counterproductive. Recall the difference in volatility between a hedged and an unhedged portfolio in Equation 1.34. Empirical evidence indicates that currencies usually do not provide enough diversification to overcome their contribution to total portfolio volatility.

6. *If currency returns cancel out over the long run, why should currency exposure be hedged?*

The notion that currency returns cancel out over the long run, thus rendering hedging unnecessary, is specious for several reasons. Little empirical evidence exists to suggest that currency returns cancel out over the long run. For example, during the past 20 years, the British pound has moved from an exchange rate of US$5.00 to the pound to (as of mid-1994) about US$1.50 to the pound, which is more than a 300 percent depreciation.

Moreover, even if currency exchange rates did revert to some long-term equilibrium value, it does not necessarily follow that the current exchange rate is close to that value. The exchange rate could depreciate or appreciate substantially from its current level.

Finally, investors' choices of portfolios reveal that they care about interim volatility. To select a diversified portfolio to control interim volatility and at the same time ignore the interim volatility that arises from currency exposure would be inconsistent. Many investors are not willing to tolerate large interim swings in exchange rates even though the swings may even out in the long run.

7. *Is a symmetrical hedge or an asymmetrical hedge better for controlling currency risk?*

A symmetrical hedge sacrifices upside potential for the elimination of downside risk. An asymmetrical hedge protects a portfolio from currency losses but preserves the opportunity to experience currency gains. The asymmetrical hedge is thus more expensive.

Which approach is appropriate depends on investor preferences and expectations. A symmetrical hedge might be preferable for a long-run policy because it controls currency risk at a lower expected long-run cost. If the investor expects exchange rates to appreciate rather than depreciate over a specific horizon, however, or if a particular threshold is relevant, an asymmetrical hedge might be more appropriate.

8. *Are forward contracts or futures contracts better for implementing a symmetrical hedge?*

When considering whether to use futures or forward contracts to implement a hedging strategy, one must keep several distinctions in mind. Table 3.3 summarized the important differences between the two types of contracts. Futures contracts are marked to market every day; hence, funds are transferred daily to cover profits and losses. Futures contracts also require margin deposits, which serve as performance bonds. Finally, futures contracts have uniform terms with respect to size and expiration.

Forward contracts are not marked to market daily, nor do they typically involve margin deposits. They are settled entirely at expiration. In addition, they are privately negotiated, with specific terms for each contract.

Perhaps the most important distinction between futures and forward contracts is the cost of trading. The futures market is affected more by market impact, whereas the forward market tends to offer volume discounts because of the size of the institutions involved. Thus, executing small trades is often less expensive in the futures market and executing large trades is less expensive in the forward market.

Finally, the forward market offers contracts on a wide variety of currencies, but futures contracts exist for only seven dollar-denominated currencies: the British pound, the German mark, the French franc, the Swiss franc, the Japanese yen, the Australian dollar, and the Canadian dollar.

9. *Should an asymmetrical hedge be implemented with exchange-traded options, over-the-counter options, or a dynamic trading strategy?*

Exchange-traded options on the major currencies are traded on the Philadelphia Stock Exchange (European convention), and options on the futures contracts of the major currencies are traded on the Chicago Mercantile Exchange (American convention). The main limitation of these options is that they are relatively illiquid beyond short horizons.

For a price, dealers will write over-the-counter options on almost any currency or basket of currencies for reasonable horizons. The investor is exposed to the credit risk of the counterparty, however, when purchasing OTC options. Also, the option payoff can often be replicated with a dynamic trading program at a lower cost than the price charged by a dealer.

The problem with a dynamic trading program is that the cost is not determined in advance because cost depends on realized, rather than expected, volatility. Moreover, price jumps can compromise the precision of the replication. Thus, the choice of an implementation strategy depends on the investment horizon, the fund's currency exposure, and the investor's price sensitivity versus willingness to incur the risk of unanticipated costs and tracking error.

10. *Should currencies be cross-hedged?*

Currencies within certain economic blocs tend to be highly correlated with each other (as much as 95 percent), but one currency might be significantly more liquid and less expensive to trade than another currency within the same bloc. The cost of hedging, therefore, might be reduced substantially by substituting more liquid currencies to serve as surrogates for less liquid currencies. This substitution is called cross-hedging.

In cross-hedging, one must take care to avoid substituting one currency for another that has a large risk of depreciation in the specific country being hedged. Using other currencies to hedge the Italian lira in 1992, as shown in Table 3.1, illustrates the dangers.

11. *Should a forward contract's discount or premium affect the hedging decision?*

The historical evidence suggests that the forward rate overestimates changes in the spot rate. If this empirical tendency persists, one can reduce the long-run cost of hedging, and perhaps even make a profit, by hedging less when a currency sells at a forward discount and more when a currency sells at a forward premium. For example, instead of assuming that a forward contract's expected return, or forward surprise, is zero (the implicit assumption if the forward rate is unbiased), the investor can condition the forward contract's expected return on the magnitude of the discount or premium. A discount implies a positive expected return, which would lead to a lower-than-normal optimal hedge ratio; a premium implies a negative expected return, which would lead to a higher-than-normal optimal hedge ratio. Note the importance of the forward premium in determining the optimal currency exposures in Chapters 3, 4, and 5.

12. *What are the implementation costs associated with currency hedging, and what are reasonable estimates of these costs?*

Five implementation costs are associated with currency hedging: transaction costs, management fees, administrative fees, opportunity costs, and in the case of options, premiums.

Transaction costs pertain to commissions and market impact in the case of exchange-traded futures and options, and the bid–ask spread in the case of forward contracts and OTC options. Transaction costs are relatively low for major currencies—on the order of 1–5 basis points (bps) per trade.

Management fees are the fees charged by investment advisors to implement a hedging strategy or, if it is implemented internally, the allocated cost of managing the program. Outside managers usually charge 10–20 bps for programs intended to control risk. Hedging strategies that also seek to enhance return are usually more expensive, 20–50 bps. Some managers also negotiate an incentive component by which they share in the profits, typically in the range of 10–20 percent.

Administrative fees are the incremental custodial charges that the investor's trustee or custodian bank charges for the portfolio accounting and performance monitoring of currency transactions. These fees are typically only a few basis points.

Opportunity cost arises from the fact that hedgers must make use of credit lines when they enter into forward contracts to hedge currency exposure. To the extent that these credit lines could have been deployed to support more profitable investments, they represent an additional cost of hedging. The magnitude of these opportunity costs are specific to the hedger.

When hedgers implement asymmetrical hedges, they must pay a premium for the option—either explicitly, in the case of exchange traded or OTC options, or implicitly, in the case of dynamic trading strategies. Moreover, the implicit premium of a dynamic trading strategy may be higher than anticipated if the currency is more volatile than expected or if its exchange rate moves abruptly, thereby preventing timely trades.

13. How much international exposure must a portfolio have to make currency exposure important?

If currency positions are treated as a separate influence within the portfolio, no international exposure is required before the issue becomes important. Currency positions, depending on their expected returns and correlations with other assets in the portfolio, can be an important source of return and diversification.

Most investors, however, are interested in this question in the context of constraints on allowable currency positions, such as prescriptions that net currency exposures cannot be greater than the respective underlying asset positions or be less than zero. For these cases, the simple illustrations presented in Tables 1.3 and 1.4 provide some insights with respect to the influence of hedging on the portfolio's risk. Note that in Table 1.4, hedging was shown to have little relative impact on the risk of the portfolio until the allocation to foreign assets exceeded 10 percent. The differential impact on the expected return from hedging will be equal to the size of the hedge times the expected forward surprise on the currency. This return differential will grow as the size of the foreign asset position increases. At what point the trade-off begins to matter depends on the risk tolerance of the investor.

14. How stable are currency correlations? Can changes be forecast with any accuracy?

We noted in Chapter 2 that the rolling five-year correlations between currency returns have been more stable for some of the major currencies than for others. The change in correlations has been especially pronounced in recent years for the Australian and Canadian dollars. In the short run, currency returns can deviate widely from their historical patterns.

Short-term changes in the covariance of currency returns have been difficult to forecast. New statistical techniques like GARCH (generalized autoregressive conditional heteroscedasticity) forecasting have shown some promise in forecasting short-term changes in currency volatilities but are generally more effective in de-

Table 8.1. The Impact of Asset–Currency Correlation in Portfolio Allocations

Asset–Yen Correlation	w_d	w_ℓ	H	$E(R)$	σ_R
A: $\lambda = 1$					
−0.2	31.4%	68.6%	93.5%	17.1%	15.1%
−0.1	32.6	67.4	76.7	16.9	15.3
0.0	33.5	66.5	60.0	16.9	15.3
0.1	33.9	66.1	43.4	16.5	15.2
0.2	34.0	66.0	26.7	16.3	14.9
0.3	33.8	66.2	10.1	16.1	14.5
B: $\lambda = 2$					
−0.2	49.1	50.9	93.5	17.1	15.1
−0.1	49.9	50.1	46.0	16.1	13.2
0.0	50.4	49.6	30.0	15.9	13.3
0.1	50.6	49.4	14.0	15.7	13.2
0.2	50.4	49.6	−2.0	15.5	12.9
0.3	49.8	50.2	−18.0	15.3	12.4
C: $\lambda = 10$					
−0.2	63.2	36.8	37.0	15.7	12.2
−0.1	63.7	36.3	21.5	15.5	12.5
0.0	64.0	36.0	6.0	15.3	12.6
0.1	63.1	36.1	−9.5	15.1	12.5
0.2	63.4	36.6	−24.9	14.9	12.2
0.3	62.7	37.4	−40.5	14.8	11.7

scribing decay patterns than in describing spikes in volatility.[1] Forecasting changes in correlations remains a challenge.

15. How correlated do currency returns have to be with asset returns to make a significant difference in portfolio allocations?

The impact of the correlation between currency and asset returns depends to a certain extent on the risk tolerance of the investor. The more sensitive the investor is to risk, the more important the correlation. For example, consider the optimal portfolio weights in Table 8.1, which is based on data from the joint optimization problem in Chapter 5 using Equations 5.3, 5.4, and 5.5.

Table 8.1 is constructed using the following assumptions about U.S. stocks and Japanese stocks (percents):

---

[1] See Sorensen et al. (1992) for an illustration of this technology.

U.S. stocks	$E(r_{US}) = 14.3$	$\sigma_{US} = 14.0$
Japanese stocks	$E(r_{JP}) = 15.6$	$\sigma_{JP} = 18.0$
Currency	$E(r_¥) = 2.4$	$\sigma_¥ = 10.0$
	$f = 1.2$	

The correlation between U.S. stocks and Japanese stocks is assumed to be 0.3. Values in the table assume that the yen correlation with Japanese stocks is equal to that with U.S. stocks.

Panel A uses a risk-aversion parameter, λ, of 1, panel B uses a parameter of 2, and panel C uses a parameter of 10. Notice that the more risk averse an investor is, the more pronounced are the effects of changes in correlation. The reason is that the change in correlation alters the risk of the portfolio but leaves the expected asset returns unaffected. The very-risk-averse investor is more sensitive to these changes than is the less-risk-averse investor and responds by changing the portfolio allocation.

16. *How might an investor establish a benchmark currency position?*

One way to establish a benchmark currency position is to use the risk–return framework we have described to choose the optimal allocations in a portfolio. The optimal allocations will depend on what the investor believes about the long-run risk and return characteristics of currency markets and the investor's risk tolerance. In the most general case, the strategic currency allocation will not be independent of the asset allocation decisions unless asset returns are uncorrelated with currency returns. Asset and currency benchmarks can be jointly determined in a mean–variance framework by using the investor's estimates of long-run expected returns, variances, and correlations for both assets and currencies. The portfolio allocations given by Equations 5.3, 5.4, and 5.5 are representative of jointly determined benchmark positions for a simple portfolio based on long-run market parameters. Optimal currency exposure will depend not only on the market assumptions for assets and currencies but also on the investor's risk tolerance. That is, the resulting benchmark will not be a universal solution for all investors. Furthermore, the benchmark positions are not likely to be the same for each currency in the portfolio.

When investors inquire about a currency benchmark, however, they generally have in mind a process that assumes the asset positions are already in place rather than a process that includes choosing optimal asset allocations. In this case, the currency exposure in Equation 5.11 can be used in the mean–variance framework to determine the benchmark currency exposure for a simple portfolio. The optimal currency exposure still depends on the composition of the underlying asset portfolio and the investor's tolerance for risk. Positive correlations between asset and currency returns will tend to reduce the currency exposure in the portfolio by hedging at least some of the currency risk. In a complex portfolio with many different currencies, each currency will continue to have a different benchmark allocation.

Benchmark currency positions will be independent of the underlying asset portfolio only if asset returns are uncorrelated with currency returns, as illustrated in Equation 5.12. In this case, the benchmark currency exposure will depend primarily on the investor's tolerance for risk and on the long-run forward surprise expected for each currency. Unless the expected forward surprise is the same for each currency, the same hedge ratio is unlikely to be optimal for all currency positions.

Two different assumptions about long-run currency returns might be used in establishing a benchmark. As noted in Chapter 2, the assumption that currency returns follow a random walk would suggest that the expected forward surprise is equal to the negative of the forward premium; that is,

$$E(r_c) - f = -f.$$

As a result, the benchmark for each currency position will reflect the cost of hedging away the currency risk. Hedge ratios will be different for each currency to reflect this difference in hedging cost.

A fully hedged benchmark for each currency is optimal if currency and asset returns are uncorrelated and the investor is interested only in maximum risk reduction, without regard for the cost of hedging embodied in the forward premium. A fully hedged position should be the benchmark also if the expected long-run forward surprise is zero. This long-run expectation is equivalent to assuming that forward exchange rates are unbiased predictors of future spot exchange rates (uncovered interest arbitrage). As we have noted, however, empirical evidence from the modern floating-rate period does not support this assumption.

Unhedged currency benchmarks are sometimes suggested as appropriate. In the context of the risk–return framework described here, however, to be optimal, such benchmarks would require assets to be sufficiently negatively correlated with currency returns or would require the expected forward surprise to be sufficiently positive as to overcome the currency variance.

Given the uncertainty in formulating long-run estimates of currency risk and return, investors in recent years have, not surprisingly, chosen partially hedged benchmarks for their currency positions. A partially hedged benchmark has the advantage of reducing the investor's regret somewhat relative to fully hedged or unhedged benchmarks. The investor can be glad that at least part of the foreign currency exposure is hedged when the home currency is strong and that at least some currency exposure is in place when foreign currencies are strong. A partially hedged benchmark also gives active currency management strategies the opportunity to add value on both sides of currency moves, whereas value can be added relative to polar benchmarks only in one direction (if no net negative exposure or leverage is allowed).

Practical considerations also enter into the choice of a currency benchmark. Some investors choose an unhedged position because currency exposure is created automatically by the asset positions and no additional transactions are needed in the currency markets themselves. A fully hedged benchmark requires the investor to make additional transactions in the foreign exchange markets. Furthermore, the hedging activity will generate losses that must be settled periodically with transfers of cash. These cash transfers are very visible, and even though the underlying asset portfolio contains offsetting unrealized currency gains, the realized losses often attract undesired attention.

17. *Based on reasonable assumptions that are consistent with historical precedent, what is a reasonable hedge ratio and how stable is it?*

Table 8.2. Currency Exposure Percentage (Hedge Percentage) versus Forward Premium

Risk Aversion (λ)	Annualized Forward Premium		
	−1.0%	−2.0%	−3.0%
A: Asset–Currency Correlation = 0.1			
1	19.7% (80.3%)	54.4% (45.6%)	89.2% (10.8%)
2	2.4 (97.6)	19.7 (80.3)	37.1 (62.9)
3	−3.4 (103.4)	8.2 (91.8)	19.7 (80.3)
B: Asset–Currency Correlation = 0.0			
1	34.7 (65.3)	69.4 (30.6)	104.2 (−4.2)
2	17.4 (82.6)	34.7 (65.3)	52.1 (47.9)
3	11.6 (88.4)	23.2 (76.8)	34.7 (65.3)

Assuming that the investor expects the currency return to be zero, the appropriate hedge ratio will depend on the investor's aversion to risk and assumption about the cost of hedging. Suppose, for example, that the investor's portfolio is exposed to only one currency, that the local assets' standard deviations equal 18 percent, and that the currency's standard deviation equals 12 percent. Suppose also that the currency is 10 percent correlated with each local asset return, including the domestic component. Table 8.2 shows how much currency exposure the investor should have (using Equation 5.11 and expressed as a percentage of the total portfolio value) for various combinations of the forward premium and risk aversion.

For example, for the correlation of 0.1 in panel A, a forward discount of −1.0 percent, and risk aversion of 1, the investor should have 19.7 percent currency exposure in the portfolio (or hedge 80.3 percent of the portfolio value). Notice that as the risk aversion of the investor goes up, the desirable currency exposure goes down. Notice also that as the forward discount becomes larger, desirable currency exposure increases. The reason is that currency exposure can be purchased at a discount as the forward discount increases (or, in other words, hedging currency exposure becomes more expensive). The trade-off between the currency risk and the cost of hedging is governed by the investor's risk aversion.

Panel B shows currency exposures under the

assumption that asset returns are uncorrelated with currency returns. Notice that the decrease in correlation uniformly results in higher currency exposure (less hedging). The lower the level of correlation between asset and currency returns, the less risk the currency exposure contributes to the overall risk of the portfolio and the more currency exposure can be tolerated.

Although currency standard deviations have been relatively stable during the modern floating-rate era, the correlations of currencies with each other and with U.S. asset returns have varied significantly, as revealed in Tables 2.5 and 2.8. The sensitivity of the optimal hedge ratio to the assumed correlations, together with the relative instability of historical correlations, suggests that the choice of a hedging policy, even in the absence of a view about the direction of the domestic currency, is a difficult task at best. Certainly, the historical record does not inspire confidence that an investor can simply extrapolate past relationships. Recent developments in the application of sophisticated econometric methods, such as GARCH models, may improve investors' and analysts' ability to forecast currency correlations.

Appendix A. Key to Notation Used in the Text

Forward and Spot Foreign Exchange Rates

S_o = current spot foreign exchange rate (home currency/foreign currency)
S = spot foreign exchange rate at a subsequent date
$E(S)$ = expected spot foreign exchange rate at a subsequent date
F = current forward foreign exchange rate
$_xS_y$ = spot foreign exchange rate between currencies x and y (quoted x units/y units)

Percentage Rates

f = forward premium or discount implied by the forward foreign exchange rate
f_a = annualized forward premium or discount
f^*, f_a^* = continuously compounded forms of f and f_a
r_c = change in exchange rates using the domestic (direct) perspective (home currency/foreign currency)
r_f = change in exchange rates using the foreign (indirect) perspective (foreign currency/home currency)
r_c^*, r_f^* = continuously compounded forms of r_c and r_f
$R, E(R)$ = return and expected return, respectively, on a portfolio
R_{UH} = unhedged return on a portfolio
R_H = fully hedged return on a portfolio
R_B = return on the benchmark portfolio
$\Delta R = R - R_B$ = differential return between a portfolio and its benchmark
r_ℓ = foreign asset return expressed in local currency terms
r_d = domestic asset return
R_c = average interest rate earned on cash reserves set aside for margin requirements
$_xr_y$ = change in the exchange rate between currencies x and y using the direct quotation convention from the perspective of a currency x investor
$_xr_y^*$ = continuously compounded form of $_xr_y$

129

Currency Management: Concepts and Practices

i_d = annualized domestic short-term interest rate
i_ℓ = annualized foreign short-term interest rate
i_d^*, i_ℓ^* = continuously compounded forms of i_d and i_ℓ
π_d = annualized domestic inflation rate
π_f = annualized foreign inflation rate

Risk Notation

σ_R^2 = variance of portfolio returns
$\sigma_{\Delta R}^2$ = variance of the differential return between a portfolio and its benchmark (tracking error)
σ_d^2 = variance of domestic asset returns
σ_ℓ^2 = variance of foreign local asset returns
σ_c^2 = variance of currency returns
$C_{d\ell}(\rho_{d\ell})$ = covariance (correlation) between domestic and foreign local asset returns
$C_{dc}(\rho_{dc})$ = covariance (correlation) between domestic asset and currency returns
$C_{\ell c}(\rho_{\ell c})$ = covariance (correlation) between foreign local asset returns and currency returns
$\text{cov}(r_A, {}_x r_z) = C_{Az}^x$ = covariance between asset A and currency z from the perspective of a currency x investor
β_ℓ = beta coefficient of the foreign local asset return regressed on the currency return
β_d = beta coefficient of the domestic asset return regressed on the currency return

Portfolio Weights

$w_d(w_d^B)$ = portfolio (benchmark) proportion held in the domestic asset
$w_\ell(w_\ell^B)$ = portfolio (benchmark) proportion held in the foreign asset
$\Delta w_d = w_d - w_d^B$ = incremental portfolio proportion in the domestic asset relative to a benchmark proportion
$\Delta w_\ell = w_\ell - w_\ell^B$ = incremental portfolio proportion in the foreign asset relative to a benchmark proportion
$h(h^B)$ = currency hedge ratio of a portfolio (benchmark)
$H(H^B)$ = currency exposure proportion of a portfolio (benchmark)
$\Delta H = H - H^B$ = incremental portfolio currency exposure relative to a benchmark
$\Delta h = h - h^B$ = incremental currency hedge ratio relative to a benchmark

Other Notation

t = proportion of a year to the maturity or expiration date
λ = investor's trade-off between expected return and variance
γ = investor's trade-off between expected incremental return and tracking error
C = price of a European call option
P = price of a European put option
K = exercise price of an option.
$N(\cdot)$ = cumulative normal distribution function
$E(\cdot)$ = denotes expected value

Appendix B. Summary of Basic Currency Relationships

European quotation convention	S	$= \text{FX/USD}$
American quotation convention	S	$= \text{USD/FX}$
Forward premium	f	$= F/S_o - 1$
Discrete currency return	r_c	$= S/S_o - 1$
Continuously compounded currency return	r_c^*	$= \ln(S/S_o) = \ln(1 + r_c)$
Hedged asset return	R_H	$\approx r_\ell + f$
Unhedged asset return	R_{UH}	$\approx r_\ell + r_c$
Forward rate relationship (covered interest arbitrage)	F	$= \dfrac{S_o(1 + i_d t)}{(1 + i_\ell t)}$
Forward premium relationship (covered interest arbitrage)	f	$\approx (i_d - i_\ell)t$
Expected portfolio return	$E(R)$	$= w_d E(r_d) + w_\ell [E(r_\ell) + f] + H[E(r_c) - f]$
Portfolio variance	σ_R^2	$= w_d^2 \sigma_d^2 + w_\ell^2 \sigma_\ell^2 + 2 w_d w_\ell C_{d\ell} + H^2 \sigma_c^2 + 2H[w_d C_{dc} + w_\ell C_{\ell c}]$
Minimum-variance currency exposure	H	$= -\left[\dfrac{w_d C_{dc} + w_\ell C_{\ell c}}{\sigma_c^2}\right]$
Efficient currency exposure	H	$= \dfrac{E(r_c) - f - 2\lambda[w_d C_{dc} + w_\ell C_{\ell c}]}{2\lambda \sigma_c^2}$
Expected relative return	$E(\Delta R)$	$= \Delta w_d E(r_d) + \Delta w_\ell [E(r_\ell) + f] + \Delta H [E(r_c) - f]$
Tracking error	$\sigma_{\Delta R}^2$	$= \Delta w_d^2 \sigma_d^2 + \Delta w_\ell^2 \sigma_\ell^2 + 2 \Delta w_d \Delta w_\ell C_{d\ell} + \Delta H^2 \sigma_c^2 + 2 \Delta H[\Delta w_d C_{dc} + \Delta w_\ell C_{\ell c}]$
Minimum-tracking-error currency exposure	ΔH	$= -\left[\dfrac{\Delta w_d C_{dc} + \Delta w_\ell C_{\ell c}}{\sigma_c^2}\right]$
Efficient relative currency exposure	ΔH	$= \dfrac{E(r_c) - f - 2\gamma[\Delta w_d C_{dc} + \Delta w_\ell C_{\ell c}]}{2\gamma \sigma_c^2}$

Selected References: Theory and Empirical Evidence

Abuaf, N. 1987. "Foreign Exchange Options: The Leading Hedge." *Midland Corporate Finance Journal* (Summer):51–58.

Abuaf, N., and P. Jorion. 1990. "Purchasing Power Parity in the Long Run." *The Journal of Finance* (March):157–74.

Adler, M., and B. Prasad. 1992. "On Universal Currency Hedges." *Journal of Financial and Quantitative Analysis* (March):19–38.

Baillie, R., and P. McMahon. 1989. *The Foreign Exchange Market: Theory and Econometric Evidence.* Cambridge: Cambridge University Press.

Biger, N., and J. Hull. 1983. "The Valuation of Currency Options." *Financial Management* (Spring):24–28.

Bilson, J. 1990. "'Technical' Currency Trading." In *The Currency-Hedging Debate*, Lee. R. Thomas (ed.). London: IFR Publishing.

———. 1984. "Exchange Rate Dynamics." In *Exchange Rate Theory and Practice*, J. Bilson and R. Marston (eds.). Chicago: University of Chicago Press:175–98.

———. 1981. "The 'Speculative Efficiency' Hypothesis." *Journal of Business* (July):435–51.

———. 1978a. "Macroeconomic Stability and Flexible Exchange Rates." *American Economic Review*, Papers and Proceedings, vol. 75:62–67.

———. 1978b. "The Monetary Approach to the Exchange Rate—Some Empirical Evidence." International Monetary Fund Staff Papers, vol. 25:48–75.

Bilson, J., and D. Hsieh. 1984. "The Risk and Return of Currency Speculation." University of Chicago.

Black, F. 1990. "Equilibrium Exchange Rate Hedging." *The Journal of Finance*, vol. 43 (July):899–908.

Black, F., and M. Scholes. 1973. "The Pricing of Options and Corporate Liabilities." *Journal of Political Economy* (May/June):637–59.

Cornell, B., and J. Dietrich. 1980. "Inflation, Relative Price Changes, and Exchange Risk." *Financial Management* (Autumn):30–34.

Cornell, B., and M. Reinganum. 1981. "Forward and Future Prices." *The Journal of Finance* (December):1035–45.

Cumby, R., and M. Obstfeld. 1984. "International Interest Rate and Price Level Linkages under Flexible Exchange Rates: A Review of Recent Evidence." In *Exchange Rate Theory and Practice*, J. Bilson and R. Marston (eds.). Chicago: University of Chicago Press:121–52.

———. 1981. "A Note on Exchange-Rate Expectations and Nominal Interest Differentials: A Test of the Fisher Hypothesis." *The Journal of Finance* (June):697–703.

Curcio, R., and C. Goodhart. 1992. "When Support/Resistance Levels Are Broken, Can Profits Be Made? Evidence from the Foreign Exchange Market." London School of Economics, Discussion Paper No. 142 (July).

Dornbusch, R. 1988. "Real Exchange Rates and Macroeconomics: A Selective Survey." National Bureau of Economic Research Working Paper no. 275.

———. 1980. "Exchange Rate Economics: Where Do We Stand?" *Brookings Papers on Economic Activity*, no. 1.

_____. 1976. "Expectations and Exchange Rate Dynamics." *Journal of Political Economy* (December):1161–76.

Engel, C., and J. Hamilton. 1990. "Long Swings in the Dollar: Are They in the Data and Do Markets Know It?" *The American Economic Review* (September):689–713.

Fama, E. 1976. "Forward Rates as Predictors of Future Spot Rates." *Journal of Financial Economics* (October):361–77.

Frankel, J. 1989. "Flexible Exchange Rates: Experience Versus Theory." *The Journal of Portfolio Management* (Winter):45–54.

Frankel, J., and K. Froot. 1990. "Chartists, Fundamentalists, and Trading in the Foreign Exchange Market." *The American Economic Review* (May):181–85.

_____. 1987. "Using Survey Data to Test Standard Propositions Regarding Exchange Rate Expectations." *The American Economic Review* (March):133–53.

_____. 1986. "Understanding the Dollar in the Eighties: Rates of Return, Risk Premiums, Speculative Bubbles, and Chartists and Fundamentalists." Discussion Paper No. 155, Centre for Economic Policy Research, Australian National University, Canberra.

Frankel, J., and R. Meese. 1987. "Are Exchange Rates Excessively Variable?" In *NBER Macroeconomics Annual*: 117–62.

Frenkel, J. 1981. "Flexible Exchange Rates, Prices and the Role of 'News': Lessons from the 1970s." *Journal of Political Economy*, vol. 89:665–705.

_____. 1976. "A Monetary Approach to the Exchange Rate: Doctrinal Aspects and Empirical Evidence." *Scandinavian Journal of Economics*, vol. 78, no. 2:200–24.

Froot, K. 1993. "Currency Hedging over Long Horizons." National Bureau of Economic Research Working Paper No. 4355 (May).

Froot, K., and J. Frankel. 1989. "Forward Discount Bias: Is It An Exchange Risk Premium?" *Quarterly Journal of Economics* (February):139–61.

Froot, K., and R. Thaler. 1990. "Anomalies: Foreign Exchange." *Journal of Economic Perspectives* (Summer):179–92.

Garman, M., and S. Kohlhagen. 1983. "Foreign Currency Option Values." *Journal of International Money and Finance* (December):231–37.

Giddy, I. 1983. "The Foreign Exchange Option as a Hedging Tool." *Midland Corporate Finance Journal* (Fall):32–42.

Goodman, S. 1979. "Foreign Exchange Forecasting Techniques: Implications for Business and Policy." *The Journal of Finance* (May):415–27.

Grabbe, O. 1983. "The Pricing of Call and Put Options on Foreign Exchange." *Journal of International Money and Finance* (December):239–53.

Gruen, D. 1993. "Explaining Forward Discount Bias: Is It Anchoring?" International Monetary Fund Research Paper (January).

Hakkio, C., and D. Pearce. 1985. "The Reaction of Exchange Rates to Economic News." *Economic Inquiry* (October):621–36.

Hansen, L., and R. Hodrick. 1980. "Forward Exchange Rates as Optimal Predictors of Future Spot Exchange Rates: An Econometric Analysis." *Journal of Political Economy* (October):829–53.

Hodrick, R. 1987a. *The Empirical Evidence on the Efficiency of Forward and Futures Foreign Exchange Markets*. New York: Harwood Academic Publishing.

_____. 1987b. "Risk, Uncertainty and Exchange Rates." National Bureau of Economic Research Working Paper No. 2429.

Hodrick, R., and S. Srivastava. 1987. "Foreign Currency Futures." *Journal of International Economics* (February):1–24.

_____. 1984. "An Investigation of Risk and Return in Forward Foreign Exchange." *Journal of International Money and Finance* (April):5–29.

Hoffman, D., and D. Schlagenhauf. 1985. "The Impact of News and Alternative Theories of Exchange Rate Determination." *Journal of Money, Credit and Banking* (August): 328–46.

Hsieh, D. 1988. "The Statistical Properties of Daily Foreign Exchange Rates: 1974–1983." *Journal of International Economics,* no. 24:129–45.

Huizinga, J. 1987. "An Empirical Investigation of the Long-Run Behavior of Real Exchange Rates." *Empirical Studies of Velocity, Real Exchange Rates, Unemployment and Productivity*. K. Brunner and A. Meltzer (eds.). Carnegie-Rochester Conference Series, vol. 27:149–215.

Kohlhagen, S. 1978. "The Behavior of Foreign Exchange Markets—A Critical Survey of the Empirical Literature." New York: New York University Monograph Series in Finance and Economics, no. 3.

Kouri, P. 1976. "The Exchange Rate and the Balance of Payments in the Short Run and in the Long Run: A Monetary Approach." *Scandinavian Journal of Economics*, vol. 78, no. 2:280–304.

Krasker, W. 1980. "The 'Peso Problem' in Testing the Efficiency of Forward Exchange Markets." *Journal of Monetary Economics* (April):269–76.

Krugman, P. 1978. "Purchasing Power Parity and Exchange Rates: Another Look at the Evidence." *Journal of International Economics* (August):397–407.

Levich, R. 1993. "Exchange Rate Behavior: Trends or Random Walks?" Working Paper, Stern School of Business, New York University.

———. 1985. "Empirical Studies of Exchange Rates: Price Behavior, Rate Determination and Market Efficiency." *Handbook of International Economics*, vol. 2:979–1041.

———. 1980. "Analyzing the Accuracy of Foreign Exchange Advisory Services: Theory and Evidence." In *Exchange Risk and Exposure*, R. Levich and C. Wihlborg (eds). Lexington, Mass.: D.C. Heath.

———. 1979. "On the Efficiency of Markets for Foreign Exchange." In *International Economic Policy: Theory and Evidence*, R. Dornbusch and J. Frenkel (eds.). Baltimore: Johns Hopkins University Press.

———. 1978. "Tests of Forecasting Models and Market Efficiency in the International Money Market." In *The Economics of Exchange Rates*, J. Frenkel and H. Johnson (eds.). Reading, Mass.:Addison-Wesley:129–58.

Lo, A., and C. MacKinlay. 1988. "Stock Market Prices Do Not Follow Random Walks: Evidence from a Simple Specification Test." *The Review of Financial Studies*, vol. 1, no. 1:41–66.

MacDonald, R., and M. Taylor. 1992. "Exchange Rate Economics: A Survey." International Monetary Fund Staff Papers, vol. 39, no. 1 (March):1–57.

Marrinan, J. 1989. "Exchange Rate Determination: Sorting Out Theory and Evidence." *New England Economic Review* (November/December):39–50.

McCulloch, J. 1975. "Operational Aspects of the Siegel Paradox." *Quarterly Journal of Economics* (February):170–72.

McGowan, C., and H. Collier. 1993. "Foreign Exchange Rate Parity Conditions: A Pedagogical Note." *Financial Practice and Education* (Spring/Summer):77–83.

Meese, R. 1986. "Empirical Assessment of Foreign Currency Risk Premiums." In *Financial Risk: Theory, Evidence and Implications*, C. Stone (ed.), Proceedings of Eleventh Annual Economic Policy Conference of the Federal Reserve Bank of St. Louis, Kluwer Academic Publishers:157–80.

Meese, R., and K. Rogoff. 1988. "Was It Real? The Exchange Rate–Interest Differential Relation over the Modern Floating-Rate Period." *The Journal of Finance* (September):933–48.

———. 1983a. "Empirical Exchange Rate Models of the Seventies: Do They Fit Out of Sample?" *Journal of International Economics* (February):3–24.

———. 1983b. "The Out-of-Sample Failure of Empirical Exchange Rate Models: Sampling Error or Model Misspecification?" In *Exchange Rates and International Macroeconomics*, J. Frenkel (ed.). Chicago: University of Chicago Press:67–112.

Mussa, M. 1986. "Nominal Exchange Rate Regimes and the Behavior of Real Exchange Rates: Evidence and Implications." Carnegie–Rochester Conference Series on Public Policy, vol. 25:117–214.

———. 1984. "The Theory of Exchange Rate Determination." In *Exchange Rate Theory and Practice*, J. Bilson and R. Marston (eds.). Chicago: University of Chicago Press:13–78.

———. 1979. "Empirical Regularities in the Behavior of Exchange Rates and Theories of the Foreign Exchange Market." In *Policies for Employment, Prices, and Exchange Rates*, K. Brunner and A. Meltzer (eds.), Carnegie–Rochester Conference Series on Public Policy, vol. 11. New York: North-Holland:9–57.

———. 1976. "The Exchange Rate, the Balance of Payments, and Monetary and Fiscal Policy under a Regime of Controlled Floating." *Scandinavian Journal of Economics*, vol. 78, no. 2:229–48.

Peterson, D., and A. Tucker. 1988. "Implied Spot Rates as Predictors of Currency Returns: A Note." *The Journal of Finance* (March):247–58.

Roper, D. 1975. "The Role of Expected Value Analysis for Speculative Decisions in the Forward Currency Market." *Quarterly Journal of Economics* (February):157–69.

Rosenberg, M. 1993. "Currency Forecasting: Theory and Practice." Merrill Lynch & Co. International Fixed Income Research.

Shiller, R. 1981. "Do Stock Prices Move Too Much to Be Justified by Subsequent Changes in Dividends?" *The American Economic Review* (June):421–36.

Siegel, J. 1975. "Reply: Risk, Interest Rates and the Forward Exchange." *Quarterly Journal of Economics* (February): 173–75.

———. 1972. "Risk, Interest Rates and the Forward Exchange." *Quarterly Journal of Economics* (May):303–9.

Silber, W. 1994. "Technical Trading: When It Works and When It Doesn't." *The Journal of Derivatives* (Spring):39–44.

Solnik, B. 1993. "Currency Hedging and Siegel's Paradox: On Black's Universal Hedging Rule." *Review of International Economics*, vol. 1, no. 2:180–87.

———. 1974. "An Equilibrium Model of the International Capital Market." *Journal of Economic Theory*, vol. 8:500–524.

Stockman, A. 1987. "The Equilibrium Approach to Exchange Rates." Federal Reserve Bank of Richmond, *Economic Review* (March/April):12–30.

Sweeney, R. 1986. "Beating the Foreign Exchange Market." *The Journal of Finance* (March):163–82.

Taylor, M., and H. Allen. 1992. "The Use of Technical Analysis in the Foreign Exchange Market." *Journal of International Money and Finance*, (June):304–14.

Selected References: Investment Principles and Practices

Adler, M., and P. Jorion. 1992. "Universal Currency Hedges for Global Portfolios." *The Journal of Portfolio Management* (Summer):28–35.

Ankrim, E., and C. Hensel. 1994. "Multicurrency Performance Attribution." *Financial Analysts Journal* (March/April):29–35.

Arnott, R., and T. Pham. 1993. "Tactical Currency Allocation." *Financial Analysts Journal* (September/October):47–52.

Benari, Y. 1992. "Linking the International Bond Investment Decision to Hedging." *Financial Analysts Journal* (September/October):55–63.

———. 1991. "When Is Hedging Foreign Assets Effective?" *The Journal of Portfolio Management* (Fall):66–71.

Black, F. 1989. "Universal Hedging: Optimizing Currency Risk and Reward in International Portfolios." *Financial Analysts Journal* (July/August):16–22.

Celebuski, M., J. Hill, and J. Kilgannon. 1990. "Managing Currency Exposures in International Portfolios." *Financial Analysts Journal* (January/February):16–23.

Choie, K. 1993. "Currency Exchange Rate Forecast and Interest Rate Differential." *The Journal of Portfolio Management* (Winter):58–64.

Chow, G. 1995. "Portfolio Selection Based on Return, Risk, and Relative Performance." *Financial Analysts Journal* (March/April):54–60.

DeRosa, D. 1993. "Introduction to Currency Options." *The Journal of Investing* (Summer):62–73.

———. 1993. "Using Derivatives to Manage the Currency Risk in Global Investment Portfolios." In *Derivative Strategies for Managing Portfolio Risk*. Charlottesville, Va.: Association for Investment Management and Research:92–97.

———. 1992. *Options on Foreign Exchange*. Chicago: Probus Publishing.

———. 1991. *Managing Foreign Exchange Risk*. Chicago: Probus Publishing.

Eaker, M., and D. Grant. 1991. "Currency Risk Management in International Fixed-Income Portfolios." *The Journal of Fixed Income* (December):31–37.

———. 1990. "Currency Hedging Strategies for Internationally Diversified Equity Portfolios." *The Journal of Portfolio Management* (Fall):30–32.

Filatov, V., and P. Rappoport. 1992. "Is Complete Hedging Optimal for International Bond Portfolios." *Financial Analysts Journal* (July/August):37–47.

Gardner, G. 1994a. "Currency Risk Management for Non-U.S. Investors." *Russell Research Commentaries* (February).

———. 1994b. "Managing Currency Risk in U.S. Pension Plans." *Russell Research Commentaries* (January).

Gastineau, Gary. 1995. "The Currency Hedging Decision: A Search for Synthesis in Asset Allocation." *Financial Analysts Journal* (May/June):8–17.

Glen, J., and P. Jorion. 1993. "Currency Hedging for International Portfolios." *The Journal of Finance* (December):1865–86.

Green, P. 1994. "Planets and Satellites: A Paradigm for Managing Currency Risk." *The Journal of Investing* (Spring):19–23.

———. 1992. "Is Currency Trading Profitable? Exploiting Deviations from Uncovered Interest Parity." *Financial Analysts Journal* (July/August):82–86.

Hazuka, T., and L. Huberts. 1994. "A Valuation Approach to Currency Hedging." *Financial Analysts Journal* (March/April):55–59.

Jorion, P. 1994. "Mean/Variance Analysis of Currency Overlays." *Financial Analysts Journal* (May/June):48–56.

———. 1989. "Asset Allocation with Hedged and Unhedged Foreign Stocks and Bonds." *The Journal of Portfolio Management* (Summer):49–54.

Karnosky, D., and B. Singer. 1994. *Global Asset Management and Performance Attribution*. Charlottesville, Va.: The Research Foundation of the Institute of Chartered Financial Analysts.

Kawaller, I. 1993. "Foreign Exchange Hedge Management Tools: A Way to Enhance Performance." *Financial Analysts Journal* (September/October):79–80.

Kritzman, M. 1993. "The Optimal Currency Hedging Policy with Biased Forward Rates." *The Journal of Portfolio Management* (Summer):94–100.

———. 1992. "What Practitioners Need to Know about Currencies." *Financial Analysts Journal* (March/April):27–30.

———. 1989. "A Simple Solution for Optimal Currency Hedging." *Financial Analysts Journal* (November/December):47–50.

Lee, A. 1988. "International Asset and Currency Allocation." In *Asset Allocation: A Handbook of Portfolio Policies, Strategies and Tactics*, R. Arnott and F. Fabozzi (eds.). Chicago: Probus Publishing:405–24.

———. 1987. "International Asset and Currency Allocation." *The Journal of Portfolio Management* (Fall):68–73.

Levich, R., and L. Thomas. 1993. "The Merits of Active Currency Risk Management: Evidence from International Bond Portfolios." *Financial Analysts Journal* (September/October):63–70.

Levy, H., and Z. Lerman. 1988. "The Benefits of International Diversification in Bonds." *Financial Analysts Journal* (September/October):56–64.

Nesbitt, S. 1991. "Currency Hedging Rules for Plan Sponsors." *Financial Analysts Journal* (March/April):73–81.

Odier, P., and B. Solnik. 1993. "Lessons for International Asset Allocation." *Financial Analysts Journal* (March/April):63–77.

Perold, A., and E. Schulman. 1988. "The Free Lunch in Currency Hedging: Implications for Investment Policy and Performance Standards." *Financial Analysts Journal* (May/June):45–50.

Pring, M. 1985. *Technical Analysis Explained*, 2nd ed. New York: McGraw-Hill.

Ramaswami, M. 1993. *Active Currency Management*. Charlottesville, Va.: The Research Foundation of the Institute of Chartered Financial Analysts.

Solnik, B. 1991. *International Investments*, 2nd ed. Reading, Mass.: Addison-Wesley.

———. 1974. "Why Not Diversify Internationally Rather Than Domestically?" *Financial Analysts Journal* (July/August):48–54.

Sorensen, E., J. Mezrich, and D. Thadani. 1992. "Salomon Brothers Currency Basket Hedging Strategy." Salomon Brothers (April).

Sorensen, E., J. Mezrich, B. Cox, D. Thadani, F. Massey, and D. Bielinski. 1992. "Forecasting Volatility: The S&P 500 Gift Wrapped." Salomon Brothers (April).

Thomas, L. 1989. "The Performance of Currency Hedged Foreign Bonds." *Financial Analysts Journal* (May/June): 25–31.

———. 1988. "The Performance of Currency Hedged Foreign Equities." Goldman Sachs Research Paper (July).

———. 1985. "A Winning Strategy for Currency–Futures Speculation." *The Journal of Portfolio Management* (Fall): 65–69.

Weigel, E. 1993. "Are There Really Trends in Foreign Exchange Returns?" *The Journal of Investing* (Summer):33–40.